D1496242

Shelby Foote

— *and the* —

Art of History

TWO GATES TO THE CITY

JAMES PANABAKER

Shelby Foote

— and the —

Art of History

Two Gates to the City

The University of Tennessee Press / Knoxville

Copyright © 2004 by The University of Tennessee Press / Knoxville.
All Rights Reserved. Manufactured in the United States of America.
First Edition.

Quotations from David Lowenthal, *The Past Is a Foreign Country* (Cambridge: Cambridge University Press, 1985), reprinted with the permission of Cambridge University Press.

Quotations from Joyce Appleby, Lynn Hunt, and Margaret Jacob, *Telling the Truth about History*, copyright © 1994 by Joyce Appleby, Lynn Hunt, and Margaret Jacob. Used by permission of W. W. Norton & Company, Inc.

Quotations from James M. Cox, *Recovering Literature's Lost Ground: Essays in American Autobiography*, reprinted by permission of Louisiana State University Press. Copyright © 1989 by Louisiana State University Press.

This book is printed on acid-free paper.

Panabaker, James, 1957–
Shelby Foote and the art of history : two gates to the city / James Panabaker.— 1st ed.
    p. cm.
Includes index.

ISBN 1-57233-318-9

1. Foote, Shelby—Criticism and interpretation.
2. Historical fiction, American—History and criticism.
3. United States—History—Civil War, 1861–1865—Historiography.
4. Foote, Shelby—Knowledge—Southern States.
5. Literature and history—Southern States.
6. Foote, Shelby—Knowledge—History.
7. Southern States—Historiography.
8. Southern States—In literature.
 I. Title.

PS3511.O348Z79 2004
813'.54—dc22   2004005775

Contents

Acknowledgments

A study such as this cannot be accomplished without incurring a great many debts. A special thanks is due to Shelby Foote for his gracious hospitality and generous cooperation, which included granting me permission to quote from unpublished materials. Grateful acknowledgment is also owed to the Mississippi Valley Collection (Memphis University) and the Southern Historical Collection (University of North Carolina at Chapel Hill) for their assistance in my research. My sincere appreciation must be expressed to Dr. Edward Lobb and Dr. Paul Stevens, both of Queen's University in Kingston, for sharing their insights and encouragement when this material was first presented as a doctoral thesis. I am grateful, as well, for the support of Kwantlen University College during the final stages of manuscript preparation.

I cannot hope to repay the debt I owe Dr. Warren Ober, who has provided sage advice and good-natured criticisms at every stage of this project; he is the best possible mentor and a great, good friend. A "thank you" seems poor compensation for the debt I owe to family, especially my parents, John and Janet, for all manner of support during the completion of this book.

Finally, my love and thanks to my wife, Melanie, whose contribution to this project surpasses all others. She has waited a long time to read the dedication.

Abbreviations

"Art"	"Art of Fiction CLVII"
Conversations	*Conversations with Shelby Foote*
Correspondence	*Correspondence of Shelby Foote and Walker Percy*
Follow	*Follow Me Down*
Jordan	*Jordan County*
Love	*Love in a Dry Season*
"Novelist's"	"The Novelist's View of History"
September	*September September*

Material from Foote's correspondence with Walker Percy, if reproduced in the collection edited by Jay Tolson, has a double reference of date and page. When quotations are taken from the unpublished archival material, the references comprise the designation "Letters" and the date. Quotations from Foote's recorded talks at Memphis University are identified by the tape number.

Introduction

If literature—and in another mode history—does anything for us it stirs up in us a sense of existential yearning. The truths it presents come in the images of experience, and the images tease us out of thought toward truth as experience. The truth we want to come to is the truth of ourselves, of our common humanity, available in the projected self of art.

—Robert Penn Warren "The Use of the Past," 1989

When I first visited Shelby Foote at his home in Memphis in the spring of 1994, he gave me a copy of his Modern Library edition of Stephen Crane's *The Red Badge of Courage*. Taking up the dip pen with which he writes all his work, Foote placed this inscription in the flyleaf: "For James Panabaker all the way up in Canada." Leaving aside my personal delight at this courteous gesture, the phrase is evocative in a number of other ways: first, it suggests something of the distance (literal and cultural) between myself and the Mississippi Delta, the region that lies at the heart of Foote's fictional world; second, it reminds me of the absence in my own nation's history of a cultural "crossroads" on the scale of the American Civil War; and, finally, it puts me in mind of one of the more conspicuous Canadian characters in southern fiction, Shrevlin McCannon, Faulkner's "child of blizzards" (*Absalom* 285), who—like myself—wished only "to understand it if I can" (297).

As Shreve McCannon listens to Quentin Compson's recital of the Sutpen history with—at least initially—the detached ironic perspective of an outsider, Shreve is drawn inexorably into questioning the nature of the southern heritage:

> I don't know how to say it better. Because it's something my people haven't got. Or if we have got it, it all happened long ago across the water and so now there aint anything to look at every day

to remind us of it. We don't live among defeated grandfathers and freed slaves (or have I got it backward and was it your folks that are free and the niggers that lost?) and bullets in the dining room table and such, to be always reminding us to never forget. What is it? something you live and breathe in like air? (*Absalom* 296–97)

Shreve's initial bewilderment is qualified, ironically, by the fact that Quentin, a native of the South and scion of Faulkner's famous Jefferson family, confesses a similar difficulty in comprehension. Their shared bemusement demonstrates that understanding the South involves a confrontation with the particular history of the place and its people, as well as an engagement with more general issues of time, memory, and representation. Fiction and history, North and South, black and white, specific and universal, Faulknerian and Hemingwayesque: such pairings are the "two gates" through which we must pass in pursuit of an understanding of the work of novelist and historian Shelby Foote.

In response to a question raised during a series of talks he gave at the University of Memphis in 1966–67, Foote remarked: "Most of the best writers I know of, and some of those that you'd least likely think this about . . . the really exciting work they write is their complete works" (Lecture, 2:26/24). Citing the example of Henry James, Foote goes on to suggest how, from this broader perspective, one begins to see novels such as *The Wings of the Dove* and *The Ambassadors* as chapters in a lifelong work, whose value—leaving aside their particular merits—lies in the contemplation of how "they're all [demonstrative of] the writer becoming a great artist" (Lecture 2:26/24). A truism, to be sure; yet one with a specific bearing on Foote's own work, which is too often compartmentalized into the separate genres of fiction and history. As Foote himself acknowledges, "My book [*The Civil War: A Narrative*] falls between two stools: academic historians are upset because there are no footnotes, and novel readers don't want to study history" ("Art" 56). Such attitudes tend to limit critical appreciation of Foote's career as a whole. If, as novelist Walker Percy remarked and several critics have since repeated, *The Civil War* is indeed an "American *Iliad*," then Foote's six novels, with their carefully developed interconnections, are his *Odyssey*. Where the *Iliad* is concerned primarily with a long and costly military campaign, whose action is leavened by brief glimpses of the commonplace world through Homeric similes, the *Odyssey* concentrates, in the fashion of a novel, on the adventures and sensibility of an individual character beset by the trials and travails of circumstance. The cumulative vision of both epics conveys a multifaceted picture of ancient Greece and, in a sense, provides a model for the reciprocal relationship between particular and universal, factual and mythical, found in Foote's writing; for both Homer and Foote, the whole proves greater than the sum of the parts. As in the case of the writers he admires, Foote's complete work is the "really exciting" one.

My comparison of Foote and Homer may not be as presumptuous as it seems. Ken Burns, one of America's most noted documentary filmmakers and an accomplished storyteller in his own right, invokes a similar comparison in defining his role as a historian and a custodian of cultural memory: "I believe that history ought to be sung," he asserts, and that "the Homeric mode is an important one, that you need to sing the epic verses, and the way we do that is around the 'electronic campfire' [of television]. And it is an inclusion of myth as well as fact, because myth tells you much more than fact about a people. But you have to distinguish between myth and fact" (749). As another "popularizer" of history (a term I am using in no way pejoratively), Foote also offers the reader "two gates to the city" (*Odyssey* XIX), two ways of approaching the past—through fiction and through history.

Foote's six novels—*Tournament* (1949), *Follow Me Down* (1950), *Love in a Dry Season* (1951), *Shiloh* (1952), *Jordan County: A Landscape in Narrative* (1953) and *September September* (1977)—and the three volumes of *The Civil War* (1958, 1963, 1974) are an attempt, as he says of Faulkner, to "communicate complexly the complexity of life" (Lecture 2:26/14). Read as a whole, Foote's oeuvre—in which historical detail underpins the fictional subject matter and fictional techniques enrich and enliven the history—represent, on the levels of both theme and technique, his ironic insights into the human comedy. His vision begins with scrupulous attention to the small "postage-stamp" world of Jordan County and expands, through the application of his craft to the writing of history, into an epic treatment of the Civil War. In fiction, he addresses the repercussions of the southern past (race, war, and honor) and the modern era on the psyche and attitudes of the inhabitants of Jordan County; in history, the nature and scope of the war occupies center stage, and Foote explores its formative influence on America as a modern nation. Through the practice of his narrative art in both spheres, Foote seeks, as Robert Penn Warren suggests, to "stir up in us a sense of existential yearning. The truths it presents come in the images of experience. The truth we want to come to is the truth of ourselves, of our common humanity, available in the projected self of art" (48). Warren goes on to elaborate the Proustian implications of history written to convey a sense of time:

> In other words, in a primal way, in a gut way, the study of the past gives one a feeling for the structure of experience, for continuity, for establishing location on the shifting chart of being. And it might be argued that without this gut-feel for overarching time, as contrasted with fractured time, there can be no true sense of identity. As for the sense of community, it is clear that the placing of the individual in time automatically accomplishes much toward establishing his relation to others. He is, to begin with, established as a part of the general human story. By the same token, man, seeing himself in time as time-perceived-as-experience, was aware of himself in the context of nature, of nature-as-the-matrix-of-experience, and was aware of his brotherhood with other men in nature. (50)

All Foote's writing considered on these terms resonates with a quality of vision that he admires in writers such as Geoffrey Chaucer, William Shakespeare, and Marcel Proust (and, for that matter, Tacitus and Edward Gibbon): the characteristic abilities of these artists "to see even the worst misery as part of the human comedy" (Lecture 2: 26/16–17).

Commenting on the distinctions between northern and southern writers, in the context of a talk on Carson McCullers, Foote remarks how it is "often cited that Northerners are tremendously concerned about people in the plural and Southerners are concerned about people in the singular" (Lecture 2:26/26). While acknowledging that such generalizations have a limited application, Foote raises an important point about his own achievement as a writer from the American South: that his fiction and history work to overcome this sort of regional parochialism. From his earliest treatment of life in the Mississippi Delta, through his historical narratives, to his latest novel, Foote's work demonstrates the broadening and deepening of a mature vision (informed by Proust on the aesthetics of harmonization, Faulkner on the nature of time, Jan Vermeer on the drama of stillness, and Ernest Hemingway on authenticity, to name but a few). His writings work to overcome the regional distinction between northern and southern views of the past posited in C. Hugh Holman's *The Immoderate Past: The Southern Writer and History* (1977): "In his concern with linear time and with the past in terms of a sequence of events, the southern novelist remains essentially in the tradition of Hegelian process, as [Sir Walter] Scott and his successors developed it, and not with the contemporary [Nietzschean] mythic writers" (100). Foote's work, when *The Civil War* is assigned its proper place, assimilates both traditions and signals an end to the polarized perspective Holman articulates. In both his fiction and his history, Foote demonstrates a deeply humanistic perspective—ironic and sympathetic in equal measure—a vision of the *comedie humaine* with something of the complexity of Proust's *A la recherche du temps perdu* (1913–1927), or even, one may dare to suggest, of the humanism of the last great plays of Shakespeare. Foote's presentation of the Civil War, relying as it does on a self-conscious aesthetic order to offset the chaos and mutability of time, is a view of history in keeping with the highest principles of modernist art and a fitting endnote for the accomplishments of the Southern Renaissance.

With his implicit rejection of the heritage of the New South Creed— the myth of the southern Cavalier grafted onto Victorian morality that Daniel Singal identifies as the bane of William Faulkner and other "intellectuals of transition" (112)—Foote frees his writing from the restrictive culture of enforced innocence that led to the ambivalent attitudes found in the work of his immediate predecessors. Foote, instead, highlights the fallacies of the southern "culture of memory" (Sullivan, *Brazen* 242) and ironically engages its pieties in both his fiction and his historical writing. By placing his own sense of modernist relativism within clearly demarcated, almost classical, narrative structures—an approach I call his aesthetic of limitations—Foote transforms the daunting influence of his immediate literary predecessor (Faulkner) into a unique style of ironic historiography. While his southern heritage stresses place and the formative influence of the past, Foote's work admits little of the continual flux between the polarities of idealism and realism that condition Faulkner's myth of the South. Instead, drawing on alternative modern literary traditions (particularly the lineage that extends from Conrad to Crane, Hemingway, and Warren), Foote's "dramatization of the past" (Rollyson 179) contains the Faulknerian ambivalence in an aesthetic closure and translates the unstable past into formal self-conscious narrative art—what Appleby, Hunt, and Jacob call "practical realism" (248). His writing offers an astringent corrective to some of the excesses of the Southern Renaissance and asserts an inclusive, rather than parochial, vision of the Civil War.

The poet James Merrill, in a work called "Lost in Translation," a poem whose Proustian antecedents are clear in its representation of the paradoxes involved in love and language, time and memory, suggests that confronting the reality of the human condition in art brings with it an answering compensation: "Lost, is it, buried? One more missing piece? / But nothing's lost. Or else: all is translation / And every bit of us is lost in it / Or found" (10). Like the escaping pearls of air that rise above Beulah Ross as she drowns in *Follow Me Down,* or like the impact of the "missing" (unrecorded) speeches of Lincoln and Davis in *The Civil War,* Foote's writing conveys the paradoxical blend of loss and discovery offered by an artistic rendering of the past. Understanding that the human condition inevitably involves a recognition of our roles as "victim[s] of the egocentric predicament" (Lecture 2:26/28), Foote also asserts the human capacity to redress that condition—whether in art (as with Proust, Vermeer, and Faulkner) or in action (as with Lee, Lincoln, and Hemingway)—by the exercise of the imaginative and creative abilities, the insights possible through an adherence to an individual "quality of vision." As Foote remarks of Shakespeare and his consciousness of evil in the world: "Shakespeare . . . wants us to know how to live with our sins. He's not a moralist in the Victorian sense. He doesn't want to remove your sins. He wants you to be a poor sinful creature and get through this world and not turn it into something frightfully evil just because you're sinful" (Lecture 2:26/28). By exploring the human condition in relation to the inexorable process of time, first in his fictional world and later on the epic scale of his history, Foote moves toward the universality of perspective he admires in Shakespeare's later plays, plays in which the artist's vision of the human condition is "freer and freer of making those last problems particular" (Lecture 2:26/28). The particular is never abandoned; instead, Foote's vision is enlarged through an exposure to the wide spectrum of human experience embodied in the events of the war. More exactly, Foote's writing demonstrates a capacity for acceptance and recognition akin to his conception of the nature of wisdom: "I would like for people to become so wise, in the way that a novelist is wise. . . . I would like for [them] to be familiar with the workings of man's nature so that, under strain, [they] would be comforted by [their] knowledge" (*Conversations* 101).

What Foote's work as a writer of fiction accomplished, prior to his embarking on *The Civil War,* was to provide him with a style and a theme, a way of seeing the world. "History, like literature," Appleby, Hunt, and Jacob suggest, "speaks directly to curiosity about human experience, but it takes concrete details to open the door into an imaginative recreation of the past. . . . The effect of this new capacity to vivify the characteristics of countless mundane lives is moral. It sparks a human connection" (152). While Foote's work reflects little of the "progressive national spirit" (Reardon 99) found in Bruce Catton's histories, and manifests only an ironic representation of the "tournament concept of war" (Gignilliat 165) present in the Virginia parochialism and hero-worship of Douglas Southall Freeman, and eschews the prominent focus on "political, social, administrative, cultural and economic history" (McMurry 324) of Allan Nevins's *The Ordeal of the Union* (1947–1971), what Foote does share with all three of these Civil War historians is a trait Nevins called "the cardinal requirement" of good history—that it must not be dehumanized and that it should be narrated "in terms of living men and women" (McMurry 322). On this theme, *The Civil War* outdoes them all. Louis D. Rubin Jr. is fulsome in his praise: "In objectivity, in range, in mastery of detail, in beauty of language and feeling for the people involved, [*The Civil War*] surpasses anything else on the subject" (45). It does so because Foote's vision—from the moment Jefferson Davis rises in the Senate until his last words, bittersweet and somewhat plaintive, "Tell them—Tell the world that I only loved America" (*CW* III.1060), reverberate at the close—never wavers from his focus on the human dimension of history. Foote's narrative succeeds because this humanistic vision is supported by the rigorous application of the artist's devotion to his craft.

C. Vann Woodward also admires the comprehensiveness of scale and sensitivity to human concerns found in Foote's history. He suggests the narrative is a reminder to "psychohistorians . . . cliometricians . . . [and] crypto-analysts busy with their neat models, parameters and hypotheses . . . [of] the terrifying chaos and mystery of their intractable subject" and serves to "disabuse them of some of their illusions of mastery" (12). Remarking on the centrality of military history to his own treatment of the Civil War era, James M. McPherson writes (perhaps with the example of Foote's narrative in mind): "Most of the things that we consider important in this era of American history—the fate of slavery, the structure of the society in both North and South, the direction of the American economy, the destiny of competing nationalisms in North and South, the definition of freedom, the very survival of the United States—rested on the shoulders of those weary men in blue and gray who fought it out during four years of ferocity unmatched in the Western world between the Napoleonic Wars and World War I" (x). The value of history written by artist-historians such as Tacitus or Gibbon—and I would add Foote—is, as Robert Penn Warren suggests, that one is "struck anew by the irony of good and evil interfused in our nature. It is hard enough, at best, to remember our humanity, but history helps us, at least a little" (37). With literary techniques devoted to creating for his readers a sense of the "lived experience" (Cox 198) of the war, Foote's narrative contributes more than "a little" reminder of the nature of our humanity. Commenting on the impact of the intricate and comprehensive "web of inclusion" in Foote's narrative, James M. Cox remarks that it leaves the reader, "or this one at least . . . perpetually astonished at how little he knows and at the same time profoundly gratified by his mounting grasp of the largeness, fullness, and pervasiveness of the Civil War" (199).

Shelby Foote and the Art of History: Two Gates to the City is an exploration of the richness and complexity of Foote's vision; as well, this study demonstrates the integral role played by the reciprocal nature of fiction and history in his work. Indeed, the title of this critical examination is modeled on the title of Foote's unfinished magnum opus—"this big novel" ("Art" 65)—on which he has been working for forty-odd years, *Two Gates to the City*. The phrase—taken from Homer's *Odyssey* XIX and referring to the gates of horn and ivory that lead to the "impalpable land of dreams" (*Correspondence* 53)—is a fitting image to represent Foote's accomplishments. While undoubtedly applicable to his projected southern family saga, the phrase also aptly reflects the author's conception of narrative. My appropriation seems justified, because it acknowledges that Foote is one of a rare breed of artists who combine the tools and sensibility of a writer of modernist fiction with the discipline of a historian. Out of this material he shapes his vision of life in the South in the first half of this century and also his insights into the seminal national experience of the American Civil War. Foote's mammoth undertaking, with its deliberately ambivalent status in relation to the genres of fictional and historical writing as they are conventionally understood, coincides with a turning point in the evolution of the literary culture of the South in the twentieth century.

This study of Foote's writings traces the reciprocal relationship between his fictional techniques and his treatment of historical materials. Chapter 1 considers Foote's writing in the context of his immediate social and literary heritage—primarily how his exposure to the influences of William Alexander Percy and the milieu of Greenville, Mississippi, helped to shape his vision. In addition, the chapter examines the relationship of Foote's work to the long shadow cast by William Faulkner. Foote's vision of the human condition in the light of southern society and the inroads of modernity is the focus of chapter 2; the discussion is based on a reading of the Jordan County novels and is organized around a series of pivotal historical moments in the history of the Delta world. Of primary concern is Foote's treatment of time, consciousness, and language and the role these issues play in shaping his vision of how aspects of the southern past "cast their shadows on the present" (*Jordan* 108). The narrative strategies and the architectonics of Foote's novels—what I call his aesthetic of limitations—are discussed in chapter 3. These ideas about the interplay of content and form in the fiction help lay the groundwork for examining Foote's historical narrative. The close reading of Foote's novels included in these chapters establish how his treatment of fictional material anticipates his success as a historian intent on making the past "live in the world around [us]" ("Novelist's" 220).

By employing selected textual illustrations (an unfortunate necessity given the quality, integrity, and size of the whole), the discussion of *The Civil War: A Narrative* in chapters 4 and 5 highlights Foote's successful combination of the discipline of the historian with the techniques of the practiced writer of fiction. Each of the these chapters opens with a discussion of aspects of Foote's historical novel, *Shiloh*. His treatment of the Battle of Shiloh as a template for his exploration of historical material offers a succinct point of entry for examining Foote's masterpiece, *The Civil War*. Chapter 4 focuses on the application of Foote's vision of the human condition in his narrative history. The first section discusses the insights *Shiloh* (and its historical equivalent) offers about Foote's treatment of the experience of combat; the discussion in the second section centers on the tension between individual existential questions and the concept of fate as it influences Foote's treatment of character in his role as an ironic historian. Chapter 5 also begins with a comparison of his two treatments of the Battle of Shiloh; at the heart of this discussion is Foote's approach to narrative form and the role played by his aesthetic of limitations. After this introduction to Foote's plotting of history, the next section turns to Foote's use of structure and his treatment of time—what critics have called his "temporal dialectic"—as illustrated in his presentation of the Gettysburg campaign. The last section of chapter 5 extends the examination of Foote's aesthetic to the thematic elements of irony and paradox evident in his treatment of the motif of fraternity.

The title of the conclusion, with its homage to the enriching vision of Vermeer (a painter whose capacity for "drama" in still life Foote admires), shifts the discussion back to the author's role of self-conscious artist and narrator (where and how he appears, and the implications of his "quality of vision"). As I suggest in the conclusion, the genius of this writer's work lies in his ability to establish a reciprocity between two jealous and demanding muses. His writing in both genres involves a complex "double view" (Cox 192); the novels and the narrative history constitute an ongoing, living, reciprocal exchange between seeming absolutes. Foote, in keeping with his bedrock principle of balance—a sort of cosmic settling of accounts that is eventually attributed to Anaximander in volume 3 of *The Civil War*—brings into play an elemental contrapuntal method that joins a host of differing perspectives and values. His aim, as both an "*honest* novelist" (true to his craft) and an "honest historian" (true to the disciplines of research), is to combine the matter of the past with his "quality of vision" and so make the past live again as art ("Novelist's" 220). Foote's ambitions in this respect make his work an intriguing case study for current ideas about the nature of historiography. Accepting that an engagement with the past is, paradoxically, both a limitation and an enlargement, Foote's writing offers unique insights into the nature of both the artist's and the historian's search for truth.

Chapter 1

"The Condition of the Tournament"

Foote, Faulkner, and the Matter of the South

The only reason for the existence of a novel is that it does attempt to represent life. . . . But history also is allowed to represent life; it is not, any more than painting, expected to apologise. The subject-matter of fiction is stored up likewise in documents and records, and if it will not give itself away. . . . it must speak with assurance, with the tone of the historian. . . . To represent and illustrate the past, the actions of men, is the task of either writer, and the only difference that I can see is, in proportion as he succeeds, to the honour of the novelist, consisting as it does in his having more difficulty in collecting his evidence, which is so far from being purely literary.

> —Henry James, "The Art of Fiction," 1884

The South is a metaphysical construct, born of the interaction of an intellectual tradition, historicist Romanticism, with social and political history. Indeed the Southern mind may be quite the most metaphysical on the North American continent.

> —Michael O'Brien, *Rethinking the South*, 1988

1

"*I*t was a Monday in Washington, January 21; Jefferson Davis rose from his seat in the Senate." So begins Shelby Foote's *The Civil War: A Narrative*; the temporal and spatial coordinates (day, place, date) are succinctly related, and then the focus quickly shifts to Foote's favorite catalyst, a man in motion. Having established the immediate present of the story, the narrative moves without delay into the past events that precipitated Davis's action. The next sentence continues:

> South Carolina had left the Union a month before, followed by Mississippi, Florida, and Alabama, which seceded at the rate of one a day during the second week of the new year. Georgia went out eight days later; Louisiana and Texas were poised to go; few doubted that they would, along with others. For more than a decade there had been intensive discussion as to the legality of secession, but now the argument was no longer academic. A convention had been called for the first week in February, at Montgomery, Alabama, for the purpose of forming a confederacy of the departed states, however many there should be in addition to the five already gone. As a protest against the election of Abraham Lincoln, who had received not a single southern electoral vote, secession was a fact— to be reinforced, if necessary, by the sword. (CW I.3)

These rapid-fire glances backward and forward in time convey the bewildering volatility of events—Davis, in effect, rises into a whirlwind. Foote's readers quickly understand that the nature of time is also a subject of the narrative. As well, the text presents us with images that mingle departures and arrivals, endings and beginnings. The final sentences of the paragraph return to Davis, still ascendant: "The senator from Mississippi rose. It was high noon. The occasion was momentous and expected; the galleries were crowded, hoop-skirted ladies and men in broadcloth come to hear him say farewell. He was going home" (*CW* I.3). Two paragraphs later, Davis is on his feet; Foote's history of the war has begun; and the narrative, in a tone that mingles sorrow with expectancy, is under way.

The mixture of emotions ascribed to Davis was also appropriate, it turns out, for the author of the volume. The move into formal narrative history was a new departure for Foote. He began *The Civil War* in 1954 after a dazzling start as a writer of fiction—four novels and one collection of stories published in the five years following the end of World War II. After *Shiloh* appeared in 1952, Foote was ready to plunge straightaway into the next stage of his career; his apprenticeship was over, and the time had come to tackle "the big one" (*Correspondence* 57), the novel by which he would write his way to greatness, a projected tour de force to be called *Two Gates to the City.* Yet, with the end of his second marriage, and with the difficulties he experienced trying to get *Two Gates* under way, Foote was undergoing in 1953–54 a period of intense self-doubt. Questioning his future as a novelist, he decided to accept an offer by Bennett Cerf of Random House to write a "short history" of the Civil War, something "about 200,000 words long" (*Conversations* 201). Having accepted the challenge, he set about the task in his usual fashion by developing an extensive outline for the plot—he has stated elsewhere that the narrative of the war was "a gigantic exercise in the handling of plot" (*Conversations* 119). Foote recounts the transformation of the project from a stopgap between novels to a Gibbon-like epic:

> [I]t started off to be a short history of the Civil War. Random House wanted me to do it and Bennett Cerf was happy about it and I signed a contract for a short history of the Civil War. It was going to be about 200,000 words, not a long book at all. But I hadn't any more than started before I saw I wasn't the one to write any short history of the Civil War; just a summary of what happened didn't interest me. But I was enormously interested in the whole thing. So, about the time I got started—in fact, I hadn't done much more than block out what I call the plot. . . . I saw it was going to take a lot more space than that. My editor at Random House then was Robert Linscott, a very nice man, and I wrote him and told him I'd like to go spread-eagle, whole-hog on the thing. It must have been a terrible shock to him, but he saw Cerf and whoever else he had to see and made his recommendations; they considered it, I suppose—I never heard any of that; he just wrote back and said, "Go ahead." So I did. What was really upsetting to them, this was supposed to be the first volume in an historical series they were going to do: one on the Civil War, one on the Revolution, and so forth. This one turned into a gigantic trilogy, so they didn't try any more. (*Conversations* 170)

It hardly seems an accident, then, that the project replacing his magnum opus begins with a farewell to the old and an embrace of the new and is resonant with suitably conflicted emotions. The palpable sense of relief evident in letters to Walker Percy after Foote began work on *The Civil War* suggests that he sat down to write with much the same sense of release with which Jefferson Davis rose to the call for action. In relinquishing the novel, though, Foote was gaining much: a fresh canvas, a stellar cast of characters, and an epic subject suited to his maturing artistic vision.

This pivotal juncture in Foote's career was the climax of a series of changes for the thirty-seven-year-old novelist. He had recently settled in Memphis—unofficial capital of the Mississippi Delta (according to David Cohn)—after moving north from his hometown of Greenville, Mississippi. The year 1954 marked the publication of *Jordan County*, a collection of stories (or historical moments) in reverse chronological order that charts pivotal aspects of his fictional Delta county. *Jordan County*, in this broad historical sense, is the culmination of Foote's vision of the major influences on his southern heritage. In a narrower sense, the book is a farewell to the idea of the novel, combining as it does older material and some parts of the stalled *Two Gates to the City*. The collection seemed to mark the end of his role as southern novelist and the beginning of his life as a Civil War "narrative historian" ("Art" 56). Instead, Foote fused the techniques of the former with the disciplines of the latter to create a narrative masterpiece.

Foote, Greenville, and the Percys

Foote's beginnings as a writer, his "quality of vision," are intimately connected to the ambience and attitudes of his home state of Mississippi. His experience growing up in Greenville and in the South, he suggests, "means a great deal to me. It means that I have been in touch with the grass roots of American life" (*Conversations* 40). The southern heritage is a unique kind of American experience, as Foote takes pains to point out: "Southerners who are at all aware of their history—and even if they aren't it's part of their heritage—are among the people on earth who know best what defeat is, and it has a great deal to do with the way we see the world. We are also thoroughly familiar with injustice, which can be recognized at a hundred yards from our treatment of the blacks over the century, so that a lot of American ideals are bound to sound pretty absurd to an observant Southerner who has been in touch with the underside of the American character" (*Conversations* 177). This sense of duality extends, as well, to Foote's conception of his particular place—the small town of Greenville. In response to an interviewer's question, Foote once noted that "[s]mall town America in 1910 is still my notion of the happiest time on earth," and yet it is also a time "when men stood and looked in both directions" (*Conversations* 92), toward the past with nostalgia and regret and toward the future with fear and excitement. Given that Foote was born in 1916, and that he and his mother only permanently settled in Greenville after his father's early death in 1922, when Foote was six years of age, his comment about small-town America in 1910 is itself an intriguing imaginative projection. The point, though, is that Foote's worldview is composed of equal parts of his southern heritage and his well-developed sense of modernist skepticism.

In many respects, Greenville in 1910—the "Athens of the Delta"—was a progressive southern town of about fourteen thousand inhabitants (over half of whom were African Americans). In many ways, Jay Tolson remarks, the town's spirit was a result of the influence of men such as LeRoy Percy and his son William Alexander Percy: "Greenville became a pocket of enlightenment," Tolson suggests. "One striking instance of this was the remarkable tolerance of minorities, particularly of Jews" (36). During the first two decades of the twentieth century, the town was noted for its resistance to the racist politics of the revived Ku Klux Klan. Greenville also boasted a vibrant artistic and cultural community. A strongly supported educational system—at least for whites—contributed to the town's "emergence as the Delta's . . . cultural Mecca" (Tolson 67). Greenville, Foote readily acknowledges, "fit the stereotypes in some fairly superficial ways and departed from them in the most important ways" (*Conversations* 219–20). While the town was, to an extent, a "great melting pot" (*Conversations* 36) of different racial and cultural influences, and more tolerant to difference than the southern norm at the time, it was no social or racial utopia. In the post–World War I years, Greenville's virtues, "its tight sense of community, the supportiveness and tolerance among its citizens," were being tested (Tolson 74). The increasing population of poor whites, together with a rise in fundamentalism and resentment of the cheap labor pool embodied by the blacks, all challenged the stability (that is, the paternalistic hierarchy) of the place. Foote's mixed sentiments about the nature of southernness and modernity, then, are caught up in the nature of the setting of his formative experiences, a nexus of love and loss.

While his personal beginnings in Greenville were less those of a scion and more those of a waif, Foote's family heritage can be traced back through a plantation-owning grandfather (Huger Lee Foote) to a great-grandfather (Hezekiah William Foote) from Macon, Mississippi, who fought at the Battle of Shiloh. Foote's father, Shelby Dade Foote Sr., was a dilettantish planter's son who turned himself around after assuming the responsibilities of marriage and family with Lillian Rosenstock. The writer's maternal heritage—his mother's father was a Viennese Jew of somewhat mysterious origins who married a planter's daughter—is the source, Foote speculates, of his aptitude for language and interest in the arts. Shelby Foote Sr.'s reformed lifestyle, though, was tragically short-lived when he died of blood poisoning in Mobile, Alabama, in 1922. The newly widowed Lillian Foote decided to return to Greenville with her son.

Tolson draws an evocative portrait (circa 1930) of the young Shelby Foote in *Pilgrim in the Ruins: A Life of Walker Percy* (1994). At the time, Will Percy was lining up some teenage companions for his soon-to-arrive "kinsmen"—his newly fatherless young cousins, Walker, LeRoy, and Phinizy:

> Shelby would not have been the first choice of many Greenvillians. He put off many people with his manner—brash, cocky, sometimes rude. The consensus in town was that his mother and aunt had spoiled him, and there was doubtless some truth to the charge. An only child, he was strikingly handsome, with a shock of dark hair and deeply set eyes, and his easy self-assurance must have struck many adults as insufferable vanity. But Will had good reasons to think that Shelby would make a good companion for his cousins. He was an intelligent boy, for one thing, quick and clever. Though not prematurely bookish, he was certainly alive to the possibilities of good literature. Will was drawn to a boy with such a fine and promising mind. (83)

Foote fulfilled Will Percy's expectations beyond all measure—he became a friend to all the Percy boys and enjoyed a particularly close and lasting friendship with the eldest, Walker. Around about this time, Lillian Foote also contributed one of the more significant influences to her son's future career. On his seventeenth birthday, she presented him with a copy of Marcel Proust's *A la recherche du temps perdu* (1913–1927), and, Foote says, "That's what, if anything, made me a writer. The other strong influence was the Percy family" (*Conversations* 157).

The Percy family and the cultural and political history of Greenville are inextricably linked. The influence of both on Foote's development as a writer cannot be overstated. In particular, William Alexander Percy was a figure with whom to be reckoned. He represented a prominent family with considerable local history; he was a planter, a lawyer, a war hero, and an adoptive father to his three orphaned cousins; he was also a published poet and, later, the author of a much lauded memoir. Will Percy was an important role model for both Walker Percy and Shelby Foote. The Percy household, Foote suggests, provided "my principal connection with a literary home" (*Conversations* 78). In time, the younger men would come to disagree with the aesthetics (chiefly Romantic) and political values (paternalistic and conservative) that Will Percy held dear; however, both men freely acknowledge the significance of his influence. "[H]e was something quite rare," Foote says: "he was a very good teacher . . . by example" (*Conversations* 158). In his introduction to the 1973 edition of Will Percy's memoir, *Lanterns on the Levee: Recollections of a Planter's Son* (1941), Walker Percy remarks that "he was more than a teacher. What he was to me was a fixed point in a confusing world. This is not to say I always took him for my true north and set my course accordingly. I did not. . . . But even when I did not follow him, it was usually in *relation* to him, whether with him or against him, that I defined myself and my own direction" (xi). Foote echoes these sentiments: "*Lanterns on the Levee* is a beautiful book in many ways. . . . It is, however, a plea for and a summation of the conservative position, and as such, it's not hard to discredit it. Many of the evils that I grew up with are defended in that position. The most persuasive thing about it is his gentleness, his honesty, and his fairness. I don't mean to shortchange any of those qualities in him" (*Conversations* 165). Bertram Wyatt-Brown's investigations come to the same conclusions about Will Percy: "Unpretentious and self-effacing, he exercised an extraordinary influence upon those around him" (192). Percy's attitudes of paternalism and noblesse oblige are represented in his memoir and similar documents such as David Cohn's *God Shakes Creation* (1935). What these memoirs reflect is the milieu of Foote's formative years, the attitudes of his most-immediate literary models, and the world against which he would define his own vision and values.

As a man and a writer, Will Percy was a powerful influence on those who grew up with his example before them (even if the result precipitated a movement toward positions antithetical to his). In his "commitment to duty and self-control" (Tolson 87), Percy embodied a Victorian moral code supported by the virtues of a personal adherence to the Stoic philosophy of Marcus Aurelius. As Wyatt-Brown notes, Percy "claimed that he would not equip the boys with obsolete instructions for following the code of medieval knights. Yet he came very close to doing exactly that—in the Victorian interpretation of that code—under the rubrics of rectitude, honor, justice, and truth" (293). Percy maintained these attitudes as a personal credo despite his pessimism about the society that emerged after the First World War. Commenting on Percy's reaction to the horror of the trenches, Wyatt-Brown points out: "Thereafter Will Percy spoke the language of honor in Victorian innocence no more. When he invoked the old precepts it was to complain that while he would remain faithful to the ethic, his was a dying cause. . . . his reaction to the great, shattering conflict of his life was to claim for the prewar years a legendary grandeur, of moral principle and uprightness to contrast against the tawdry present" (216). Biographical material about Percy and evidence in his own writing suggest his personal division between a yearning for the kind of moral certainty and ability to act that he identified with his father—LeRoy, the archetype of the planter-aristocrat-hero—and his despair of finding such an ideal in himself or in his world. The sort of moral quandary that Percy symbolized becomes a major theme in Foote's work and the condition—to a greater or lesser extent—of some of his most intriguing characters, who are caught between the opposing values of alienation and responsibility.

In the face of his sense of the meaninglessness of modern life and the decline in values, Will Percy set his stoicism, his romantic idealism, and his conservatism. "The two central tenets of his philosophy of life" reflected in his memoir were, according to Tolson, the basically solitary nature of human existence and the idealization of blacks (as "noble savages" or "innocents" who lived solely in the present). While he refused to ignore his responsibilities and exhibited considerable empathy for the alienated and oppressed, Percy's attitudes were not free of paternalism. As Wyatt-Brown points out: "Like Thomas Jefferson and many other intellectuals throughout Southern history, he could not examine the subject without first complaining how Southern whites suffered both morally and emotionally from the heavy yoke of superiority that God in His wisdom had thrust upon their reluctant shoulders" (265). He could not, in a sense, escape his heritage. *Lanterns on the Levee,* the memoir that Wyatt-Brown sees as a southern counterpart to Henry Adams's *Education* (1907), reveals all of Percy's contradictions and his uneasy situation in a limbo between inherited values and modern pressures. Percy's work represents a divide between the old and new orders; his sensibility was, essentially, Romantic, idealistic, and directed toward the virtues of a southern past, yet his experience was modern, and this bred a certain skepticism and disillusionment. As Tolson suggests, the pride in southern virtues (coupled with a consciousness that they are past) "would ultimately issue in disillusionment during the 1930s, when writers like Percy realized that the old order was gone for good and that the code of honor could apply to personal conduct alone" (76–77). In this sense, it is interesting to note that Foote, when responding to a question about theme during an interview, identifies this same "basic loneliness of man" ("Art" 66). In a similar parallel, Percy countered his sense of the rootlessness of modernity and the horror of daily life with his commitment to Greenville (Tolson 73), while Foote chooses to center his own fiction on the clash of old and new values in Jordan County.

Reading *Lanterns on the Levee* in conjunction with Percy's poetry, Michael Kreyling sees the author enacting "a constant search for a place to brace himself for action in a post Christian, post heroic, and now 'post southern' world. A constant theme in his writing is the uncertainty of heroic action as a possible, let alone prescribed, response to the disintegration of the world order of the past. He feels outside the pageant of meaning in the past, estranged from the degraded present, forever excluded from the circle of heroes where contingency never undermines the purity of action and where bravery is unmixed with 'the business of being brave'" (154–55). Percy performed an important role in his representation of the "twilight of the old world" (Kreyling 155). He asks, as a poet, a memoirist, and a man, questions about the definition of morality in the new century and the nature of authentic being; he identifies, indeed embodies, issues that would be addressed by both Walker Percy and Foote in their writings. In particular, Foote engages Will Percy's assumptions about the heroic figure of the planter-aristocrat and the idea of honor as a chivalric code and tests these tenets of southern society against the realities of his post–World War II perspective and against philosophical questions about authenticity and action. As well, and perhaps even more importantly, Foote explores Percy's conception of human solitude amid social obligations to family and community—solitude that, Tolson tells us, "could almost be described as a dulcet anticipation of the core idea of existentialism" (65). In their shared ambivalence between the past and the modern world, Will Percy and William Faulkner figure prominently in helping to define the nature of Foote's attitudes toward his southern heritage and the existential dilemmas posed by life in the twentieth century.

The Heritage of the New South

Foote, in an interview, talks about the strong mixture of feelings evoked when he contemplates his relationship to the world of the Mississippi Delta: "The Mississippi Delta was a splendid place to have grown up and I have enormous affection for it which will be with me as long as I live, but that doesn't keep me from seeing the great ills. . . . You grow up in a thing and you're not inclined to see the evil as clearly as you would if you were visiting that place. It seems so much a part and parcel of the life, especially when it contributes to your comfort as it did to mine" (*Conversations* 130). The heritage Foote is articulating, a mixture of affection and rejection, guilt and complacency, is a reflection of his own experience of the South. One hears an echo of the values of Will Percy (paternalistic responsibility, etc.) yet also a recognition of the fundamental need for change—a radicalism that Percy would deplore. Foote's vision of the South, then, is informed by the time of his own mature experience of the place. As he suggests, "I was born during the First World War, spent my adolescence in the Great Depression, and I came of age in the Second World War. Now that is a hell of a thing" (*Conversations* 47). A "hell of a thing," indeed! And a tacit recognition of how his own experience of the South is shaped by the apocalyptic nature of the times.

The South—subject to a "cultural lag" (Gray, *Writing the South* 123) because of its post–Civil War experience and, as a result, manifesting a "terrific compression" (Cobb 310) of cultural progress—exemplifies in vivid form the cultural movement from Victorian precepts to the modernist worldview. Forms of idealism, as Joel Williamson suggests in *William Faulkner and Southern History* (1993), were dominant even in the antebellum period, and while "[t]he experiences of Civil War and Reconstruction certainly dampened Southern idealism[,] . . . clearly in the succeeding decades it was rising again, evolving, and finally flourishing. Indeed, idealism (and a concomitant romanticism) became one of the great tools by which the New South in the turn-of-the-century years levered up the Old South and made it beautiful" (356). Here, Williamson echoes C. Vann Woodward's observation that "[o]ne of the most significant inventions of the New South was the 'Old South'" (*Origins* 154–55). The legend of the Cavalier and the myth of the Lost Cause embodied a locus of security for southerners confronting (or denying, depending on one's perspective) the collapse of the Confederate dream. Their response to the sense of defeat and humiliation, Richard Gray suggests, "was perhaps predictable: defensiveness turned gradually into defiance and a proud determination to tell *their* story, their side of things. And crucial to this was their reinvention of the past in terms that provided them with a moral defence and an emotional refuge: as a Great Good Place, the site of patriarchal virtues, which had effectively been swept away by the barbarian hordes from the North" (*Life* 26). A novel such as Faulkner's *The Sound and the Fury* (1929), characterized by Daniel Singal as a "radioscopy of the Southern Mind" (*William* 135), reflects how the "emergence of the New South created a nostalgically fictional version of the Old South that could thus be both honored and replaced" (Matthews 97). After the Civil War, the myth of the Cavalier tradition of the Old South becomes wedded to the New South creed of progress and the notion of the gentleman as businessman, capitalist, and philanthropist, embodying all the virtues of the Victorian model: optimism, material success, diligence, and practicality (Singal 22). Thus, the New South rests on a central ambivalence brought about by its "aggressive refurbishing" (Matthews 99) of the image of an agrarian utopia run by benevolent planter-aristocrats.

Noting the attractiveness of such ideological constructs, Kreyling reminds us that "[t]he power of directed myth to establish unity where history supplies only contingency was still felt a century and more later . . ." (29). Writers such as Ellen Glasgow, Faulkner, Allen Tate, and the Agrarians all register the difficulties involved in emerging from the "restrictive culture of enforced innocence" (Singal 8) that was the New South legacy. Such mythologizing represents, for C. Hugh Holman, a typically southern "Tory nostalgia for a lost good world" (10). Reinventing the figure of the planter-aristocrat and refurbishing the image of the plantation world helped to keep at bay the psychological reality of the enormous postwar cultural changes. Such concern for controlling and determining the definition of the southern hero, Kreyling remarks, is indicative of a society looking for a "theory of culture and history that transcends contingency" (4). In the context of the Mississippi Delta, the planter-aristocrat fulfilled this projection of a cultural need—that the image rested on a fallacy was beside the point. As Singal explains, the aristocratic image was largely an exercise in wishful thinking. Beneath the veneer of aristocratic civility lurked a fierce and violent frontier mentality: "Believing in their own mythology, [these self-made aristocrats] kept these strong passions hidden from themselves, instead projecting their anxieties onto the supposed violence of their slaves and backwoods neighbors. In the end—as some of their twentieth-century descendants would later perceive—the social volcano they thought they were sitting on may not have been as consequential as the secret volcano that rumbled inside" (20–21). The aristocratic ideal becomes, in effect, a cultural repository for repression and self-deception. Upon closer inspection, John T. Matthews asserts, the development from old to new "turns out to be the disguised, partial reinvigoration of the dominant ideology. The mercantile capitalism of the New South obscures its affinity with the agrarian, slaveholding capitalism of the Old South precisely because it rests on the same foundation of economic and racial exploitation" (97).

Ritchie Devon Watson, in *Yeoman Versus Cavalier: The Old Southwest's Fictional Road to Rebellion* (1993), stresses the reactionary nature of this mythologizing and romanticizing in the South. Rather than an expression of "cultural stability and harmony," it was, both before and after the war, "a fabrication by a culture that felt its very foundations being undermined" (75). The New South culture exhibited characteristics that seem particularly Victorian in its determined defense—on the basis of what Walker Percy calls the "old alliance of Negro and white gentry" (*Signposts* 84)—against the attacks of the "populist barbarians." This defense involved a glorification of the middle-class elite and a denigration of the "rednecks," or lower-class whites, the class associated with violence and irrationality. Similarly, the New South intellectuals supported segregation as a morally justified measure necessary for public order. Ironically, the "progressive" civilizing influence that informed this ideology carried with it the means for perpetuating the social divisions and tensions that a war had been fought to resolve. As Singal suggests, "Although New South thinkers genuinely wanted to 'uplift' the lower class of whites, they remained contemptuous and fearful of them. As for blacks, New South intellectuals regarded them with a mixture of traditional paternalism and Victorian moralism, sympathetic with their plight but preoccupied with preserving a strict separation between civilization and savagery" (32). Foote, as we noted earlier, grew up under this complex equation of paternalism and noblesse oblige. The contradictions of such values constitute the elements of southern society reflected and brought under critical scrutiny in his work.

Dodging the Dixie Special:
The Influence of William Faulkner

Born in Mississippi, and coming to maturity in the late 1930s and early 1940s, an ambitious young novelist such as Foote could not escape living in the shadow of William Faulkner. Indeed, on this subject Foote likes to paraphrase Flannery O'Connor, "who said that when the Dixie Special [Faulkner] is coming down the track everybody's got to get off" (*Conversations* 87). When Foote sat down at his desk in Memphis in 1954 to pen the opening lines of *The Civil War*, he was, in a manner of speaking, doing just that—clearing a new path away from the genre of fiction, without abandoning its techniques, and away from the subject matter of the South, without relinquishing Faulkner's insights into the nature of time and the inescapable presence of the past. Foote said to an interviewer in 1971 that he thought the Southern Renaissance was over, and that Faulkner had "killed it with superiority" (*Conversations* 87). In the light of this feeling, Foote's challenge as a novelist and southern writer following in Faulkner's footsteps was to open up a space in which to demonstrate his own mastery and to complete the process of stylistic individuation he had begun with his fiction. One way to avoid the "Dixie Special" was to approach the past from a new vantage, to apply the innovations and skills of a modern novelist—learned during his apprenticeship as one of the "tribe of Faulkner"—to the writing of formal history, a genre that Faulkner never attempted or (if one counts the essay "Mississippi") that he subverted by fabrication. Foote's new beginning can be seen, in retrospect, as an act of liberation and renewal.

Speaking at a series of informal discussions on Faulkner, published in *The South and Faulkner's Yoknapatawpha: The Actual and the Apocryphal* (1977), Foote observes that, beginning with *Sartoris* (1929), "Faulkner wanted to write about these two sides of his homeland, the aristocrats and the peasants. Well, just as there aren't any peasants, there aren't any aristocrats. I think when he came back to the aristocrats, eventually, he found they had vanished, pretty nearly. He wound up writing about middle class people" (Harrington 50). Foote's comments reflect how Faulkner's work depicts the contradictions of the New South—a situation that Matthews describes as a simultaneous forfeiting and re-avowal of the Old South (99). Foote finds a similar ambivalence in the sentiments expressed by Faulkner in his acceptance speech for the Nobel Prize for literature: "Faulkner

13

warned about writing of the glands, because you would never understand the heart. Mr. Faulkner wrote better about the glands than any writer I know of and most of his bad writing came when he was writing about the heart" (Harrington 41). For Foote, these contradictory impulses became a corrupting influence on Faulkner's work:

> I really think that the Nobel speech is—I'll try not to use ugly words—a misrepresentation of Faulkner's art. I feel that strongly. I do not admire the speech except as a noble statement by a man. . . . I think that in some ways that Faulkner sought in his later work to reinforce what he said in the Nobel speech. I like the Faulkner who believes you are going to get the black jack at the end. I believe the dark diceman is waiting there and he's going to cut you down. I like the Faulkner of *Light in August,* and he is not characterized by the Nobel Prize speech. It seems to me to underrate the thing he did best and to overrate the thing that caused whatever flaws there are in his later work. (Harrington 162–63)

In his succinct way, Foote points out a fundamental aspect of the Faulkner heritage—the attempt to reconcile a deeply felt yearning for an ideal coupled with the despair-inducing knowledge of its absence or failure in the present time.

The "Faulknerian Universe," Joel Williamson observes, constitutes "two connected continuums" (355): one of which "stretches between extremes . . . labeled perfect idealism and perfect realism" (355), and the other in which men live "in a state of nature on one side and in modern society on the other" (358). In both cases, Faulkner's work depicts the give-and-take between "what Is [and] what Ought To Be" (358), with Yoknapatawpha County as the testing ground in which to act out "the drama of man's emergence from nature—from the Garden of Eden—into the modern world" (358). Faulkner's characters, then, negotiate their way between these competing extremes often "off balance and at war within themselves" (359), caught up in what Singal calls, in reference to Thomas Sutpen, a "disabling innocence" (190)—an allegiance to the myth of the Old South totally at odds with the modern economic and cultural reality. Richard Gray, in *Writing the South: Ideas of an American Region* (1997), reads Faulkner's "postage stamp" world in a similar way, referring to the Yoknapatawpha saga as an exploration on Faulkner's part of the "illusion of ownership" (168), both literally and in terms of humanity's relation to the past. Faulkner's ambiguous situation, Gray suggests, is as a "double agent" (171), playing the dual roles of insider and outsider with respect to the southern world and its mythology.

Faulkner's writing depicts southern heritage as, ultimately, a moral and intellectual trap. The nature of this curse, and its effects on the individual psyche, are captured most vividly in the paradoxes surrounding a character such as Quentin Compson (*The Sound and the Fury* and *Absalom, Absalom!*); for him, to perceive and move toward the ideal is to leave this world, yet to acknowledge and live in this world is to suppress many of the spiritual qualities in humanity and, therefore, to doom oneself to chase frantically after an ever-shifting social and material universe. "In his own life," Williamson suggests, "Faulkner knew the paradox intimately, and it runs through the weave of his writings to the very end like some dark and somber thread. For Faulkner virginity symbolized the ideal: the virginity of women, the virginity of men, the virginity of the earth. To possess the woman, the man, the earth was inevitably to violate their purity, to reduce, ruin, and dissolve them" (364). In his depiction of figures such as Colonel Sartoris and Thomas Sutpen, Faulkner registers the problematic heritage of the southern mythology, and the unresolvable ambivalence of his own feelings about the past. This duality leads Singal to include Faulkner in a group he calls the "intellectuals of transition," those who "remained attached to the South's traditional mythology even as they acted to vitiate it" (112). These writers—George Cotkin calls a similar group "reluctant modernists" (xi)—reflect what Lewis Simpson refers to as the "culture of memory" (242) central to the southern experience, where "[t]he pathetic figure of the defeated South, maintaining the historic high tone—that is to say, the memorial high tone—against historical fate, may be taken as the quintessential image of the restraint imposed by the piety of memory on the capacity of the southern literary and artistic psyche to comprehend historical reality" (*Brazen* 237). By challenging this southern "piety of memory," and the transitional or reluctant nature of Faulkner's or Percy's modernism, Foote transforms their ambivalence into a fully modernist aesthetic and an ironic and self-conscious historiography.

As a writer at this transitional point, Faulkner sets his modernist exploration of human consciousness, with its potential for evil, against the idealizing tendencies of the New South tradition. "Faulkner's literary project," Gray remarks, "grew out of the tension between the tradition of old tales and talking he took from his region and the disruptive techniques of modernism: just as his historical project (in so far as the two can be distinguished) issued out of his involvement with a traditional society in transit" (*Life* 78). What results is Faulkner's vision of the South as self-destructively tied to a chimera of its own creation (Singal 154). A novel such as *Absalom, Absalom!* illustrates how the Cavalier ideal acted as a lure and a goad when "imposed on a raw southwestern social structure just emerging from the frontier, a society that one would have thought thoroughly impervious to aristocratic ideals" (Watson 42–43). Sutpen is ensnared by this idealized version of the past, and his blind allegiance to the myth dooms both him and his offspring. Indeed, Faulkner's novel is populated by characters who feel incomplete, and whose urges for wholeness or absolutes lead to catastrophe. As Singal notes, "the portrait of antebellum life revealed in *Absalom, Absalom!* . . . constitutes a refutation, almost a parody, of the familiar conception of the South as a stable, well-structured organic society" (193). In the attitudes of the two generations of storyteller-historians found in the novel (Rosa Coldfield and Mr. Compson and Shreve and Quentin, respectively), Faulkner displays the conflicting worldviews of nineteenth-century fatalism and twentieth-century relativism. Indeed, in later novels (those that Foote suggests attempt to conform to the dictates of the sentiments of the Nobel speech), Faulkner returns to a less critical depiction of the Sartoris ideal; in effect, he retreats to the comforting nineteenth-century mythology of the chivalric code and aristocratic ideal that, while challenged and found wanting, proved "too comforting for him ever to let go" (Singal 197).

The relationship of Foote's work to this dichotomy between civilization and savagery, the tension between a yearning for the Cavalier ideal and the acknowledgment of the unpalatable realities of southern society, helps to establish his unique position as a southern novelist writing on the eve of the Second Reconstruction. Gone is the "ideological certainty" that informed the perspective of Douglas Southall Freeman in his celebrated biography of Robert E. Lee, a work that in Michael Kreyling's view depicts Lee as a man who "from within the capsule of heroic selfhood controlled every facet of his life . . . abolish[ing] ambiguity and contingency" (106). Gone is the world of Victorian morality and Stoic virtue articulated and exemplified by William Alexander Percy; what is left is the "extraneous man" (Kreyling 162), whose disillusioned reaction to the present was to idealize the past (Wyatt-Brown 216). Gone, too, is the tortured ambivalence of Faulkner, whose examination of "the human heart in conflict with itself" found ample material in the "pathological identity" (Singal, *William* 200) inherited by

twentieth-century southerners. Foote, who asserts that he is "more inter-
ested in sociology" (*Conversations* 49) than Faulkner was, also distances
himself from the conservative idealism of Allen Tate (and like-minded
Agrarians), who viewed the Old South as a genuinely aristocratic society
and advocated a return to its values as a defense against the debasements
of the modern industrial world. Where the speaker in Tate's famous "Ode
to the Confederate Dead" (1937) stands wistfully outside the cemetery
wall, yearning for a connection to the heroic dead to offset the encroachments of the modern world, Foote's work rejects such nostalgic or sentimental notions about the matter of the South.

For writers such as Robert Penn Warren and Foote, the Faulknerian
heritage of tormented dualism between the ideal and the real, the ambivalence of the reluctant modernists, is largely over. Authors such as Warren,
Singal suggests, started by assuming "that man was the human animal,
that the universe was inherently irrational, that morality was embedded in
history and not in immutable natural laws" (261). Indeed, as Mark G.
Malvasi points out in *The Unregenerate South: The Agrarian Thought of
John Crowe Ransom, Allen Tate, Donald Davidson* (1997):

> Unlike Ransom, Tate, and Davidson, Warren concluded that to
> overcome the spiritual anarchy of the twentieth century, modern
> men had to endure it alone. They could not draw a sense of iden-
> tity, value, and meaning from the society in which they lived, for,
> properly speaking, the social bonds that had once provided such
> cohesion no longer existed. Rather, modern men, severed from the
> past and the future, could only create a place, a purpose, and an
> identity for themselves in the present. (11–12)

Similar skepticism about traditional southern mythologies and "Hollywood" Christianity is reflected in Foote's novels and correspondence. In a
letter to Walker Percy, Foote outlines these sentiments:

> How in God's name can Faith, no matter how desirable, be possi-
> ble in this day? It seems to me to have gone out of existence, or
> even the possibility of existence, with the automobile and Arrow
> collars. God painted himself back into a corner and inconsider-
> ately disappeared. It's inconceivable that he could have the
> slightest interest in what's going on on this miserable cinder. If he

had, he wouldnt stay his hand; or else he'd help. What I do is I deny him. I put my faith in the human virtues, which at the worst are merely improbable, not impossible. I see God as History—the example he set while he was with us. (Letters, June 18, 1959)

As explorers of both history and consciousness, freed from the ambivalence of the earlier generations, Warren and Foote tend to reject the dominant tropes of southern writing. As C. Vann Woodward suggests of Warren in a comment that could apply equally well to Foote, particularly in the light of his use of Stephen Crane and Ernest Hemingway in his history: "he was somewhat closer to Joseph Conrad that to William Faulkner. Warren was a master of the ironic and the oxymoronic. He is constantly reminding us of the contrast between the intent and the result of human motives and plans, between expectation and the outcome" (284). When Singal suggests, however, that these "fully Modernist southern writer[s]" (259) gained freedom by narrowing their focus in an "effort to achieve empirical honesty" (Singal 262), Foote proves the exception. *The Civil War: A Narrative* stands as a refutation of Singal's assertion that "[m]inute detail frequently absorbed them, while grand visions typically eluded them" (Singal 262). In an anecdote that serves to highlight the uniqueness of Foote's achievement, L. Hugh Moore Jr. says that "At the Fugitives' reunion in Nashville in 1956 a recurring question was why, with all their promise, none of the group had attempted an epic, the creation of a myth for society, the task Homer performed for the Greeks" (21). Foote's articulation of that grand vision in his historical narrative, begun two years before the reunion, suggests that the "disabling innocence" bequeathed by the New South that hindered this earlier generation was now at an end. The cycle that started as the literary reaction to Reconstruction was now complete, and the beginning of a new vision for southern writing was under way.

Taken all together, Foote's fiction explores the period immediately after the first Reconstruction (*Tournament* and much of *Jordan County*), through the New South and the modern era (*Follow Me Down* and *Love in a Dry Season*), culminating in events on the eve of the Second Reconstruction, the beginning of the Civil Rights movement (*September September*). While his fiction registers the effects of the Civil War on the South and the century-long aftershocks of that cultural trauma, his history seeks, from a centenary perspective, to move past a southern parochialism toward a national and humanistic vision of the war. *The Civil War* revisits the origins of the Lost

Cause itself, the source of the mythologizing of the New South and the culture of memory it inaugurated. Foote turns from the regional preoccupation with the repercussions of the war to a narrative engagement with the whole matter of the war. His writing amounts to an act of literary reconstruction, an attempt to heal the divided southern consciousness (so tellingly outlined in W. J. Cash's seminal 1941 *The Mind of the South*) and to reconcile the parochial northern and southern versions of the conflict. In this respect, Foote's corpus of work provides a fitting conclusion to the era of southern modernism dominated by Faulkner's writing. It is appropriate, then, that the writers who follow Foote (e.g., Walker Percy, John Barth, Cormac McCarthy) reject or parody specifically southern cultural assumptions. Current critical writing about the region also generally accepts the end of a uniquely southern literary perspective. That both these developments coincide with the completion of Foote's treatment of the Civil War suggests a symmetry that this classically oriented writer would fully appreciate.

Foote as an Ironic Historian

From *Tournament* on, Foote's aesthetic of limitation—sharply delineated narrative structures containing multiple and restricted points of view—is increasingly pronounced in his fiction and plays an important role in his approach in *The Civil War*. Faulkner, in *Absalom, Absalom!*, subtly implicates the reader in the historiographical complications involved in trying to fix the events of the Sutpen household. Even while giving credence to Quentin and Shreve's conclusions, the reader, in the end, is left suspended in a web of speculation, conjecture, and uncertainty. Foote's approach to writing the past, on the other hand, contains this modernist relativity within a clearly demarcated aesthetic structure. Commenting on a single paragraph describing the moment of Lincoln's assassination in Foote's history, Carl E. Rollyson Jr., in *Uses of the Past in the Novels of William Faulkner* (1984), suggests that Foote "perhaps comes as close as possible in a work of formal history, based on a copious assortment of primary and secondary sources, to Faulkner's dramatization of the past" (179). Foote's paragraph in question deftly situates his reader as a member of the audience at Ford's Theatre at the start of that fateful evening's performance of *Our American Cousin:*

Then it came, a half-muffled explosion, somewhere between a
boom and a thump, loud but by no means so loud as it sounded in
the theater, then a boil and bulge of bluish smoke in the presidential box, an exhalation as of brimstone from the curtained mouth,
and a man coming out through the bank and swirl of it, white-faced
and dark-haired in a black sack suit and riding boots, eyes aglitter,
brandishing a knife. He mounted the ledge, presented his back to
the rows of people seated below, and let himself down by the hand-
rail for the ten-foot drop to the stage. Falling he turned, and as he
did so caught the spur of his right boot in the folds of a flag draped
over the lower front of the high box. It ripped but offered enough
resistance to bring all the weight of his fall on his left leg, which
buckled and pitched him forward onto his hands. He rose, thrust
the knife overhead in a broad theatrical gesture, and addressed the
outward darkness of the pit. "Sic semper tyrannis," he said in a
voice so low and projected with so little clarity that few recognized
the state motto of Virginia or could later agree that he had spoken
in Latin. "Revenge for the South!" or "The South is avenged!" some
thought they heard him cry, while others said that he simply mut-
tered "Freedom." In any case he then turned again, hobbled left
across the stage past the lone actor standing astonished in its center, and vanished into the wings. (*CW* III.980)

Rollyson examines the minutiae of this paragraph to reinforce his thesis
that Foote's method illustrates Faulkner's belief that narrative alone could
"bridge the gap between facts and truth" (177) by demonstrating the mul-
tiplicity of possible truths. Rollyson continues:

The tension in this scene between what is known and not known is
reminiscent of *Absalom, Absalom!*. Did Booth "cry" or did he "mut-
ter"? And what exactly did he say? Phrases like "somewhere
between" and "but by no means so loud as" convey the subtle shifting between precise and not so precise assessments of atmosphere,
which verges on staged melodrama. . . . The momentousness and
inevitability of the assassination have reached such a pitch of
expectation in Foote's narrative that he has only to say "then it
came," and to carry us in a long sweeping sentence a third of the
way into the paragraph, the deed already done as swiftly as in real-

ity. Sentence by sentence there is a fine blend of immediacy and retrospection, as there always is in the best of Faulkner. The alliteration and onomatopoeic effects are balanced by the language of surmise. Image and metaphor are countered by supposition and analogy. Foote conjectures "an exhalation as of brimstone from the curtained mouth," which is a kind of bridging phrase between fact and fiction, for his "as of" is akin to Faulkner's "as if." As in Faulkner, the narrative is cumulative, basing itself on authorities but breathing with its own life, its own management of the past, sustained by the incremental nature of its tropes. (179–80)

Rollyson's identification of the studied ambiguity of Foote's presentation is convincing. Yet, this Faulknerian sense of the past works because of the balance Foote establishes between the contingencies of immediate experience and the larger patterns, the overt aesthetic ordering, in the narrative as a whole. As he remarked once to Walker Percy: "I don't think I'll ever be satisfied to represent vagueness by being vague, or irrational to represent the un-understandable complexity" (Letters, September 21, 1951).

Within the clearly defined limits of his narrative frameworks, and the restrictions imposed on him by historical documentation and factual material, Foote stresses the Faulknerian sense of the past as an absent presence, paradoxically both fixed and malleable at once. Foote's "dramatization of the past" (Rollyson 179) takes on a subtlety in *The Civil War* because it works within our expectations of objectivity in the domain of historical writing; it offers both "the facts" and the fact of Foote's reanimation. Foote's work continues to acknowledge his debt to Faulkner and to Proust; yet the style and structure of his narrative, as well as its philosophical orientation, remain distinct. Foote extends literary technique into formal historical narrative and takes his modernist sensibility into the world of "fact." He manifests little of Faulkner's ambivalence with respect to the New South mythologizing. What haunted and ultimately defeated the fictional historians Quentin and Shreve (and, perhaps, Faulkner himself)—the unbridgeable chasm between the ideal and the real, between the southern past and the modern present—is subordinated to Foote's acceptance of the paradox of reduction and enlargement that is narrative art. By deliberately highlighting the architectonics of his form and the consciously limited palette of symbols and images he employs, Foote underscores the artifice of narrative, whether it be historical or fictional. This aesthetic of limitations that Foote creates so clearly in his fictions, when practiced in relation to the factual materials of historical writing, allows him the fullest exercise of that sympathetic imagination integral to the creation of history as art.

On the basis of the fluidity and indeterminacy of the past in novels such as *Absalom, Absalom!*, Rollyson remarks that history for Faulkner was "a permanently unsettling phenomenon" (10). While particularly appropriate given Faulkner's ambivalence about the South and his conception of the nature of time, Rollyson's statement also applies to current discussions of the role and function of narrative in history. In recent decades, the discipline of history has become increasingly aware of its "epistemological fragility" (Jenkins, *Re-Thinking* 11). The collapse of the scientific absolute, following modernist attacks on conventional moral verities and the acceptance of "the linguistic turn" that suggests all knowledge is, at base, a form of discourse, has unsettled the foundations of the traditional thinking and practice of history. As the authors of *Telling the Truth about History* suggest, "given the issues about truth and relativism that have been raised late in this century, historians cannot pretend that it is business as usual. It is essential to rethink the understanding of truth and objectivity" (194). The practitioners of historical study must confront the Faulknerian ambivalence of their assumptions about historical representation: "Since the scientific enterprise involved drawing a fixed boundary between the objective reality of things-as-they-are and the subjective realm of things-as-we-would-like-them-to-be, historians were loath to explore the subjective component of history-writing. Fact had to be distinguished from opinion, documentary evidence from interpretation. In this intellectual milieu of the nineteenth and early twentieth centuries, the historian's practice of merging the two remained in a conceptual limbo, undiscussed and unacknowledged" (Appleby, Hunt, and Jacob 242–43). Where conventionally three components were assumed in a historical account, "the story, the historian and the event," Peter Murray, writing in *Companion to Historiography*, now suggests we can assume only two, "the historian and the story" (855). Current critical thinking, led by theorists such as Hayden White (in *Tropics of Discourse: Essays in Cultural Criticism* and *The Content of the Form: Narrative Discourse and Historical Representation*, 1978), has forced an acknowledgment that historical narratives are "what they most manifestly are: verbal fictions" (*Tropics* 82). History as the story of past truths is now history as a form of discourse, and historiography "the attempted imposition of meaningful form onto a meaningless past" (Jenkins, *On "What Is History?"* 137). Such attempts are not measured by their objective vision of the past (an impossible task) but by the validity of their aesthetic form (how much they succeed in "imposing upon the chaos of the world a momentary form" [*Tropics* 44]). This being the case, the imagination and skill of the writer play an increasingly significant role; note how White's definition of historical writing echoes Wallace Stevens's remark on the function of poems as "necessary fictions" and how his statement on the role of form is analogous to Robert Frost's saying that poetry is a "momentary stay against confusion."

The reassessment of the nature of historical writing focuses on narrative; as Appleby, Hunt, and Jacob suggest, "'narrative' has become one of the charged code words of the current struggles over history" (231). Narrative as the nexus of such controversy is fitting because it remains "the only literary device available which will reflect the past's time structure" (Murray, "The Historical Narrative" 851) and so retain the power to "mimic the unfolding of reality" (Fulford 15). Yet, contemporary historical narratives must now incorporate some acknowledgment that time itself may be an illusion—a component of the textuality of human discourse. Discussing the necessarily artificial nature of narratives and explaining the central role that unstated or implicit generalizations play in their construction, Murray outlines how the "Covering Law Model" represents the most minimal structure in the narrative framework. This model contains three propositions: one general and two particular propositions that stand in a causal relation by virtue of the generalization (a Delta image appropriate for Foote). The model, Murray writes, "establishes the historical element in all explanations and it is this fact which enables us to use this arrangement as the minimum standard of explanation in history and as the model for the construction of narratives. This model of explanation does justice to the arrow of time because it reflects the temporal sequence of the explaining and explained facts" (859). The sequence of facts in the narrative, and the criteria for deciding which facts are admitted, are determined by the generalizations employed. Such generalizations exist at the root of all narratives but are not necessarily stated—one can see them manifest at a variety of levels (e.g., genre). The emplotment—White's term—of facts in a narrative framework is what creates in historical writing "an appearance of necessity and predictability" (Murray 861). The study of history, then, is merging with what were previously thought strictly literary concerns. The focus of postmodernist history, Appleby, Hunt, and Jacob remark, is "self-reflexivity and . . . problems of literary construction: how does the historian as author construct his or her text, how is the illusion of authenticity produced, what creates a sense of truthfulness to the facts and a warranty of closeness to past reality (or the 'truth-effect' as it is sometimes called)? The implication is that the historian does not in fact capture the past in faithful fashion but rather, like the novelist, gives the appearance of doing so" (227).

The prevailing concern with the literary dimension of historical writing bespeaks a surrender of the conventional authority of the historian; yet, it also raises new possibilities about how historians explore and represent the past. Dominick LaCapra, commenting on the necessity for integrating a critical consciousness of the textuality of historical writing into its production, suggests that such innovations and experiments have "rehabilitated [narrative] as a way of representing the past" (118). In fact, he goes on to suggest that "the most telling question posed by the novel to historiography may be whether contemporary historical writing can learn something of a self-critical nature from a mode of discourse it has often tried to use or to explain in overly reductive fashion" (132). By concentrating on the literary nature of historical production, historians manifest a very relevant interest in the techniques and structural devices of the novelist. "In point of fact," Hayden White suggests, "history—the real world as it evolves in time—is made sense of in the same way that the poet or novelist tries to make sense of it, i.e., by endowing what originally appears to be problematical and mysterious with the aspect of a recognizable, because it is familiar, form. It does not matter whether the world is conceived to be real or only imagined; the manner of making sense of it is the same" (98). This is a point Foote has maintained throughout his career: "There is no reason why the historian should not be an artist, too; and all art is mutual. . . . [The historian] can learn even from a writer of fiction, who is nothing if he is not an artist in pursuit of truth" ("Novelist's" 224). Articles such as Peter Burke's "History of Events and the Revival of Narrative" demonstrate the increased attention of historical writers to literary techniques and narrative strategies: "[M]any scholars now think that historical writing has also been impoverished by the abandonment of narrative, and a search is under way for new forms of narrative which will be appropriate to the new stories historians would like to tell. . . . If they are looking for models of narratives which juxtapose the structures of ordinary life to extraordinary events, and the view from below to the view from above, historians might be well advised to turn to twentieth-century fiction . . ." (245). Arguing that historians should embrace techniques such as heteroglossia, self-reflexive narration, and Clifford Geertz's "thick description,"

Burke suggests that such attention to matters of narrative technique may "help historians in their difficult task of revealing the relationship between events and structures and presenting multiple viewpoints. Developments of this kind, if they continue, may have a claim to be regarded as no mere 'revival' of narrative . . . but as a form of regeneration" (246). White goes further: "In my view, history as a discipline is in bad shape today because it has lost sight of its origins in the literary imagination. In the interest of *appearing* scientific and objective, it has repressed and denied to itself its own greatest source of strength and renewal" (*Tropics* 99). Foote, writing history with the techniques and from the perspective of the novelist, finds himself—somewhat ironically, given the abiding academic distrust of "amateurs"—in the forefront of current scholarly fashion.

Seeking to provide a workable methodology for contemporary historians by striking a balance between the polarities of nihilistic postmodernism and discredited historicism, Appleby, Hunt, and Jacob offer what they call "practical realism" (248). These historians deny a belief in the "myth of correspondence" (247), admitting they exist in a contingent world, yet refuse finally to surrender history utterly to fiction: "The historian is someone who reconstructs a past pieced together from records left by the past, which should not be dismissed as a mere discourse on other discourses" (250). In novels such as *Follow Me Down* and *Shiloh*, Foote's narratives suggest the multifaceted nature of historical "truth" and the inevitable ironies generated by the juxtaposition of limited individual perspectives in the assumed present. In *The Civil War*, he includes a Faulknerian sense of contingency and indeterminacy within a self-conscious aesthetic narrative structure. Foote's work, in both his chosen genres, is "practical realism." His assertion of the potential of limitation as a fundamental aesthetic principle is a definition of the artist's role that corresponds to C. Vann Woodward's identification of the southern writer's ironic stance toward history. In a seminal essay, "The Irony of Southern History," Woodward develops the regional implications of a thesis advocated by Reinhold Niebuhr in his *The Irony of American History* (1952):

> Yet the ironic interpretation of history is rare and difficult. In the nature of things the participants in an ironic situation are rarely conscious of the irony, else they would not become its victims. Awareness must ordinarily be contributed by an observer, a nonparticipant, and the observer must have an unusual combination

of detachment and sympathy. He must be able to appreciate both elements in the incongruity that go to make up the ironic situation, both the virtue and the vice to which pretensions of virtue lead. He must not be so hostile as to deny the element of virtue or strength on one side nor so sympathetic as to ignore the vanity and weakness to which the virtue and strength have contributed. Obviously, the qualifications of the ironic historian are pretty hard to come by. (Woodward, *The Burden of Southern History* 193–94)

Although Woodward does not refer to him specifically, Foote certainly deserves such an accolade. His qualifications as ironic historian include his skeptical distance from the mythologized South and the idealized planter-aristocrat; his awareness of, and commentary on, the attractions and dangers of the observer's role; his status as a keen and sympathetic student of human nature and the egocentric predicament; his investigations, following Proust and Faulkner, into the nature of memory and time; and, finally, his mastery of the techniques of the novelist and his consummate skill in the use of paradox and counterpoint. In short, he deserves it by virtue of the quality of his "quality of vision."

Foote is, as Walter Sullivan suggests, a Faulknerian with a difference: "[Foote's] is fiction on a grand scale . . . reminiscent of Faulkner. What makes [Foote's works] different is the tightness of [their] structure" and their dependence on a "philosophical foundation . . . older and better-established than any Southern code" (378–79). Of course, Foote reveals his southern heritage in his choice of his subject matter and in his preoccupation with the past as absent presence. Yet, in contrast to Faulkner's South, where cultural myths are continually negotiating between the polarities of idealism and realism, Foote's exploration of the past is based on the assumption that necessary closure can be achieved and that a conditional sense of the past can be salvaged, but only through the ordering agency of an artist-narrator. We can engage the past, that is, only when it is brought to life through the exercise of an artistic imagination. "History," Appleby, Hunt, and Joyce explain, "fulfills a fundamental human need by reconstituting memory. Memory sustains consciousness of living in the stream of time, and the *amour propre* of human beings cries out for the knowledge of their place in that stream. Westerners have learned how to externalize this curiosity about the past. They even distance themselves from its impertinent subjectivity by directing questions to such objects as the rise of the nation state or the impact of the printing press, but the renewable source of energy behind these inquiries comes from the intense craving for insight into what it is to be human" (258–59). To be fully human is to love, and Foote is fond of quoting a saying that he attributes to his "other favorite modern writer, Keats" (November 8, 1955; *Correspondence* 104) (Proust, of course, is the first): "A fact is not a truth until you love it" (*Conversations* 248). Foote goes on to declare—giving due credit to Francis Butler Simpkins for this insight—that "a historian can't make a more serious mistake than to equate facts with truth. It's what you do with them that counts . . ." (*Conversations* 226). It is the nature of this love, which empowers the imagination of the artist-narrator to refine fact into truth, that we will explore in the following pages.

Chapter 2

Jordan County

The South and the Birth
of the Modern

*Jordan County, if it is a novel, is a novel which has place for its
hero and time for its plot. It is the main character in the novel—
the land itself. And you go backwards through time to find out
what made it what it is.*

—Shelby Foote, *Conversations*, 1989

*D*aniel J. Singal, in his book *The War Within*, finds that the traditional
values of the South (agrarianism, conservatism, social hierarchies, and
moral certitudes) are, in fact, slightly exotic variations of the nineteenth-
century precepts called Victorianism. The South, in Singal's view, provides a particularly clear model of the tension between Victorian order
and optimism and modernist chaos and skepticism. In the wake of the
devastation of the Civil War, the southern psyche was increasingly invested in maintaining the self-image of a lost aristocratic culture. The Cavalier myth, Singal explains, ". . . embodied traits of order, stability, and
cohesion that southern society stood in desperate need of. The result was
what Paul Gaston has called the New South Creed, a transposition of Cavalier mythology onto the framework of Victorian belief in morality and
industrial progress, a fusion of ideological elements so formidable that it

effectively blocked the arrival of intellectual Modernism in the region through the First World War" (8–9). While "intellectual" modernism may have been delayed, modernity was not; and Foote's novels recount the transformation of Jordan County into what Paul Johnson, in his book *A History of the Modern World from 1917 to the 1990s,* calls a "relativistic world" (1).

Modernism, as the term is generally understood, refers to the impact on Western society of ideas articulated by Karl Marx, Sigmund Freud, and Albert Einstein. It is a world where "Marxist and Freudian analysis combined to undermine, in their different ways, the highly developed sense of personal responsibility, and of duty towards a settled and objectively true moral code, which was the centre of nineteenth-century European civilization" (Johnson 11). Reflecting on the ambivalent heritage of the modernist movement in a letter to Walker Percy, Foote suggests that the modern condition amounts to "a gain of individuality. Thats whats done us in."

> [D. H.] Lawrence said, "The opposite of love isnt hatred, the opposite of love is individuality." The more we gained in individuality, the more we lost in personal satisfaction, in love. Marx and Freud, by identifying us to ourselves, have cost us more than we'll perhaps ever be able to pay. Gone is the brimful joy of the cathedral worker of the Middle Ages, working away at something he would never see finished and with which no one would ever connect his name. Instead we have this lifelong wrestling match with the over demanding Self, which always wins and collects his due in dissatisfaction. . . . I dont blame or even regret these two; I think what they found was the truth; only we cant stand it, even the approximation of the truth they pointed out. Jesus's truth could be lived with (and even *by*) but not Freud's, which puts too much on us, more than we can bear, and gives us no relief. (November 7, 1974; *Correspondence* 196–97)

Foote's sense of the moral anarchy generated by the collapse of seemingly immutable natural and moral laws—the onset of relativism (in the popular cultural application of Einstein's theory of relativity)—forms the basis for his conception of the modern condition. Against this sense of individual alienation and moral chaos Foote offers, like other modernist writers, a conception of value resurrected by the saving grace of an artist's "quality of vision" (individual style as a self-conscious, if qualified, idea of order).

Near the middle of "Child by Fever," the longest story of Foote's *Jordan County: A Landscape in Narrative* (1954), the tone of the narrative shifts from that of a stark Gothic fable to a lyric paean to the Delta country. Foote's lyric meditation calls to mind the cadences of the opening pages of D. H. Lawrence's *The Rainbow* (1915), which chronicles another rural, almost feudal, society in the throes of modernization. "I see it as a time," Foote suggests, "when men stood and looked in both directions" (*Conversations* 92). In the transition from Old South to New South to Modern South (accomplished between 1850 and 1920) one finds, C. Hugh Holman suggests, "a greatly accelerated instance of the classic historical novelist's ideal historical moment" (39). Such moments are rife with change and conflicting cultural myths and differing ideas of regional identity. Richard Gray maintains that if one looks closely enough, even the most hegemonic of societies manifest such conflicts.

> After all, as Fredric Jameson has argued, historical epochs are not monolithic integrated social formations but complex *overlays* of different methods of production that serve as the bases of different social groups and classes and, consequently, of their world views. It is because of this that, in any given epoch, a variety of antagonisms can be discerned, conflicts between different interest groups. One culture may well be dominant, but there will also be—to borrow Raymond Williams' useful terms—a residual culture, prescribing new meanings and practices. The writer, in effect, like any other member of any society, is not the victim of some totalizing structure, since—to quote Williams—"no dominant culture ever in reality includes or exhausts all human practice, human energy and human intention." He is therefore able to insert himself in the space between warring interests and practices and then dramatize the contradictions the conflict engenders. (*Writing* 294)

In Foote's novels, however, the identity issue is less involved in defining southernness and more concerned with the vacuum formed by the collapse of Victorian (or chivalric) value systems. The testing ground for Foote's depiction of the onset of modernity is Jordan County and the town of Bristol, a fictional version of Washington County and Greenville, Mississippi. The following discussion introduces Foote's vision of the moral decay of the South (past and present) and the relationship of the southern heritage to the changes demanded by the modern world. The chapter is patterned on the paradoxical (forward yet backward) structure of *Jordan County,* the last fictional work Foote published before beginning his narrative history. Each historical moment involves the presentation of characters caught in a web of opposing values. Out of such material, Foote reflects his unflinching vision of the human condition and the upheavals of history; inseparable from this vision is his conception of the redemptive potential of an aesthetic and imaginative order with metaphor at its heart.

Historical Moment I

"The Sacred Mound" and the Original Sin of Conquest

The concluding story of Foote's long backward glance in *Jordan County* is "The Sacred Mound," a parable about the beginnings of modern alienation and the possibility of artistic redemption. Both a beginning (in terms of the European experience in Mississippi) and an end (of an independent aboriginal culture and, literally, of the collection itself), "The Sacred Mound" is a tale of white conquest and native disenfranchisement. Set in the Spanish-controlled "Province of Mississippi" (*Jordan* 283), the story depicts the events surrounding the ritual torture and sacrifice of two European traders atop a sacred mound near the future town of Ithaca. The Choctaw Indian Chisahahoma's "confession" recounts the exploration of the area by the Spaniard Hernando de Soto in 1541–1542 and the history of trading, conquest, and settlement up to 1797. Told in his "own words" (they are transcribed by the Spanish notary during interrogation), Chisahahoma relates the mutual incomprehension of dissimilar cultures and the effects of European encroachments on the native populace. Language, as a tool for communication, is ironically implicated in the themes of disjuncture and blindness.

The different approaches to narrative that emerge between Chisahahoma and his European inquisitors reflects a fundamental clash of cultures. The oral tradition of the native involves a seamless interchange between the past and the present. The legalistic and limited approach to narrative employed by the Europeans has no such fluidity. The past of Chisahahoma's people is alive to him, even when it extends back five generations and beyond. His consciousness of a living past (before the white presence) is antithetical to the experiences of those who have appropriated the Choctaw lands and who settle the region over the next 150 years. The six stories preceding "The Sacred Mound" establish the fallout of this failure on the subsequent generations. The native speaker's story is enveloped by the legalities of a European judicial proceeding and framed by the concerns of nationalism and imperialism embodied by the Spanish governor and the scrivener. Foote's narrative frame is designed to illustrate how the past is forever reduced and enlarged, recounted and distorted.

The history of Jordan County, then, begins with a parable of displacement, cultural genocide, and narrative dispossession. "The Sacred Mound" marks both an end and a beginning—like the turning of an hourglass. The story presents southern history as a Eurocentric creation—built around ambiguous questions of identity and ownership. The narrative engages the ironies that lie behind the inquisitor's question, "of what country is he a native?" (*Jordan* 284), and Chisahahoma's response as he begins his "confession," that "all men are brothers" (*Jordan* 284). The white man's inability to recognize or acknowledge the shared myths of Christ and the Indian "Corn God" (*Jordan* 296) points up the willful and defensive blindness of the Europeans. European ideas of ownership clash with the native belief in stewardship: "No man owns the land," the Indian leaders say, "take and live on it; it is lent you for your lifetime; are we not brothers?" (*Jordan* 287). Their question resonates ironically throughout the story, particularly when the authorities free Chisahahoma and reveal the self-serving threefold grounds for his reprieve: 1) as a Catholic convert and a prospective missionary Chisahahoma (newly christened John Postoak) is now valuable because he will spread the true faith; 2) the two victims of the Choctaw tribe were "neither of our Nation nor our Faith" (*Jordan* 298) and consequently beneath consideration; 3) the Spanish are leaving this "barbarous land" (*Jordan* 298) to the Americans anyway and need concern themselves no more with its problems. Chisahahoma's alienation from his place and the past of his people reflects the individual legacy brought about by European exploitation and subjugation.

Foote's development of the trope of displacement leads us to the symbol of the sacrifice—the incident of retributive justice at the climax of "The Sacred Mound." Chisahahoma's tale chronicles the loss of a unified relation between man and the land—a heritage of alienation that is evident in Foote's white Delta characters. By converting to Christianity, Chisahahoma

33

internalizes this disjunction. The reaction of the tribe to the sacrifice also suggests a fundamental loss of self-identity: first comes a feeling of satisfaction, then one of shame. "Were [we] savages, barbarians," he asks, "to come to this?" (*Jordan* 294). The two forms of ritual mutilation (the cutting out of Tyree's living heart and Fink's castration) reinforce this idea of internal division. Symbolically, the mutilations represent moral character and sexuality—the two most vulnerable aspects of the human psyche and the archetypal sites for spiritual and psychological malaise. Unexpectedly, the short, fat trader, Tyree, is revealed, in the Indians' eyes, as the "brave" (*Jordan* 293), while the tall, more imposing figure of Lancelot Fink suffers a humiliating death. Symbols related to this primal scene are played out again and again in Foote's investigations of human nature—at Shiloh during the heat of battle, in characters such as Hugh Bart (*Tournament*), Luther Eustis (*Follow Me Down*), and Rufus Hutton (*September September*), and in *The Civil War* with respect to the unpredictable nature of human reactions under duress. Witnessing the tortures—simultaneously the climax of the story, the end of the novel, and the beginning of Delta history—the reader is forced to reconsider the history of *Jordan County* that preceded the story of the sacrifices, retracing in the narrative the figurative manifestations of this original legacy.

The legacy of "The Sacred Mound," the heritage of alienation, echoes through all of Foote's texts as oppression is extended and internalized. The joint legacy of the native and the black figures forms a political subtext for the white psychological malaise. The descendants of the aboriginal culture exist in the white world as alienated outcasts, silent witnesses, debased representatives of the native sense of a holistic connection between man and nature. These figures begin with the mixed-race butler, Edward Postoak—presumably a descendant of Chisahahoma—who stands as silent witness to the burning, in 1864, of the plantation house Solitaire. Still later, in "Child by Fever," it is the nurse Emma, "gangling, limber-jointed . . . with amber eyes . . . and . . . Indian blood" (*Jordan* 98)—a "bit 'touched,'" yet a natural story-teller—who perceives the innate corruption in Hector Sturgis's soul. The same combination of traits is evident in smallpox-afflicted Miz Pitts (misfits?), who recognizes the divided nature of Luther Eustis in *Follow Me Down*. Her ability to give form to the story of her own life marks her connection to the native culture and sets her apart from the disjointed world that bedevils Eustis. In "Ride Out," it is the intuitive genius of the black jazz trumpeter Duff Conway—whose itinerant musician father has

Choctaw blood—that creates a music capable of reanimating the primal voice silenced by white civilization. And, finally, the haunting spirit of the Indian mound itself, and all it represents of a lost power and connection to the land, stands as an emblem of missed potential in the eyes of Reeny Perdew, the female kidnapper of *September September*. Reeny's share in this debased heritage is bequeathed her by her father, Reverend Jimson. Jimson, who presides over a "mass sanctification" in *Follow Me Down* by standing like a "calendar Indian" in a way that "showed off the bulge in his crotch . . . that was part of what he meant when he spoke of the strength of the Lord" (*FMD* 79), represents the corruption of Christian belief and the debasement of the aboriginal heritage (and, perhaps, a degenerate strain of the "aristocratic" Jameson family, first introduced in *Tournament*). Through this intricate weave of images, Foote reinforces the heritage of alienation. The narrative also affirms his belief that nothing is lost to the world, no past is ever completely absent; rather, the past remains as ironic residues and traces affecting events and individuals in the present (regardless of the participants' awareness, or ignorance, of their past).

Central to Foote's conception of human history is the image of an eternal return, a primordial balance of opposites existing under the "ordinance of time." Intimations of this law—identified later as Anaximander's in *The Civil War*—are offered in a brief passage in "Pillar of Fire," in which Isaac Jameson, in 1864, muses on human history while walking through the remnants of a Choctaw village near Solitaire. Reflecting on the native peoples as "casualties not of war but of progress" (*Jordan* 269), Jameson contemplates his own people's ultimate demise: "Was it all for nothing, the distances, the ambition, and the labor? . . . If so, where was the dignity of man, to be thrown aside like this, a worn-out tool?" (*Jordan* 269). His answer, it seems to me, sums up Foote's own perspective on the relative importance of human endeavors; it is a statement, like the place itself, never far from the center of his fiction:

> He remembered the land as it was when he first came, a great endless green expanse of trees, motionless under the press of summer or tossing and groaning in the winds of spring and fall. He ringed them, felled them, dragged them out; he fired the stumps so that the air was hazed with the blue smoke of their burning, and then he had made his lakeside dream a reality; the plowmen came, the cotton sprouted, and he prospered; until now. The earth, he thought, the

earth endures . . . and the earth goes back to the sun; that was where it began. There is no law, no reason except the sun, and the sun doesnt care. Its only concern is its brightness; we feed that brightness like straws dropped into its flame. Fire! he thought suddenly. It all goes back to fire! (*Jordan* 269–70)

The final image is clearly apocalyptic—a disavowal of human "law" and "reason." What is left is the counterpoint of circularity, pattern, and completion—a Promethean vision of artistic power suggested by Foote's attention to the "landscape in narrative."

Historical Moment II

"Pillar of Fire" and the Collapse of the Planter Ideal

"Pillar of Fire," the penultimate story in *Jordan County*, is Foote's vision of the Old South. Here, Foote addresses the myth of the Delta (and, by extension, America as a whole) as a land of untold promise and possibility. The time frame of Isaac Jameson's story parallels the growth of the nation; it begins with his birth in 1776 (during the Revolution) and concludes with his death during the Civil War in 1864. He represents the frontier phase of the Delta settlement. Told from the perspective of Lieutenant Adam Lundy, a Union officer attached to enforce order in the Mississippi region after the fall of Vicksburg, the tale anticipates the themes of conquest and subjugation raised in "The Sacred Mound." (Foote's ironic subtext, however, is that in this case the society to be suppressed is the Old South—the planter-centered culture based on a vision of a slavery-based agrarian utopia.) Lundy—as an Adamic figure who represents the northern utopia of equality based on material prosperity and democracy—reflects Foote's skepticism about the idea of progress. Here, even as it is being presented, the American myth of progress and betterment is being subverted.

Jameson's story is the archetypal frontier legend: dreams of new beginnings, virgin spaces, political freedom, and economic opportunities. After an early life of adventure—"his name had turned up in varied connections: with the Burr conspiracy and with Jean Lafitte and Dominique You, with the Mississippi Militia fighting Creeks at Burnt Corn and with Andrew

Jackson fighting British regulars at New Orleans" (*Tournament* 31)—a wounded Jameson returns to his father's home in Natchez: "He was a year mending. Then he spent another year trying to make up for lost time. But it did not go right. There were still the cockfights and the grog shops and the women under the hill, but the old life had paled on him. He was thirty-nine, a bachelor, well into middle age, and apparently it had all come to nothing" (*Jordan* 241). Jameson's personal crisis coincides with Mississippi's entry into the Union; so he sets out to explore the Delta region recently vacated by the displaced Choctaw tribes. On the shore of Lake Jordan, in a dream-vision, Jameson sees the future:

> . . . and all that night, surrounded by lake-country beauty—overhead the far, spangled reaches of sky, eastward the forest murmurs, the whisper of leaves and groan of limbs in the wind, the hoarse night-noises of animals, and westward, close at hand, the lapping of water—he dreamed. He dreamed an army of blacks marching upon the jungle, not halting to chop but walking steadily forward, swinging axes against the retreating green wall. Behind them the level fields lay stumpless and serene in watery sunlight, motionless until in the distance clanking trace chains and clacking singletrees announced the coming of the plowmen. Enormous lop-eared mules drew bulltongue plows across the green, and the long brown furrows of earth unrolled like threads off spools. What had been jungle became cultivated fields, and now the fields began to be striped with the pale green lines of plants soon burdened with squares, then purple-and-white dotted, then deep red with blooms, then shimmering white in the summer heat. In a long irregular line (they resembled skirmishers except for the singing; their sacks trailed from their shoulders like limp flags) the pickers passed over the fields, leaving them brown and desolate in the rain, and the stalks dissolved, going down into bottomless mud. Then in the dream there was quiet, autumnal death until the spring returned and the plowmen, and the dream began again. This was repeated three times, with a mystical clarity. (*Jordan* 243–44)

Like a figure from the Old Testament (Joseph, Moses, or Isaac), Jameson leads the way to the land of plenty. Cast in biblical and mythic terms, the vision reflects the human desire for a world that is stable and constant.

More specifically, Jameson's dream reflects the bedrock components of the Delta economy—King Cotton and slavery. On this foundation, Isaac dreams of a dynasty growing up around the plantation called Solitaire (a diamond set by itself, a game of cards played alone, a hermit figure—three images that reflect the teleology of Foote's depiction as his work charts the decline and corruption of the original dream).

On a material level, Solitaire embodies Isaac's original vision of prosperity as the house evolves from spartan plainness to grandeur. In more figurative terms, it represents Foote's conception of human limitation in the face of impersonal, inexorable forces (natural or divine), which is articulated by Lundy's quotation from the Book of Job at the conclusion of the story: "Yet man is born unto trouble, as the sparks fly upward. And: Man that is born of woman is of few days, and full of trouble. He cometh forth like a flower, and is cut down: he fleeth also as a shadow, and continueth not" (*Jordan* 280–81). The original building is destroyed along with slavery and the Old South (and Jameson's vision), but his son Clive's mansion (built of brick made of clay prized by the Choctaw for pottery), the second Solitaire, survives. Furnished in the best European style, this version lacks Isaac's primal and imaginative connection to the land. This second Solitaire is a hollow structure, a monument to alien tastes, and now represents a people "dispossessed" (*Jordan* 244).

In "Pillar of Fire" Foote traces an ideological progression from the frontier idealism of Jameson, through the secessionist and aristocratic politics embodied by his son, to the pragmatic and limited vision of the self-made men of the later part of the century. On first seeing Lieutenant Lundy, Isaac observes that his "face had been baked in the same crucible that had hardened and glazed the face of his son Clive—and he thought: It's something the war does to them; North and South" (*Jordan* 271). The attributes of Isaac as a frontier hero are gone forever, consumed in the conflagration of his house and vanished like his gentle-hearted son into the vortex of the Civil War. The inner strength that Lundy sees in Isaac Jameson is not present in the representatives of the next generation (Clive Jameson, Lundy, and Colonel Frisby): "He was old—though old was hardly word enough to express it; he was ancient—with sunken cheeks and a mass of white hair like a mane, obviously a tall man and probably a big one, once, but thin now to the point of emaciation, as if he had been reduced to skin and skeleton and only the most essential organs, heart and lungs and maybe bowels, though not very much of either—'Except heart; there's plenty of that . . .'"

(*Jordan* 238). Lacking heart, the progenitors of the modern generation are wounded, body and soul—"torn on the bias"—drawn more to the pillar of fire than to the promise of the land or the power of the original dream.

Foote's first novel, *Tournament* (his most comprehensive treatment of the role of the planter in the New South), tells Hugh Bart's story (from the late-Reconstruction period to 1914 and the onset of the First World War). Bart's life—he is a man who loses his way—is a burlesque of Isaac Jameson's. He shares many of Jameson's characteristics yet lacks his primal vision. After Clive Jameson's death in 1882, "ex-planter, ex-beau sabreur, ex-everything" (*Tournament* 25), the family is forced by foreclosure into a life of genteel poverty in Bristol. Five years later, penniless but "capable" (*Tournament* 26), Bart buys Solitaire. He is one of a new breed of planters, "self-made men who had risen by ability. . . . For [which] they received due credit, but they also paid a certain price. Outside the field of their endeavor they had scarcely any existence" (*Jordan* 251). As men they have limitations—in part as a result of the war, and later as a result of "Progress" (*Jordan* 180)—and are undone by their inability to think past the rigid, parochial planter society. They are neither of the past nor, ultimately, of the future; what they inherit is the spiritual confusion that comes with modern uncertainties.

At the outset, Bart shares with Isaac Jameson a capacity that elicits Billy Boy's and Judge Wiltner's admiration:

> that spark Bart carried in his breast, which made his advances possible and was the mainspring of his reaction when choice was necessary, which enabled him to reach out in the dark and touch Right when other men, lacking the spark, would not have been able to distinguish it from Wrong in broad open daylight. This inner quality, a combination of simplicity and insight—so that in a sense Bart was a sort of Billy Boy Wiltner—made him a man of action who never faltered, a man of intelligence who never erred, so long as he obeyed the spark. (*Tournament* 67–68)

Like Jameson, who was "wilderness born, conceived in a time of revolution [and] had received in his blood . . . some goading spark of rebellion, some fierce, hot distillate of the jungle itself" (*Jordan* 240), Bart manifests an innate capacity for action and accomplishment, being "born to work and risk" (*Tournament* 75) and lead. Bart's prowess as a man of action wins him—"the newcomer, the outlander" (*Tournament* 1)—the support of the men of Issawamba County and his position as the sheriff: "They believed that he embodied what they could have been if their love of leisure had been replaced by whatever it was that made them admire him, like junky horses admiring a Percheron" (*Tournament* 74). His qualities of "integrity and devotion and bravery" (*Tournament* 74) are real ones, and represent for the aspiring Delta middle class "what they believed was their intrinsic worth" (*Tournament* 74). Bart fulfils his original promise by a meteoric rise from sheriff to planter and seems destined to repeat the accomplishments of the founder of Solitaire.

Foote, though, makes clear distinctions between Jameson and Bart; and in doing so he casts an ironic eye at the myth of the Old South, the ersatz values of the New, and the pretensions of "Progress." Where Jameson's world is shattered by a war that revises the American political equation, Bart's world is destroyed by the failure of the man himself. Foote notes Bart's self-division early in his tenure as sheriff. The episode involves the murder of a planter by his tenant of twenty years (a veteran turned share-cropper who kills the son of his old regimental commander). The confrontation represents the breakdown of Old South loyalties and the collapse of a sense of moral stability; it also triggers an internal crisis in Bart when he realizes, after killing the man, that he will never settle the morality of the issue to his satisfaction:

> He never forgot this other voice inside himself, nor the men behind the railroad embankment eager for a death, the unequal, fore-decided contest, the haloed maniacal face grimacing as the old repeating rifle, pointed directly at him, clicked time after time on dud after dud until a round finally fired and missed, the double-barreled explosion blotting the whole scene, and then the rushing roar of all past time and injustice and insolent might of law and order coming through the air to set the two voices going inside his head: when? Never. (*Tournament* 9)

Bart's inner division, his lack of moral certitude, stands for failures in the society as a whole. Judge Wiltner sees the alteration: "youre different. Youve stopped changing, or youre about to stop" (*Tournament* 52). Bart ignores the Judge's advice to "keep growing" (*Tournament* 52) and abdicates action in favor of an "edifice" (*Tournament* 52) made up of plantation, position, and family. As the Judge remarks:

Youre made another way, son. If my reasoning is right (and I know men) and if youre half what I took you to be, you cant stop like the rest of them. You cant loaf on a slope, no matter which way youre heading: youve got to keep moving. If you stop youll fret; youll lash out for action. And you wont pick an action that will carry you toward the things your life points to; youll just grab the first action that comes to hand. And if it isnt the kind that will carry you along the way you were born to travel, youll snarl up the whole business. Youll undo in a hurry all youve done. Youll bungle, son; youll bungle. (*Tournament* 53)

And Bart does bungle, by forfeiting his relationship to the land that gives him strength and focus.

The contest, the tournament, is now with himself. Unlike Jameson, who knows when burying his first child "that now, with flesh of his flesh interred in [the small plot at Solitaire], he would never leave this land" (*Jordan* 250), Bart chooses, out of simple boredom, to relinquish his dream. Gaining Solitaire, Bart finds only a vacuum: "nothing was going to happen that was any different from what had happened last week or last month or last year. The frontier had caught up with and passed it; life now was no more than variations on a theme already stated" (*Tournament* 76). Confronting his eldest son's rejection of the planter heritage, Bart says, "All right. If you dont want Solitaire, I reckon Solitaire dont want you," and later thinks, "I shouldnt have said that; he didnt see what I meant. Because Bart had not meant the house, the home; he meant Solitaire, the land, the five square miles of cotton rows and the random cuts of corn and hay—as if the growing things were sentient, as if they would renege, bloom and boll clamp shut with indignation, and stalks jerk back into the ground" (*Tournament* 178). In truth, unwittingly, he is speaking a warning to himself.

Foote employs the time span of Bart's life to link his representative New South planter to other societal changes. Born in the year before the Civil War, 1859, the son of a Mississippi Unionist who farmed in the Black Prairie Belt to the east, Bart arrives in Issawamba County in 1878 and succeeds to the sheriff's job in 1883, taking over Solitaire four years later. It is post-Reconstruction, and Bart reclaims the plantation with jail labor much as Jameson had cleared the land with slaves. Bart moves into a world that was "like something out of the Middle Ages" (*Jordan* 120), a feudal society enmeshed in the seasonal cycles of the planting, the natural cycles of the river, and social rituals as fixed as either: "What was intended was the repetition of a cycle, maintenance of a static life-way" (*Tournament* 92). By linking the cycles of the planter society to his treatment of the 1903 flood (floods coming "roughly every seven years" [*Tournament* 96]), Foote gently mocks the hubris evoked by such assumptions of permanence. The irony is carried forward when Bart's death coincides with the end of the New South and the beginning of the modern era. His retirement to Bristol in 1912, exchanging land for cash, mirrors "a period of historical unrest. So much was changing, the people were bewildered. The railroads had out-done the river packets; the motion picture and the automobile had altered all conceptions of leisure and love; the electric light and the telephone no longer were gadgets—all these, and more, were part of a new and different life, unlike the life this generation had been born to" (*Tournament* 182–83). By leaving the land, Bart ties himself to an abstraction—money; after the crash, "what he wanted was money—just that alone, for the first time in his life" (*Tournament* 198–99). He is an alien figure out of place in the twentieth century, a wanderer through the suburbs of the new Bristol. While strolling through town in the last year of his life, 1914, Bart considers

> the new, tight, practical twentieth century five-room bungalows where the young married learned marital bliss, patterned their lives on the dimensions of the dollar, built their dreams on expected promotions made possible by the deaths or misdeeds of their seniors, took revenge on the denying, embattled world by nagging each other or vilifying their neighbors, and sought occasional gratification and exhaustion by revioloating one another in clumsy repetition of their wedding nights. In his mind these days Bart saw them approximately thus; he saw life as a snarl of causation. (*Tournament* 212)

The modern, for Foote, is a period of decline—a sentiment that echoes the view Will Percy articulated of his sense of alienation and displacement. From hunting for sport to trap-shooting for glory, from gambling on life to endless rounds of poker, from killing as a sheriff representing the law to defense of personal honor and an antiquated code (the Tarfeller episode), from straightforward confrontation to assassination by bank draft (the Wisten affair): Bart succumbs to the tenets of the modern world. Foote ties the diminishment of the man to the increasing falsity of the ideals associated with the planter vision of the South, and both finally collapse with the onset of World War I. Bart's story chronicles a fundamental alteration of the society's relation to the land itself, from the Reconstruction period of sharecropping to the urban, Americanized South of the mid-century. Side by side with this physical restructuring of the landscape comes the dissolution of conventional moral verities. The center cannot hold, and life becomes a "snarl of causation." Foote's tale involves not just a reassessment of the conventional view of the South, but also, and more significantly, an articulation of the fundamental alteration of how the human condition is understood—the implications for individuals of their place in a relativistic universe.

Historical Moment III

"Child by Fever" and Foote's Apocalyptic Modernity

The disillusionment and spiritual exhaustion of Bart in the closing years of his life matches Foote's other treatments of the planter class, particularly in the central story in *Jordan County*, "Child by Fever." Although a Freudian family romance constitutes the main story line of "Child by Fever," Foote's novella also explores the effects of the changing times on the Delta world. The story of Hector Sturgis, with its Gothic overtones and echoes of the style and subject matter of Edgar Allan Poe, charts the transformation of the South from the world of feudalistic plantations to twentieth-century suburbia. Extending from the earliest arrival of Hector Wingate—founder of the dynasty—in the Delta region in 1835, until the dissolution of the family with Esther Wingate Sturgis's death in 1944, the tale is an overview of the societal changes embodied by Clive Jameson, Hugh Bart, and his son. One observes a similar deterioration of moral and spiritual values: from the first Hector, who settles the land, establishes the plantation, builds the Wingate mansion, and dies at Buena Vista during the Mexican War, one moves forward to the last Hector, failed planter, husband, and artist, who dies a suicide at thirty-three in 1911. In this sense, the male line marks the diminution of the myth of the southern male from Cavalier (the first Hector), to embittered landowner who feels he has "failed his heritage" (*Jordan* 78) of military glory (the second Hector), to the third and last Hector (Sturgis), an insubstantial "dude . . . always in a hurry but going no place, an outlander, rakish and modern" (*Jordan* 127). Of equal significance are the dates associated with his mother, who is born just prior to the beginning of the Civil War, in 1860, and dies, the aged and revered "Mother of Bristol" (*Jordan* 76), at the close of World War II.

At two pivotal points in the story (the first related to Hector's childhood experiences and the second just prior to his suicide), Foote writes about the "four dominants" (*Jordan* 180) of the old Delta world. In the first instance, Foote identifies those elements, "the trees, the war, the Negroes, the river" (*Jordan* 108), that "rose out of the past and cast their shadows on the present" (*Jordan* 108); later he considers the "new dominants" (*Jordan* 180) that replace them when twentieth-century "Progress" (*Jordan* 180) overtakes the old world. These new dominants are linked to the increasing abstractness of the modern society: the cinema, where "upturned faces [drink] the frictionless shadows of a nation's desire" (*Jordan* 180); labor-saving devices (the automobile, the telephone) that "agitated [men's] brains" (*Jordan* 181); "the increasing dichotomy between the Business life and the Christian life" (*Jordan* 181) that inaugurated the age of anxiety; and, finally, the as yet unnamed malaise of existential despair. While the ethos of the modern world is the frame and the lens through which Foote views the Delta and its history, his vision evokes the paradoxes evident in this interplay of change and continuity. In defiance of the old covenant, humanity moves further into the illusion of mastery, and the result is an existence increasingly relativistic and absurd.

The Trees

The trees on Hector Sturgis's maps represent for him "the teem of life below the surface" (*Jordan* 106) and introduce an image by which Foote connects the present psychological malaise with its historical imperatives. Bristol's "live oaks, older than the town" (*Jordan* 105), are themselves reminders that "[t]his had all been forest before the white men came" and that "even today whoever grew up in Bristol grew up in their shade" (*Jordan* 106). The trees exist as a ghostly representation of the tale of Delta origins, a story of aboriginal displacement and genocide that, given the structure of Foote's collection, has yet to be revealed to his reader. Other images in "Child by Fever" reflect the presence of the past. In a reference to the results of pneumonia suffered by Hector's infant son, Foote again stresses the lingering effects of this distant, forgotten heritage. The child's damaged heart is first revealed by the blue color of his penis, a discoloration that gradually envelops his body. The link between loins and heart takes one back (or forward, in terms of the order of the stories) to the symbolic import of the sacrifices on the Indian mound. In fact, Ella Sturgis's nightmare dream-cure for her ailing child is also eerily familiar; in a kind of domestic operating theater she removes the child's heart, "shaped like the hearts on valentines" (*Jordan* 152), and massages it with liniment in an attempt at revival. The connection suggests the internalized and isolated nature of contemporary experience.

This transformation of ancient ritual into modern psychological trauma is carried forward in the episode of Florence's forced haircut in *Love in a Dry Season*. The eldest daughter of Major Barcroft, Florence is afflicted in early adolescence by an attack of asthma and subsequently confined to her home from 1912 until her death, twenty-six years later, in 1938. Her sequestered life inaugurates Florence's long decline, the outset of which is marked by the symbolic implications of a clash of wills with her father. Florence's one vestige of a doubtful youthful attractiveness is her long blond hair with the "rich sheen of cornsilk" (*Love* 15) that echoes the vanished Corn God; her hair is a focal point for her vanity and a covert means of asking for parental attention. Brooding on his failure to realize his dream of military glory, the result of a heart murmur that Florence inherits, the Major resents her coquettish complaints and her self-absorption, and he calls her bluff. In a macabre scene combining images of castration and abortion—a point underscored by Florence's subsequent nightmares of confinement in a room hung with instruments like "shears and clippers and other tools, vaguely obstetric" (*Love* 19)—the Major oversees the symbolic destruction of her sense of self, the internalization of her outward disfiguration. Shorn of her locks and confined to the lower-floor front parlor, Florence finds that her life is reduced to obsessing over "lurid headlines" (*Love* 20) about outlaw heroes and crimes of sexual perversity and her monthly celebration of the Eucharist. The act of Communion becomes for her a form of sexual fetish where, intoxicated by the fumes of the wine, she is "transported . . . [remembering] the half-naked man nailed to the wall of the church beside the altar, and she fed on him in her heart and drank his blood" (*Love* 22). The mystical is literalized, reduced, and rendered obscene. With her defective heart beating like a "tomtom . . . gone all wrong" (*Love* 23) and her isolated rapture induced by tales of violence or acts of religious ritual evoked with a disturbing literalism, Florence neglects the lesson of the accompanying biblical text: "remembrance" (*Love* 22). Like Hugh Bart, Florence manifests a crippling sense of self-division, asking: "How can I be two people?" (*Love* 19). Once again, the heritage of Jordan County is brought ironically into play—textual memory being broader and deeper than the consciousness of individual characters.

In all cases, Foote reinforces the irony by setting narrative continuity against individual disconnection with the past; his modern characters live either ignorant of their heritage or subscribe to fatal misrepresentations. Just as the death of her child marks an end to Ella's hopes of escape and fulfilment—her spiritual barrenness matches Hector's physical impotence—so too the Bristol trees are being destroyed, blasted by progress: "Many . . . had been felled to make way for widening the boulevards, and others were dying of thirst, choked by the concrete poured close about their trunks for the new sidewalks; the leafy tunnels were badly gapped, as if by shellfire, and dead leaves fell unseasonally" (*Jordan* 180). The Delta world is out of joint. In a similar example, the four majestic oak trees that grace the front of the Barcroft mansion in *Love in a Dry Season*—a number corresponding to the ill-fated inhabitants of the house—are gradually brought down, until (like Amanda) there is but a single survivor: "[t]he Barcroft oak . . . one of Bristol's landmarks," so called even "after most people no longer remembered how it got its name" (*Love* 246). With each succeeding generation, as Foote marks the process of decay, the influence of these natural elements (and their correlatives of individual memory and communal history) recedes, leading to a greater sense of isolation, spiritual abstraction, and existential despair.

The War

The history of Jordan County and the legacy of the Civil War are inseparable. Mainly, the war marks the end of the Old South dream of a pastoral utopia. As Hector Sturgis sees it, "there had been a war and a way of life that was lost when the war was lost" (*Jordan* 106), and now it is merely one more discarded myth, an irrelevant bit of the past. Formerly the war was given a pride of place in the Delta society; it generated the sustaining myth of the Lost Cause and tales of valorous exploits in a string of legendary names, "Biblical, Indian, English names . . . unimportant in themselves until the day when the armies came together, more or less by accident, to give the scattered names a permanence and to settle what manner of life Hector Sturgis, for one, was to grow up under" (*Jordan* 106). By 1910, however, there are but a few crippled veterans left, and "the battle names had been forgotten along with the cause for which they were fought, the fields themselves planted in cotton or run to weeds" (*Jordan* 180). Foote reinforces the regressive nature of this cultural atrophy by connecting it, on an individual level, to Hector's childhood desire for "a world all his own" (*Jordan* 104), and his fascination with the attic hideaway crammed with "the overflow of half a century" (*Jordan* 103), including, most notably, the Confederate uniforms, sidearms, and sabers of his dead uncles. Linked to his grandfather's bitterness over lost military glory, and a reminder of his own thwarted attempt in that direction, the attic represents an empty heritage, another form of escapism. Like Hector's increasingly obsessive character, evident in his drawings, this desire to retreat into himself finds its apotheosis in his suicide in that same attic (*Jordan* 221). The connection of individual alienation and the southern heritage is articulated by Parker Nowell in *Follow Me Down:*

> Love has failed us. We are essentially, irrevocably alone. Anything that seems to combat the loneliness is a trap—Love is a trap: Love has failed us in this century. We left our better destiny in '65, defeated though we fought with a fury that seems to indicate foreknowledge of what would follow if we lost. Probably it happened even earlier: maybe in Jackson's time. Anyhow—whenever—we left the wellsprings, and ever since then we have been moving toward this ultimate failure of nerve. Now who has the answer? The Russians? The Catholic Church? Or are we building up to Armageddon, the day they drop the Bomb? God smiles and waits, like a man crouched over an ant-hill with a bottle of insecticide uncorked. (*Follow* 31)

The lawyer suggests that Lost Cause thinking dovetails into Cold War angst; his skepticism provides a nihilistic vision of the final degeneration of southern, and by extension American, idealism. Nothing remains but individual self-immolation transferred onto a global scale; or, in Parker's case, a retreat into stoicism and a cynical version of narrative art.

Two other examples of Foote's treatment of the influence of the Civil War are interesting in connection with the Lost Cause as a debilitating individual retreat. The first is found in the familial heritage of Luther Eustis in *Follow Me Down*. Luther is the grandson of Luther Dade, the private in the Sixth Mississippi regiment initiated into the realities of war at Shiloh (Dade's is the third monologue of Foote's historical novel *Shiloh*). During Eustis's crisis of faith—or midlife crisis, depending on one's perspective (another ironic connection of heart and loins)—he turns for solace and escape to the memory of his grandfather at a veterans' reunion on a secluded island in the Mississippi. Seeking to leave behind the worldly cares of the life of a sharecropping farmer on Solitaire, Eustis (with his youthful inamorata, Beulah Ross) turns to the idealized past of his childhood memory. It is a version of Eden, and also an image of the heroic age of the South: "All the veterans were officers by then. They were old beyond time, and seemed bigger than life in their gray full-skirted coats and wideawake hats with plumes" (*Follow* 95). Like Hector's attic, the island is where Eustis learns the attractions of solitude: "A man alone here . . . would be like the only person left alive on earth" (*Follow* 97). This memory is connected in Luther's mind to an Edenic vision of utopia: "I never went back again in all those years. I kept it in mind, though, and the more time went by, the more beautiful it seemed. I used to dream about it, green and peaceful, shining in the sunlight: a promised land. Later, reading of Adam and Eve when the world was new, I understood what the Garden was like before the Serpent snaked in and corrupted it" (*Follow* 97). Note how the individual past is tied to the idealization of historical reality; even the drummer boys achieve rank as the years pass, promoted by Time. Such self-serving abstractions, Foote stresses, result in dangerous distortions of both the past and the present.

Major Barcroft in *Love in a Dry Season* provides a second illustration of the corruptive power of embracing an illusory heritage. Barcroft dies at sixty-seven in 1939, "an institution in Bristol, one of the final representatives of what the town had progressed beyond" (*Love* 3). The son of a Confederate veteran, Barcroft inherits a "courteous old-world manner" (*Love* 3), a capacity to act the "cavalier, Old South . . . *galant*" (*Love* 181), and an enduring interest in military history and strategies. As a youth, his fascination with military glory leads him to an adulation for heroes such as Stonewall Jackson—even to the extent of impersonating the general's eccentric mannerisms. Yet his war remains literary, an extension of his younger passion for tactics manuals:

To these . . . he brought an enthusiasm and appreciation which some young men his age were devoting to Keats. He found them exciting, and not only for their subject matter—the language itself enchanted him. The mission of the infantry in attack, as defined by the text: "to close with the enemy and destroy him," had a wild, triumphant, almost lyric beauty, while the mission of the infantry in defense: "to maintain the integrity of the position," was nothing less than the finest phrase in literature. His scalp would tingle when he read such things; the hair on his neck would bristle. (*Love* 4–5)

Barcroft's sole exposure to military life is service as a company commander during the Spanish-American War, in which, ironically, "embalmed beef" was the chief enemy and reflected "no glory on the men who fought it" (*Love* 6). He receives his majority in 1899 and clings to it through the rest of his life; fixing his hopes for military glory career on his only son, Malcolm, Barcroft's obsession eventually leads to the boy's death in a shooting accident. With the outbreak of the First World War, his last "chance at glory" (*Love* 15) is frustrated by a weak heart. Foote's Major Barcroft declines into a parody of the heroic ideal; he becomes a "middle-aged old man" with the "septuagenary dignity, the stiff, sway-backed carriage, the grizzled hair and slightly tufted eyebrows he was to take to the grave" (*Love* 24). Like Hector Sturgis before him, Barcroft retreats into a world of abstraction, carefully charting the troop movements of 1939 on a "large-scale map of western Europe . . . [where he marks] the positions of the armies with . . . swarm[s] of black- and red-headed pins" (*Love* 176). Like that of other watchers and mapmakers, the Major's activity reinforces the dehumanizing distortions of his megalomania. His final role in the novel's black comedy of sexual warfare is as a matchmaker for his daughter Amanda. Donning "the obsequious, false joviality of a procurer, a pander, and attendant even—lacking only the basin and towels, a jar of petroleum jelly and a box of coffin-shaped bichloride tablets" (*Love* 186)—Barcroft performs his final betrayal in the name of family honor. Even his face in death—a grotesque black mask resulting from the suffocation caused by heart failure and two days of lying undiscovered in his study during the month of May—confirms his spiritual corruption. The impulse toward abstraction, the transformation (and degradation) of the legacy of the war, reflects a kind of cultural *angina pectoris,* a modern constriction of the soul.

The River

The river—a Heraclitean image of time—constant but always changing, either benign provider or flood-tide destroyer, is an integral part of Foote's landscape in narrative. As central as the Mississippi seems, though, even the river is being displaced from the consciousness of the modern South. Once again, Foote marks the beginning of these two roles of the river in "The Sacred Mound." The Choctaw Indians understood their entire world in relation to the river and fought to avenge its "Desecration" and "Pollution" (*Jordan* 284) after de Soto's remains are buried in its waters. The natives' reverence is a stark contrast to the Europeans' impulse to fear and control the river—a point Foote underlines when juxtaposing the cycles of planter society and the cyclical flood tides in "The River" chapter of *Tournament*. The arrogance of the planters leads them to disregard the lessons of the past and to rebuild the landing in the face of a rising river. The power of the Mississippi becomes abundantly clear when the river floods. All the planters can do after the levee breaks is to move to the highest ground and wait for the water to advance "like an immense plate being slid over the ground, shallow, opaque, innocent looking" (*Tournament* 103), slowly invading their houses, "rippl[ing] over the door sill and onto the polished hardwood floor in little reaching rivulets, blunt fingers of brown water creeping toward the staircase as if it knew that was the way upstairs" (*Tournament* 104). The denizens of Foote's Delta are at their most vulnerable when attempting to create an insular world, "a static life-way" (*Tournament* 92).

At one time the river existed as a vital part of human life, "dark . . . brooding . . . inscrutable" (*Jordan* 107)—the "strong brown god" of T. S. Eliot's "The Dry Salvages" (205). This primal relation decays rapidly in the postwar era. At one time, the riverboat captains could look down from their wheelhouses at "the very heart of the delta" (*Jordan* 108) and sneer at the "land-going, malodorous, railbound mechanism" (*Jordan* 108); now the once proud packets lie "bleaching their ribs on mudflats all the way from Cairo to New Orleans, the pulsing throb and rumble of their whistles drowned by the piercing, one-note shriek of locomotives" (*Jordan* 180). In a short passage near the center of *Follow Me Down*, when Luther Eustis is wrestling with his conscience in solitude on the Arkansas side of the island paradise, the "terrible bellering screech" (*Follow* 122) of a steamboat whistle, like a voice from the past—perhaps like a distant echo of the now lost rebel yell, but to Luther's mind more like "God or Satan roaring out of the whirlwind" (*Follow* 122)—underscores his decision to murder. The whole episode on the island, bracketed as it is by an arrival and a return by train, is a fitting emblem of the exhaustion of the old dominants. Luther returns (like Rip Van Winkle) to a modern world, one that no longer hears the voice of the river or, for that matter, the voice of God. And yet this modern world too shall pass. The projected opening sentence of Foote's unfinished novel, *Two Gates to the City*, stresses the demise of the railway itself: "Three years ago they took it off; but up till then, since back beyond the memory of any man now living, there was a midnight train out of Memphis, south one hundred fifty miles to Bristol; the Cannonball they called it, in inverse ratio to the compliment implied, for the trip was scheduled at just under seven hours and even so the thing was always late, stopping at every station along the line, backing onto spur-tracks to reach others, and panting on sidings—not so much from impatience as from age—while faster trains ran past without even a hoot" (November 10, 1951; *Correspondence* 63). It is a similar equation (part of those "ordinances of time") that links the moral degeneration and aimlessness of the characters in *September September* to their automotive mobility.

The Negroes

Foote's investigation of change in the South includes his depiction of the black population (and by extension the legacy of slavery and Reconstruction and the future of the Civil Rights movement) in the life of Jordan County. Initially presented as the silent majority of the Delta population, the blacks live apart and seem to possess hidden knowledge behind their "dark masks" (*Jordan* 107), as well as an intrinsic vitality glimpsed in the Saturday finery they wear downtown: "the women in gored skirts and bright red shirtwaists, carrying india-rubber sponges to sop their faces, and the men in swallowtail coats and button shoes, sporting horseshoe tie pins and big-link watch chains" (*Jordan* 107). They also embody, to the white mind, an unspoken threat as "a fuliginous backdrop against which the town, mindful of Haiti and John Brown and Reconstruction, played out its life" (*Jordan* 107). An important element of the social matrix, the blacks seem, early on, to possess a reservoir of energy and vitality, even in their legally and socially marginalized existence—a reservoir confirmed by the victory of Jack Johnson, a black fighter, over Jim Jeffries in the Fourth of July heavy-weight title bout of 1910, an event whose symbolic value flies in the face of the racist complacency of the Delta world. Yet, the grinding poverty brought by progress is a drain on their spirit: "the gay-colored shirtwaists and swal-lowtail coats" were not replaced, "for they were too poor; their faces no longer resembled masks, for they knew no secret; Haiti and John Brown had no connection with such as these" (*Jordan* 180).

The ebbing fortunes and moral integrity of white characters dominate the first four published novels devoted to Jordan County. Not until the story "The Freedom Kick" does Foote address the emerging voice of the hitherto silent black presence. Set in the period of Reconstruction, the story recounts the experiences of a black woman who tests the reality of the freedom osten-sibly won during the Civil War. The speaker is her son, born on "the day after Vicksburg fell on the Fourth [of July 1863]" (*Jordan* 226). This short piece reflects a central tenet of Foote's vision of the human condition: the near miraculous ability of some individuals to adjust to a changing world. "It was the times," says the narrator, "the whole air swirling full of freedom and danger; it was catching, you see, and Mamma already had it bad in the first place" (*Jordan* 228). What is remarkable about Esmeralda is not that she triumphs over the entrenched racism of the whites—indeed, her re-ward for challenging the system in the name of "freedom and justice and the vote" (*Jordan* 228) is a severe beating—but rather that she perseveres in her dream, passing on the hope of its realization to her son. Like Isaac Jameson, or Hugh Bart (early on), Esmeralda possesses a spark that marks the onset of a new form of vitality in the region. By preserving a symbol of this dream (the teeth she lost as a result of the kick), she asserts her free-dom and, as a consequence, acts "like she'd sued and won. She held her head high, showing the missing teeth and the sunk-in cheek. You couldnt down her" (*Jordan* 229). The ironic undertone to the story—the paradoxi-cal relationship between past time and present consciousness that fasci-nates Foote—is found in the subdued voice of her son, recipient of the very freedoms Esmeralda prized. He muses: "But I dont know. It was true, I got them, but it seems like they dont mean so much as they did back then with the Kluxers riding the roads to take them from you. Thats how it is, even with freedom" (*Jordan* 229).

Foote explores this paradoxical connection between complacency and resistance, between acceptance of the status quo and active protest, in his major treatment of the black experience in the Delta, *September September*.

In this novel, he traces the emergence of a new American dream through the awakening of a political sensibility in Eben Kinship, a middle-class black man living in Memphis. Eben's marriage to the daughter of a wealthy real-estate speculator, Theo Wiggins, re-creates in a different racial context the typical Delta patriarch-dependent relationship. (As the speaker of "The Freedom Kick" notes, the black population is not immune to the class consciousness of white society. The speaker's maternal grandfather, a free man and a barber, whose proximity to the whites guaranteed him a certain social status, evinces considerable disappointment at Esmeralda's marriage to an ex-slave: "he had looked a good deal higher for her than that" [*Jordan* 225]. This transgression against his "blood-pride" [*Jordan* 226] is treated somewhat ironically by his grandson, who "never put much stock in all that talk. You used to hear lots of such claims among the colored. If it wasnt [African] chiefs it was French blood. Maybe we caught it from the white folks" [*Jordan* 226].) In Eben's case, what begins as a staunchly conservative position bred out of subservience and fear (of the political power of the whites and of the economic clout of Wiggins) ends in an assertion of individual integrity and mutual respect. The gradual divergence in the views of the two men, over how to confront segregation and political disenfranchisement, represents Foote's charting of a new frontier. The transformation of Eben's attitude from conservative quietism to a determined political activism embodies—at this endpoint in Foote's Jordan County chronology, the month of September 1957—the emergence of a new consciousness in the Delta world. While the relationship between the elder Wiggins and the younger Kinship echoes Foote's other depictions of dysfunctional planter patriarchies, the alterations they undergo as a result of the traumatic kidnapping of their child resolve into hope for a new social and familial vitality.

• • •

In political terms, Eben changes from a disciple of Booker T. Washington and his "accommodation philosophy" (*Encyclopedia of Southern Culture* 390) to the political activism of the Civil Rights movement represented by Martin Luther King. Wiggins is a Booker T. Washington man. Soon after his arrival in Memphis in 1909, he heard Washington speak: "'Let down your buckets where you are,' [Theo] liked to quote, if only to himself" (*September* 57). Wiggins builds a real-estate empire by recognizing the existing racial divisions in institutions such as the law: "It's been a longtime rule of mine to stay clear of the law whenever and wherever the two colors are involved. You got to remember, the law is first of all the white man's law. He wrote it, he enforces it, and he sits in judgment on it. . . . It's his, not ourn, and nothing but trouble can come of not facing up to the fact that that's the way it is" (*September* 146). Similarly, Theo describes—in a statement of political strategy that echoes Foote's descriptions of Abraham Lincoln's character and methods—how he "used [the system] against itself, and beat it" (*September* 288):

> I long since learnt to live with them and expect still worse with every go-round: especially where the law, the power, is concerned. All them other scrabblers, black and white, I dealt with as they come along. You can catch more flies with honey than with vinegar, by a long shot. What I did, right down the line, was pretend to be on their side so I could get them on mine, unbeknownst. You think I ever minded some man having a low opinion of me? No indeed. That give me the best of all advantages over him. He wouldnt even take the trouble to look at my position and think what I might do: especially a white man. Handkerchief Head, Uncle Tom—what do I care what he thinks I am, so long as I know I'm me? (*September* 248)

Eben absorbs Theo's philosophy without possessing his inner conviction; indeed, it is this attitude he parrots at the outset of the novel. Sitting comfortably at home, ensconced in his middle-class rituals of an orderly home, regular work, nightly news, and weekly sex, Eben reflects on the confrontation in Little Rock, Arkansas, over desegregation of the school system. Launching into a conservative tirade about "Those damn people" (*September* 18) that reminds Martha of her father, Eben dismisses the aims of the agitators: "And what follows? I'll tell you. Lost jobs, foreclosed mortgages, white resentment; all that. Like that city-bus business last year in Montgomery, that preacher's son, King—a preacher himself, I understand; some kind of preacher anyhow. Lord God. Who cares which end of a bus he rides on, just so it gets him there? The thing to do, and everybody knows it, is hump hard inside the system, so youll own your own car and wont even have to think about busses, let alone ride one" (*September* 18). What Eben comes to realize, after being brought face to face with his vulnerability within such a system, is the necessity of reaffirming the higher principles instead of accommodating himself, and his children, to a diminished existence.

The corollary to Eben's politics of accommodation is found in Martha's internalization of racist values. She lives in a personal wasteland, suspended between the two races and cultures—a condition symbolized by the contrasting parental photographs on the walls of the Kinship living room. Theo's image is described as Buddha-like, with echoes of the masked countenances of other black figures in Foote's fiction, as well as an inscrutable and brooding power:

> Dominant on this wall . . . was a large oval portrait in a burled walnut frame of a man so altogether solid-looking, despite his more than sixty years, that even looking at him from dead ahead, as you did here, you could tell he had thick folds of fat across the back of his neck but absolutely nowhere else. The small round eyes peering intently out of the otherwise uninterrupted dark expanse of face contained a sentience beyond interpretation on short notice. He wore a hat, a heavy watch chain linking the bottom pockets on his vest, a snub bow tie, and square in the notch of the V of his starched shirt-front, which had the glazed, milky look of mother-of-pearl, one tiny polished gleam of gold so central to his aspect that he might have been built around it. (*September* 16–17)

Theo is, in fact, constructed around gold. His orientation to the gold standard, ironically, results in the re-creation in his household of the planter paternalism, most noticeably in the figure of his niece, Dolly, who serves as the family's help: "Lincoln they say freed the slaves almost a hundred years ago, but Dolly never got the word: unless, that is, emancipation didnt apply within the family" (*September* 52). Theo's connections with the planter heritage are also evident in his choice of wife, Lucinda:

> Aristocratic of mien, with skin a good bit lighter and paler than high yellow, she had intelligent eyes and a high-bridged nose, aquiline in contrast to his broad flat one with its two fuliginous nostrils, black on black, that put you in mind of a double-barrel shotgun trained on a point exactly midway between your eyes. In the juxtaposition of their two photographs, as different in style as they were in subject, she might have been some distant forebear in an old-time ambrotype; a quadroon or octoroon great-grandmother, say, whose white blood had been abolished in his and his father's

and grandfather's veins by some progressive, highly virulent form
of male genetic domination. (*September* 17)

Child of these parents, Martha lives at odds with her black heritage and in
rebellion against her own nature.

A result of this reproduction of white social values is that Martha
reflects the dysfunction found in Foote's other planter households, mimick-
ing the society from which she is excluded by her color: "Most everything
I was, and am," she muses, "came from getting my daddy's looks and not
my mamma's. If I'd been born willowy like her, high-nosed and light of skin,
instead of squat and froggy, dark like him, I wouldnt have had to spend so
much time rising above my appearance" (*September* 150). Indoctrinated
with the values of Miss Endicott's Finishing School for Young Ladies of
Color in Saint Louis, Martha spends much of her time perusing beauty magazines for tips and adopts various methods, such as straightening her hair,
in an effort to accommodate her appearance to their dictates. Even her
approach to sexuality bespeaks a kind of self-loathing. After her brief experience of sexual awakening under the tutelage of Snooker Martin, cut short
by her father's intervention (in the form of two thugs who run him out of
town), Martha ties her sense of gender shame to her racial heritage: "In my
shame I decided what I felt went back to Africa, jungle doings, and we
really were animals, the way some people said of those who did the things
that got them lynched—wild animals deserving of being cut and blow-
torched, not only for what we did, but for what we were, deep down in the
blood brought here from Africa two hundred years ago" (*September* 157). In
her continued denial of her race and her father's social pretensions, Martha
enters her marriage with Eben, keeping "a tight rein on myself, and on
Eben too" (*September* 159), and accommodating her sense of self, both
racially and sexually, to her definition of middle-class propriety. The result
is a passionless existence of conformity. Martha's situation is as debilitating
as any of the white relationships where the dominant planter patriarch
attempts to dictate his children's future: "Nothing we had didnt come from
him, and we both knew it. Job, house, promotions, expectations, all tied
in to Daddy and what he wanted, what he thought. In bed it was that
way, too . . . and it led me to think a terrible thing, no less clear for being
terrible: Eben has the prick but Daddy pumps it" (*September* 159). Under
the shock of her son's kidnapping, and the heightened racial tension

fomented by Governor Orval Faubus in Little Rock, Martha responds in a manner appropriate to her sense of subjugation:

> I felt about it . . . something like the way we felt in the old days when a lynching came along. We tended to blame the one who got himself cut and burnt for doing what he'd done, not the whites, who after all were doing exactly what they said theyd do if he crossed the line. We held it against him, even while he hung there burnt and cut on, for proving to the whites that theyd been right all along in saying we were animals: not just the low-life killer or raper who got what he had known he'd get, but the rest of us as well—animals out of Africa. (*September* 148)

This Wiggins and Kinship world of ritual and quietude, of accommodation and self-blame, of careful distancing from the realities of their compromised situation, collapses under the impetus of direct contact with their powerlessness. Yet, rather than suffering dissolution, these characters in Foote's last novel emerge with a clearer sense of their individual self-worth, and a new taste for political activism.

One other significant picture hangs on the Kinship living-room wall. It is a "gilt-frame chromo of a girl-faced Christ" (*September* 16), a guiding spirit in the family's absorption of white middle-class values. As Eben begins to alter his perspective under the stress of the kidnapping, his response to this particular image changes: "Ugly, he told himself in quick reaction to the rage that had been with him since the day before" (*September* 214). Now the message of the picture reflects Eben's sense of isolation in his time of need: "From time to time he looked at the framed chromo on the wall above his head, but it seemed to him that Jesus, who was also looking upward, was too occupied with his own concerns to be troubled much about what might be happening down below. No doubt his problems were white ones, Eben thought, since he himself—like his Father before him, invisible somewhere in the direction he was gazing beyond the gilt upper limit of the frame—was a white man" (*September* 214). Indeed, from his first response to Martha's frantic call a week earlier, Eben is stymied by the system—he cannot even take the first cab he hails when rushing home because it is for whites only (*September* 76). But the rage builds with his increasing consciousness of his dilemma:

He was part of a system which asked certain things of him—things he gave, if not gladly then anyhow willingly; taxes, for one, and close to four years in the army for another—yet which turned out to be unavailable when he got around to needing something in return; in this case, assistance in the recovery of his son. There was no refusal, not even the occasion for refusal, since, knowing as he did that almost nothing worse could happen than for him to be granted that assistance, he did not ask it. (*September* 217)

What Eben realizes is that his rage, like his wife's sexual desire, has been "festering inside" (*September* 240) for a considerable time—a direct challenge to his sense of being unmanned by accommodation to Theo's power, and in a larger sphere to the racial injustice of the society. He comes to deny the Washington credo: "'Let down your buckets where you are,' old Booker T. advised, and I believed him, along with Tio [Theo], until I let my bucket down, the way he said, and found it had no bottom" (*September* 241). Out of this revelation comes Eben's desire to "change things" (*September* 287), first by asserting his rights in relation to Theo, and later by addressing the injustices of the society in which he lives: "'It *is* my time,' Eben told [Theo]. . . . 'I can begin to square away what's around me; or start trying'" (*September* 288). The final discussion between Theo and Eben marks a new departure in Foote's vision, a dialogue across generations couched in terms of mutual respect. In a compromise nearly unique in the Jordan County novels—its closest equivalent being Isaac Jameson's demand for his legacy in order to finance the clearing of Solitaire and realize his, not his father's, dream—Theo recognizes the justice of Eben's goal and agrees to support him: "I decided you were right about a lot you told me, yesterday and last week, under all that pressure. Right for you, I mean; not me. I did what I did, in my way and in my day, and I outdid them. It could be I gave you a kind of base to stand on, you and others like you still to come; to stand on and say, 'He done it his way in his day. Now the time is come for us to do it our way'" (*September* 289). In this respect, the history of the Delta region comes full circle and moves toward a new beginning. The fact that the vision is articulated by one of the dispossessed highlights the pivotal nature of this next era in the region's history. Foote's novel marks the emergence of these marginalized figures and reflects the ironic displacement of the surviving white characters westward in search of easy Las Vegas money (the ultimate abstraction).

Historical Moment IV

"Rain Down Home"—Love and Alienation

The first story in Foote's *Jordan County* collection is "Rain Down Home"; it is the tale of Pauly Green, a returning Korean War veteran whose troubled state of mind is reminiscent of the Nick Adams character in Ernest Hemingway's "Big Two-Hearted River" (1925). Unlike Nick, who returns from the First World War to immerse himself in healing retreat into nature, Pauly discovers nothing of his own lost world. Instead, he returns to a hometown that has forgotten him, an urban world of traffic lights whose "lidless glare" and mechanical changes suggest "some central brain, peremptory, electric, and unthinking" (*Jordan* 5); a town of imitation marble facades and parking meters "each with its clockwork entrails ticking off time between now and the red flag of violation" (*Jordan* 5). Exploring Bristol, Pauly encounters only isolated individuals and examples of missed connections—a wasteland where the past, like the statue of the Confederate soldier before the courthouse, stares sphinxlike with "blank stone eyeballs" (*Jordan* 13) across the landscape. In search of meaningful human contact, Pauly discovers only feelings of defeat and hopelessness, most clearly articulated by an old man who attributes the current malaise to a people who have "got away from God" (*Jordan* 12). Recounting his wife's horrific death by cancer, the old man asserts: "It dont mean a thing. Nothing. Why should it mean anything?" (*Jordan* 13). Horrified, Pauly reacts to this enervated environment with an act of seemingly meaningless violence; he calmly shoots up the inside of a café—a gesture of despair and resistance. Pauly's story marks the exhaustion of an era and the beginning of the reader's odyssey into the Delta past. In a typically understated fashion, this initial story in Foote's *Jordan County* includes oblique references to places of significance in the following tales and in all of the novels. As the reader moves back into the history of Jordan County, it is clear that Foote is stressing how knowledge of the past offers greater understanding of the present, although, ironically, the cure for the present malaise is found in the old values of self-awareness and compassion—traits possible only through a recognition and acceptance of humanity's limited existential condition.

In the novels set between the late 1920s and the late 1950s (*Love in a Dry Season, Follow Me Down,* and *September September*), Foote presents the alienation arising from an exhausted heritage and the loss of a moral center through debased familial and sexual relationships. The primary statement of this theme is in "Child by Fever": "that biblical verse which tells of the children's teeth being set on edge by grapes the parents ate" (*Jordan* 76). Much of what Foote explores in this context can be introduced by quoting from the monologue that comprises "A Marriage Portion":

> I sometimes think I married him just to get him out of my system. Not that I didnt admire him; who wouldnt? He was so much older, twenty-four to eighteen, and such a sheik. He played the ukulele, wore wider-bottomed trousers than anyone, had a car and all those things. Also his folks had money, lots of it, and Daddy had lost our money on the market years ago. I knew if I didn't marry him I'd regret it all my life. Then, too, everyone kept saying he could "handle" me, get me "tamed" as Daddy said. That was what I wanted, after what had happened between my parents; I wanted what my mother didn't have. (*Jordan* 73)

The speaker's perspective in "A Marriage Portion" also indicates the dangerous implications of what Hugh Bart calls "romance" (*Tournament* 29). Time and again in Foote's fiction, idealistic self-delusion plays a central role in the personal dissatisfaction experienced by the characters (such as Bart, his daughter Florence, Amanda Barcroft, Luther Eustis, Hector Sturgis, and Rufus Hutton). Foote's depiction of generations is, in fact, the story of a fall from the world of romance (another way of considering the myth of the Old South and the American frontier) into the world of Freud and Nietzsche. The nature of this modern failure is stated precisely in Foote's letter to Walker Percy (November 7, 1974; *Correspondence* 196–97) when he aligns himself with D. H. Lawrence in identifying individuality as the endemic sickness of the modern age. Foote's consideration of the history from "Old Dixie" to modernity—the backdrop against which the individual relationships are set—conveys this loss of community, and love, most clearly in his depictions of sexual relationships. As the world moves further into the twentieth century, the excremental aspect of Foote's vision becomes more pronounced—though it is never Swiftian—and the debilitating effects of moral and social alienation become more extreme.

Concentrating on the dynastic element in southern families, Foote chronicles the effects of broad societal changes on successive generations.

In the case of Solitaire, it is Bart's wife Florence, granddaughter of Isaac, who retains a sense of the importance of the land at the crucial juncture in their lives. After Bart sells the plantation, with "the decisiveness of a snake when it casts its skin; he had taken the cash and let the worry go" (*Tournament* 183), he seeks to impress Florence with their considerable bank balance, mistakenly proud of a meaningless abstraction. "What do you want for your birthday?" he inquires, ironically unaware that what she desires is the return of her birthright: "Solitaire, she almost said. But she just sat there" (*Tournament* 183). While Florence recognizes the importance of this connection to the land and the familial heritage, her children share none of her enthusiasm. The eldest son, Hugh Jr., drifts aimlessly; he lacks both his father's "spark" and its accompanying drive and ambition. Hugh tries law, farming, and marriage, each an unsatisfactory attempt either to escape or to reconcile himself to the dynastic imperative of the planter world. Only belatedly does he recognize that the family "ought to be there [at Solitaire], ought never to have left" (*Tournament* 186). The difference in outlooks of father and son lies at the heart of their inability to communicate: "Bart, who had worked so hard all his life, always with his goal set plain before him, whose every move had been shaped by what was ahead and tempered by what was behind, could not imagine a life without its aim in full view, could not conceive of a dormitory filled with boys who were not spending all their time planning their future. A person who had time to plan and yet was planless was like a loaded rifle without a firing pin" (*Tournament* 142). Part of the son's reluctance is a result of the debilitating influence of the planter paternalism, but another part is the erosion of stable values as the twentieth century begins.

Bart's ambitions to found a Delta dynasty, to re-create the essential pattern of planter society that was "laid out and waiting for Bart's three children as they entered the new century" (*Tournament* 95), runs afoul of the modern world and the corruptive influence of his own material success. As his grandson Asa, the narrator of Bart's history, wryly points out, "No lifeway could have been more completely unlike the one he had been raised under, back in East Mississippi. He might have reminded himself at the outset to expect a different product" (*Tournament* 95–96). Bart's children—Hugh, Florence, and Clive (namesake of the general—in whom perverse recklessness takes the place of daring)—all exhibit the sickness of the new age, which is reinforced by the move to Bristol. City dwelling is Bart's last disastrous attempt to adjust. Asa sums up: "Clive who was still a boy but who even Bart now knew, in the phrase of the time and place, was not worth the powder it would take to blow him up, because he had no interest in means but in results, because he lacked what the educators call application and what sportsmen call heart; Florence who was foreign to this land because she cared nothing for a living soul she had ever known, least of all herself, who was running hard even now toward no one knew what catastrophe: and Hugh, who had failed" (*Tournament* 177). The younger generation embodies the "historical unrest" (*Tournament* 182) tied to the new urban setting. They share the outlook of the "'town' people," of whom Bart thinks: "People here . . . were unlike those he had lived among up to now. The farming activity, which absorbed the lives of the men he had known on the lake, had been replaced by a zeal for other things; they said Money with a tone of reverence, and when they used the personal pronoun they gave it a capital I" (*Tournament* 182). The complete alienation of Bart from his children, and his grasping after a connection with the young Asa— the grandson he has hitherto ignored—establishes the fundamental model for the relationships between parents and offspring in Foote's fiction. Familial communication, like most other treatments of language in Foote's books (with the exception of the Wiggins and Kinship reconciliation in *September September*), is hopelessly flawed, corrupted by the incompatibility of the Delta heritage and the vexed issue of self-knowledge in the modern world.

Foote's depiction of the decline of the New South and the modernization of the region is constructed around the male figures associated with the planter society—figures such as Hugh Bart, Hector Sturgis, and Major Barcroft. These representations of the Delta patriarchy are, however, only half of the equation when it comes to examining his treatment of this society. Just as the previously marginalized voices of the black community find more complete expression in the Kinship family of *September September*, so too the female voice emerges as Foote's history moves beyond the watershed year of 1910. When Parker Nowell articulates his bleak vision of this century, in which "Love has failed us" and "We are essentially, irrevocably alone" (*Follow* 233), he represents the exhaustion of a worldview that originates with the attitudes of the earliest European figures. What is important to note is that Foote turns to the voices of Beulah Ross, Reeny Perdew, and Martha Kinship, and the bedrock values they represent, to fill the vacuum. Certainly, the presence of the female voice was not always so strong, although Foote outlines, early on, the contribution of the women to the Delta way of life.

The female characters are presented, initially, as largely silent adjuncts in a male-ordered society—pleasing abstractions contained in a chivalric code. A case in point is Foote's depiction of Katy Jameson, wife of Isaac. While the story is constructed around Isaac's role in the settlement of the region, and his status as larger-than-life frontiersman in the Jordan County pantheon, it is the figure of Katy who anchors the dream in reality. Her youthful vigor and command of organization convert the settler's shack into a proper home: while Isaac watches "with amazement her transformation from girl-bride into mule skinner and section boss (all that was missing was the cursing). . . . He watched with no less amazement, when the work was done and the house was to her liking, his wife's re-transformation back to the girl-bride she had been before the steamboat blew for the landing" (*Jordan* 247). The children she gives him, living and dead, sanctify his relation to the place. Indeed, it is Katy's death that precipitates Isaac's recognition of the finite nature of human existence; he is "bewildered at last by mortality, by a world in which a person could sneeze and say, 'God bless me: I feel dizzy,' and then be dead" (*Jordan* 263).

The vitality of the female characters (initially presented in images related to matrimony and the procreative) is, over time, reduced by planter culture into empty social ritual. Much of Foote's depiction of the planter society Hugh Bart knew demonstrates this point. The women are the silent anchors for the Delta world (like the unspoken vitality of the blacks) and are, finally, "what made planter society hold together as long as it did" (*Tournament* 95). The nature of this strength is articulated in Foote's consideration of the virtues of Katy Jameson's granddaughter and Hugh Bart's bride:

Taken as they had just emerged from girlhood (the average bride was eighteen) they called their husbands Mister all their lives. They lived in a lambency of inexperience but were able in times of crisis, war or sickness or death, to choose and decide for the good of the family by drawing upon some antediluvian feminine reserve, like the mother spider or spawning salmon which strives constantly and apparently with all its strength, yet when faced by an unexpected condition, draws upon a hidden well of undefeat to produce the action which surmounts the obstacle and allows continuance of the bland unruffled striving. They bowed their heads to their husbands' slightest whim—allowing the male, brute blunt instrument for providing, to be the intelligence in all decisions which, apparently world-shaking, were of small import in fact—but asserted themselves and handed down irrevocable decisions in matters which were basic and therefore vital. They did this without alarming their husbands or even putting them on the defensive, for the decision was always given such a manner, spoken in the male-mate language, that it appeared to the husbands as echoes of their own thought, like a stone that had been polished or dipped in gold. They wore clothes which gave inch for inch as much covering as medieval armor and yet were able, laced and stayed as they were, not only to be willowy and tender but also to bear large numbers of children and to raise those who lived (many were stillborn; many died in infancy: every plantation burying ground had its cluster of small anonymous headboards) in the strict formula whereby life was simple because conflicting thought did not cloud it and no battle raged between conception and execution. (*Tournament* 35–36)

The last of the statements here is the most telling: the suggestion that the female characters in planter society retain a version of the "spark" that first animated Isaac Jameson, and then Hugh Bart. The increasing rigidity and hollowness of the planter world (when faced by the challenges of the modern) lead to a distortion of this vitality in female characters such as Bertha Tarfeller, a "romantic, violent girl" (*Tournament* 39), whose ill-considered romance with the gambler Downs Macready leads to the death of her father in a pathetic and farcical gunfight, or Hugh Bart's daughter Florence, whose younger "rough-and-tumble hoyden ways" (*Tournament* 133) develop into the aestheticism and lesbianism that break her father's spirit.

In "Child by Fever," the female characters, most notably Mrs. Wingate, Mrs. Sturgis (her daughter), and Ella (Hector's wife), reflect the changes in traditional planter hierarchy. Mrs. Wingate embodies the static ideal of the plantation-society status quo, the changeless ritual of working the land and maintaining a stable power structure. Her daughter, in rebellion against the restrictions of that environment, first attempts escape through marriage, only to be frustrated by her chosen husband's capitulation to the Wingate wealth and power. Relying on her own indomitable will, a capacity her husband recognized as "formidable, even inexorable" (*Jordan* 88), Esther Sturgis survives them all and comes to represent the dictates of Progress as it sweeps away the old dominants of the planter life in the twentieth century. The complementary nature of the gender roles is now dissolved. The perverse nature of the relationship between Hector and Ella reinforces this decline. Hector pursues the same route for escape as his mother did; lacking her strength of will, however, his attempt is more a feverish form of naive romanticism: "Love was his release from the burden coming-of-age had thrust upon him; Love was his consolation for all failures, all shortcomings; he perceived now that nothing could ever be really unbearable if a man had love to turn to. Also, she needed him. This alone, in Hector's mind, was enough to recommend marriage" (*Jordan* 138). Ella, in fact, possesses this potential for escape and redemption—having engineered it once on her own behalf with her rejection of an earlier penchant for promiscuous behavior, and her transformation from "Lilith on the lookout" to her present "mournful, slightly soured expression of Magdalene redeemed" (*Jordan* 137). The failure of the relationship lies more on Hector's head, a result of his inability to move out from under Mrs. Sturgis's domination.

The crisis in Hector's marriage involves his loss of nerve when confronted by the traumatic birth of his son. Unable to reconcile the ecstasies of conception with the painful realities of delivery, Hector is shocked into impotence. When Ella turns to him in need after the death of the child, she finds "no resurrection of the flesh" (*Jordan* 155) and is forced to look elsewhere for sexual comfort. Ironically, Hector can only realize his love after Ella's death when she has become a malleable part of his imagination, an abstraction in whose company he effectively "seceded from the human race" into a self-constructed "universe within a universe" (*Jordan* 205). In the daylight world of the ten remaining years of marriage, their relationship deteriorates to the point where violence replaces sexual gratification: "Experienced from within, there was something terribly degrading about [his striking her]; yet seen . . . impersonally, it gave him a strange, vicarious pleasure" (*Jordan* 156). Where earlier the strength of familial relationships was founded on a unity "between conception and execution" (*Tournament* 35–36), the figures drawn from the present are able to achieve only a bleak parody of this unity by violent means.

As the novels move into the modern age, the depiction of relationships becomes more violent and grotesque. The story of Hector Sturgis is one example; the family history of the Barcrofts is another. The alienation of the characters transforms conventional values into destructive abstractions. Major Barcroft, for example, out of his infatuation with the family honor, destroys the potential for happiness in each of his children. Foote's depiction of the modern South follows this process of decline and dissolution to its logical conclusion. In *Follow Me Down,* Luther Eustis's dual heritage of lust and murder—his mother's infidelities and his father's violent retribution that consumes the homestead in a "pillar of fire" (*Follow* 203)—leaves him spiritually and emotionally adrift. In his portrait of the three white kidnappers in *September September,* Foote suggests a state of almost complete moral dissolution.

The most extreme example of this malaise is Rufus Hutton, a character whose past is made up of absent figures and missed connections and who, as a consequence, fabricates a history (creating a fictional past continually subject to revision according to his whims in the immediate present). Rufus is not even convinced that his surname is real, suggesting that all his father "left [him] was his name, if it was his name, and even that turned out to be a burden" (*September* 73). Spurred on by this lack of connection, as well as his bookkeeper grandfather's deathbed teachings, "Dont trust 'um. . . . Honest always, I was. . . . Never touched so much as a dime, one thin dime. . . . Mistake. Mis-take. You take um, Rufus, hear me? Take um. It's the only way youll get justice. Steal 'um blind" (*September* 74–75), Rufus invents not only a past, but also his own self-serving morality. What was for Luther Eustis an unwitting strategy of denial and evasion is for Rufus an entirely conscious process of redefining the world on his own terms—a procedure conditioned by the books he has read and the films he has seen. Rufus reveals his self-awareness when commenting that his life is "a pattern of failure rushed to completion as soon as I saw failure looming. I saw now where I'd been headed; 'Die young and make a handsome corpse,' as the fellow said in the Bogart movie" (*September* 76). Rufus exercises a self-serving freedom in crafting a web of lies as a substitute for history; he lives a fiction that leads his accomplice, Podjo (who refuses to romanticize his lot in life) to think "There's worse things than a liar, by far, but Rufus had gone beyond lying to become the things he told. He wasnt just a liar. He was a lie" (*September* 45). Rufus is not "any part of a whole man" (*September* 208) but rather a pastiche of desires and impulses gathered around a vacuum. Once again Podjo offers the most succinct assessment of Rufus's psyche:

> Nothing is as dangerous as a coward when he's crossed and cornered; that is if he's got some angle he can work to get back at you, never mind what's likely to come down on his own head afterward;

especially when he's as keyed-up as Rufus was all through that
time. . . . There's no top to that ladder for men like him, built
around their privates with a brain that ticks like a time bomb in the
shape of a clenched-up cunt. If it was big enough, and you could
smoke in there, theyd live in it. And the lies; my God, the lies. Instead of making a life for himself, he made one up. (*September* 252)

Lacking the character to translate his "joy of invention" into anything positive ("I should have been a writer, except I could never really get down
to it as a trade like any other; bank-robbing say, or carpentry, if I'd only
had the patience" [*September* 76]), Rufus sustains himself by the excitement of the moment, whether it be the thrill of the kidnap, the throes of
orgasm, or the imagined anguish a brutal ransom note will generate. As
Reeny remarks in connection with his obsessive lovemaking, "None of it,
such as it was, was really for me, no matter how much I wanted or enjoyed
it. It was all for him, a kind of wrestling, a struggle to get outside himself
by catching his excitement from mine; feeding on me . . ." (*September*
174). Rufus dies, literally consumed by the material world, in the explosion of his cherished Thunderbird. Burning like "a grasshopper caught in
the flame of a blowtorch," he finally "fold[s] inward on himself" (*September* 298) in tacit recognition of the hollowness within.

The second male conspirator, Podjo Harris, recognizes and accepts
his inadequacy in the face of past models and lost certainties. Podjo is
aware that his life of crime (gambling and manslaughter) makes him a
lesser man than his father: "Only half of me is my father, and I'm half the
man he was" (*September* 263). Having rejected his mother's wish that he
become a priest, and acknowledging that "All religion did for me was
make me scared to death of God" (*September* 49), Podjo consoles himself
with the truth that "we're not very smart, those of us who go in for crime.
We have to make up in risk for what we lack in skill and insight" (*September* 48). Podjo retains, though, a degree of self-awareness in his admission of the limitations of his chosen existence; more importantly, he
demonstrates an integrity in his final commitment to Reeny—his willing-
ness to "take unto [himself] a millstone" (*September* 261), to break out of
his isolation and cherish her "good-hearted [nature] . . . combined with
friendliness and caring" (*September* 261–62). The third kidnapper, Reeny
Perdew—only daughter of a preacher whose sermons tie "[i]t all . . .
in—lust and the Lord" (*September* 135)—survives past exploitation and

exhibits an honesty, clear-sightedness, and a genuine sympathy for other humans. Shortly after talking to Martha on the telephone, reassuring the frantic mother of her son's health and well-being, Reeny demonstrates these qualities by accepting responsibility for her actions: "I felt strange from having talked with her after all we'd done and were doing to her. She seemed a lot realer . . . and somehow I seemed less real; that is, I had an even harder time believing we'd done what we had done—what we were doing. But we had; we were" (*September* 162). These traits, combined with an honest self-awareness, enable Reeny to effect a series of rebirths or new beginnings. She realizes, albeit in an unintended way, the hopes implicit in her proper name, Renée (reborn); and, in a sense, embodies the regeneration of the original Jameson spark in the debased Jimson line.

Historical Moment V

"Ride Out"—A Conclusion

The paradox of opposing values simultaneously sustained is central to Foote's "quality of vision." In this way, the artist (poet, novelist, painter) attempts to redeem the experience by translating it through the filter of imagination into art. Chaos acquires form; the past is regained; meaningless experience becomes meaningful. The work of art (whether generated through metaphor or narrative, brush or chisel) is always greater than the sum of the parts. In Foote's story "Ride Out," this conjunction of opposites is represented by Harry Van, "son of a New England choir master and a sea captain's daughter, advanced student at one of the nation's leading music institutions" (*Jordan* 48), and Duff Conway, "the son of an itinerant guitarist and a Mississippi servant girl, horn man in a Harlem gin-mill" (*Jordan* 48). The combination of classical training and jazz improvisation reflects a similar combination of aesthetic values in Foote's work: "An inferior art by virtue of its limitations, [Conway's jazz] involved great drive and marvelous technique and little else; but jazz men . . . never let technique be anything but a means to an end. This was what [Van] mainly got" (*Jordan* 49). Such generative oppositions inform Foote's work as an ironic historian, where detachment and sympathy are held in balance; being "double-sided" in this way, these oppositions play a crucial role in his investigation of human frailty, whether physical or moral. One might even expect to find this seminal tension in the condition of being at once southern and modern.

In a letter written after reading Walker Percy's essay about the significance of language, "The Delta Factor," Foote develops his own view on how a writer constructs reality:

> Something of this carries into writing. Its glory is the metaphor, whether a simil[e] or a more subtle form of comparison, an equaling of two very different things whose comparison makes each of them far realer than before. "All flesh is grass" is one of the great statements, reaching well down into our very bones; even though, as you say, it is patently false in fact, it is superbly true in its application, in our response to the words themselves and the thoughts they provoke. All flesh is grass, and it is the aptness of the metaphor that makes it so much truer than the simple statement that all flesh is mortal. (Incidentally, I don't think you should leave out the all, which makes it even truer by wider application.) In other words, the metaphor is what makes it truer. Metaphor, if it is right, always makes everything truer. Proust called it finding the true way to explain or demonstrate a thing, provided it was encased in a "fine" style. (December 4, 1974; *Correspondence* 198–99)

In all his work, Foote applies this principle to further his artistic representation of the complexity of experience and perception. His goal is reflected in the following quotation, from a letter to Walker Percy, in which he again refers to Proust:

> For Proust, every work of art is a harmonization, a kind of metaphor. It can be understood only in relation to something else, for it is always in harmony with something of a quite different nature which exists only in the author's mind. For him, a work of art is not an aspiration: it is not a fulfillment of desire or an expression of faith; it is not a means to any end whatever; nor is it a discovery of something new, since it only reveals a discovery which necessarily precedes it. It is none of these things. It is the concrete equivalent of a reality belonging to another order: an order perceived because it confers upon things the enigma of a new and autonomous beauty.

What he discovers is what all artists are seeking: inner reality.
Without it there can be no esthetic beauty, for it is itself the source
of beauty. Artistic sense (so called) is insep[a]rable from submission
to that inner reality. (Letters, October 29, 1955)

Metaphor, then, is central to Foote's aesthetic ordering of opposing values.
The work of art, the narrative in Foote's case, gains its effects by means of
this harmonization—an "idea of order" that "confers upon things the enigma of a new autonomous beauty." Foote's fiction presents the psychological
and moral counterpoint created by the overlay of the southern heritage and
the modernist challenges to established verities. A similar tension is identifiable between the sense of contingency and indeterminacy within the narratives and the highly structured nature of the narrative frames. At the heart
of great writing, for Foote, is this process of harmonization; and the agency
of metaphor provides the means whereby fact is transformed into "truth."
In a sense, the transformation of chronicle into history, or event into myth,
is analogous. In speaking about Faulkner's writing, Foote suggests "that a
quality of very great writing is that it converts tales into myths. Because
myth is so much greater than fantasy, if you handle a fantasy right it will
become a myth" (Conversations 224). A central aspect of Hayden White's
analysis of historical narrative is his assertion that emplotment is a species
of metaphor providing direction in understanding a subject: "It functions as
a symbol, rather than as a sign: which is to say that it does not give us either
a *description* or an *icon* of the thing it represents, but *tells us* what images to
look for in our culturally encoded experience in order to determine how we
should feel about the thing represented" (*Tropics* 91). In this respect, the art
of description, the act of creating a narrative, the overlay and interconnec-
tion of kinds and degrees of metaphor, constitute, for Foote, the highest
form of analysis. It is by this means that he transforms a regional focus into
an exploration of the modern condition and, by doing so, sets the stage for
the masterful narrative art of *The Civil War.*

Chapter 3

The Aesthetics of Limitation

Event, Memory, and Narrative

. . . hindsight paradoxically limits our ability to understand the past by giving us greater knowledge than people of the time could have had. "Can we really be fair to men of the past," asked A. F. Pollard, "knowing what they could not know? Can we, indeed, understand them at all . . . with our minds prepossessed by a knowledge of the result?" The question raises an issue that transcends the limits to historical understanding, for it implies that bias does not merely reduce the historical past but also enlarges it.

— David Lowenthal, *The Past Is a Foreign Country,* 1985

Dont tell me you have swallowed that hokum about the writer being a Wise Man. As a matter of fact he is stupid to an amazing degree about the things that people value; he has a block that stops him short of acceptance that makes him examine what others accept; he can be fascinated by the shape of his own hand, watching it by lamplight holding the pen; for him "understanding" is merely description—that is enough. Your wise-man says "There is my hand; all right; lets get on to important things. How about the relation of God to man?" But the artist, I believe, concentrating on the hand itself, without even a thought of God, comes closer to finding the meaning simply by observing how the hand, held between his eye and the lamp, becomes semitransparent, showing the skeleton hand beneath.

— Shelby Foote, letter to Walker Percy, November 8, 1951

*A*t the end of *Tournament,* Asa Bart draws a distinction between the "unadorned statement of fact" that constitutes his "one stark memory" of his grandfather and his own reconstruction of Hugh Bart's story, which he labels "hearsay" (*Tournament* xxxiii). Bart's last words (in reality the last intelligible words Asa personally recalls) function, paradoxically, as both the beginning and the end of his attempt to reclaim Bart's story. The words reveal as much about Asa's perspective (as the one who fashioned the "hearsay" that is Bart's history) as they do of Hugh Bart. Asa's violation of chronology means that Bart's questing spirit, revealed in his *actual* last words, "I'm looking for a home," are displaced in favor of the phrase Asa privileges as "fact" only because *he* heard it: "The four walls are gone from around me, the roof from over my head. I'm in the dark alone" (*Tournament* xxxiii). These final few lines of the novel form a nucleus for issues Foote explores throughout his career: how "an unadorned statement of fact" placed in an imaginative context constitutes the milieu for human under-standing of the past. The significance of Asa as the first narrative voice in Foote's fiction is pointed out by Helen White and Redding S. Sugg Jr.: "Asa's point of view, although not specifically invoked again in the later Jordan County works, may be said to condition all of them. It is the point of view of the author's generation" (21). That Bart's statement of man's solitary condition is preceded by silence and followed by silence suggests his inability to fashion fact into truth or, as Ezra Pound would have it, make it cohere. For Asa, this vividly recollected phrase speaks to the condition of all humanity and creates the challenge the artist faces when fashioning experience (the "hearsay" of memory and time past) into a structure that makes meaning possible. At the center of Foote's aesthetic lies the ac-knowledgment of the possibility of the meaninglessness of individual expe-rience. As he remarked in response to an interviewer's question about themes, "I'm not sure . . . except something so large as the basic loneliness of man. That's always there" ("Art" 66). The apocalyptic is balanced, how-ever, by the redemptive potential of aesthetic "ideas of order." This aes-thetic order rests, ultimately, on "hearsay" and yet can rise above it through imaginative empathy and artistic skill with language.

Choosing a portion of the first line of L. P. Hartley's *The Go-Between* (1953) as the title of his investigation into man's conception of the past, David Lowenthal, in *The Past Is a Foreign Country* (1985), asserts that "[w]hether it is celebrated or rejected, attended to or ignored, the past is omnipresent" (xv). Reading Foote's fiction it is impossible to miss the carefully textured presentation of the Delta world and the integral role historical consciousness plays in his vision. Foote's subject has always been the fluid and paradoxical relation of past to present, fact to truth, and word to memory. The formal designs of his books play a significant role in his treatment of humanity's relation to the past. Unlike Faulkner, who resisted "codifying and documenting the past" (Rollyson 5) in books such as *Absalom, Absalom!* and *Light in August*, Foote presents his vision within tightly framed and visibly plotted narrative structures. As he notes in a letter to Walker Percy, "I don't think I'll ever be satisfied to represent vagueness by being vague, or irrational to represent the un-understandable complexity. The naturalists taught us much; though much of what they did is very bad, the technique is useful when it is made part of a whole. The romantics, on the other hand, taught us only to avoid romanticism" (Letters, September 21, 1951). While his fiction reflects the influence of Faulkner—"He taught me to look at the world within the close atmosphere of the novel" (*Conversations* 81)—Foote's historical narrative suggests, through its deliberate artistry, his fascination with the tension between formal structure and imaginative flight. Foote's adherence to the classic conception of plot and narrative structure ("I like to be limited by forces" [*Conversations* 23]) is supported by his references to Aristotle's *Poetics* in his essay "The Novelist's View of History": "Aristotle called the management of plot the most important element in dramatic composition. . . . He subordinated to it the ability to create character, the command over language, and all the other elements of any composition. . . . The writer, Aristotle says, acquires that mastery last, if at all. This is true of the novelist, I know, and it seems to be true of historians, as well" ("Novelist's" 223). The role played by narrative structures are central to understanding Foote's sense of the relationship between fact and fiction, the present and the past, and historical process and individual experience.

"The Novelist's View of History" includes a discussion of the importance of plot to good writing in any genre. To make his point, Foote employs an analogy to the work of the painter Jan Vermeer:

> The Dutchman Vermeer painted no "literary" subjects, no maidens sighing for lost lovers, no Susannas being spied upon, no Sebastians pierced by arrows. He painted people in their everyday

aspect, and he painted them with all the clarity he could manage, which was considerable. The drama comes from where the picture starts and stops; from where it meets the frame. The brim of a hat may be clipped off, or the gable of a house; that's all. And yet, so well does he accomplish this, that I (for one) find him not only the best (whatever that means) but also the most dramatic of all painters. ("Novelist's" 224)

Foote's appreciation of the dynamic formalism of Vermeer's paintings provides a key to his own work; this stylistic paradox is not all that different from the one Lowenthal identifies in relation to hindsight—that it is invariably both a reduction and an enlargement of the historical past. It is interesting to note, as well, that in interviews Foote often links Vermeer's style as a painter with Ernest Hemingway's style as a writer; both artists exhibit a profound "clarity of vision" (*Conversations* 83) and a mastery of powerful effects achieved within self-imposed stylistic limitations. In fact, while Faulkner and Proust supply the models for Foote's conception of time, it is Hemingway who provides the model for his style as a historian: ". . . read some Hemingway and you can learn how to write. If any historian in this country wrote a single page of history that had the clarity of a single page of Hemingway, that page of history would live forever. But he won't study Hemingway, he will think he is wasting his time if he reads Hemingway, and he is not. Hemingway will teach him how to write history" (*Conversations* 126). Whether in his fiction or his history, Foote's aesthetic of limitations, and his attention to the rhetorical potential of form, produces dramatic art of the first order.

Much of the drama Foote mentions is achieved through an understanding of the dynamics of plot. Pushing the definition past the architectonic aspects of placement, Foote suggests that plotting "includes a great deal more than the mere arrangement of events in dramatic sequence. It includes, as well, the amount of space and stress each of these events is to be accorded—and because of this, by a combination of them all, it gives a book its larger rhythms and provides it with narrative drive, the force that makes it move under its own power" ("Novelist's" 223). Foote articulates this central premise: "I learned very soon after first sitting down to write, that no one can really teach—or even tell—anyone anything; not really . . . . with luck and talent . . . a man can show another man something; that is, he can make him see and hear and maybe even feel and smell it.

But telling him something is quite another matter . . ." ("Novelist's" 225). The passage echoes Joseph Conrad's description of the artist's aims in his preface to *The Nigger of the "Narcissus"* (1898): "My task which I am trying to achieve is, by the power of the written word to make you hear, to make you feel—it is, before all, to make you see. That—and no more, and it is everything. If I succeed you shall find there according to your deserts: encouragement, consolation, fear, charm—all you demand—and, perhaps, also that glimpse of truth for which you have forgotten to ask." Louis D. Rubin Jr., in his introduction to the second edition of *Tournament*, comments on how, after the Proustian cast of this early novel, Foote's writing developed "toward more dramatic, 'objective' fiction," based on "the interaction of his characters within a known historical context" (n.p.). The influences of Proust and Faulkner on Foote have received considerable attention; now, I believe, is the time to examine Foote's aesthetic of limitations as it sets the stage for his historical narrative. This shift is reflected in the absorption of the Asa character (the foregrounded and self-conscious artist-narrator) into the seemingly impersonal structure of the narratives. It is a procedure Foote perfects in *The Civil War: A Narrative*.

Fact and Hearsay in Asa's Vision in Tournament

Asa's final confession—the somewhat belated assertion that the preceding work is largely an act of imaginative reconstruction—marks a significant point in Foote's conception of himself as a writer (and as an historian). Asa acknowledges that the past is, indeed, a foreign country, one that is domesticated, so to speak, by the Keatsian exercise of an imagination fulfilling its own agenda: that of explaining the present to itself. As Foote suggests to Walker Percy: "[Studying Keats] has made wonderfully clear to me what I want from a writing life. I want what Keats was working toward, an affirmation of spirit expressed by means of images and recollections of the world of facts, transmitted into the world of fiction" (Letters, March 15, 1953). While Asa's reconstruction of Bart's life conveys little sense of the present time of composition, Foote does establish the narrator's distance from his subject. We learn, in Asa's framing "overture" and "coda" (White and Sugg 22), that his investigation of the past began as a reaction to Billy Boy's version of Bart's "decline and fall," and that Billy Boy's tale is informed by "the rich, unreal glare of hero-worship" and dominated by his conception of Bart as the "proud tall figure . . . immense and knightly and biblical" (*Tournament* xxix). Asa's story, then, exists in the tension between these larger-than-life figures from a mythical past and the flesh-and-blood individuals of his memory. The narrative is revealed to be a tournament between myth and memory, fantasy and fact.

As the narrator, Asa is situated in what Lowenthal calls the "temporal *mélange*" (186) of humanity's sense of the omnipresence of the past: "We are in fact aware of the past as a realm both coexistent with and distinct from the present. What joins them is our largely unconscious apprehension of organic life; what sets them apart is our self-consciousness—thinking about our memories, about history, about the age of things around us. . . . But conflation and segregation are in continual tension; the past has to be felt both part of and separate from the present" (186). Asa's final assertion of the unresolved distinction between the known fact and the fictional history outlines a paradox that Foote pursues throughout his career: the sense of the past continually impacts on the present, yet its influence is discernible only through a self-conscious effort of memory (singular) or aesthetic ordering (multidimensional). Whether writing his history of Jordan County or the history of the Civil War, Foote's goal remains the pursuit, within a consciously limited framework, of a past that makes known only what can be known: in other words, a setting where memory (in its multifold guises—maps, journals, reports, diaries, for instance—and with its own measure of fallibility) can acquire, through conjunction with art, a sense of the authentic. Proofs, as scientifically defined, are only one aspect of the process. The kind of knowledge of the past that Asa affirms in *Tournament*, and that Foote pursues in both his fiction and his history, is based on an acceptance of this realm of contingency—limited by the artifacts themselves on the one side and by an aesthetic discipline on the other—a past accessible through an art tested against the ethic he refers to when speaking of the "honest novelist along with the honest historian" ("Novelist's" 219).

The narrative structure of *Tournament* represents Foote working out his position about the writer's relation to historical events that rise "out of the past and cast their shadows on the present" (*Jordan* 108). Fourteen years later, and two volumes into the composition of *The Civil War*, Foote paused to articulate, in "The Novelist's View of History," what he feels is the "basic difference" between history and fiction as each tries "to make [the past] live again in the world around them": "the historian attempts this by communicating facts, whereas the novelist would communicate sensation. The one stresses action, the other re-action. And yet the two are not hermetically sealed off from one another" ("Novelist's" 220). The tension between these two kinds of activity—call them event and memory—is presented through the characters of Hugh Bart and his grandson Asa. Given the qualification Asa makes at the conclusion of his story with regard to the factual veracity of the material, the novel reveals itself, at another level, as a tournament between Asa's mature reflections and his initial rash judgment of his heritage. The tale is an "expiation" (*Tournament* xxxii) of what Asa has come to consider an immature condemnation of the man he discovered he never really knew. The moral of the piece involves the necessity to repudiate facile judgments—those that would preempt an imaginative reanimation and reconstruction of the past. Asa's consciousness of the formal aspect of this process, and of the centrality of hindsight in formulating his vision, is underscored by his rather brutal assessment of his father's demise (Hugh Bart Jr. having died in the back-flare of an artillery piece during training in 1919): "Thus sometimes a man's death will make all the confusion of his life come clear; you cannot understand the motivations, the whys and wherefores; it is all a senseless ineffectual snarl until you see the manner in which he leaves it: death can be like a catalytic agent dropped into a cloudy liquid" (*Tournament* xxxi–xxxii). The artistic reclamation of the past celebrated in *Tournament* involves Foote's recognition of the paradoxical nature of writing about the past: his discovery that forms, patterns, and structures—the aesthetic tools for demonstrating ideas of order—constitute both an enlargement and a limitation.

The conclusion of *Tournament* reveals the story of Hugh Bart to be wholly conditioned by the viewpoint of the narrator (the one who raised the problem of history at the outset). In the last lines of the preamble, Asa summarizes what he has come to "know" after supplementing Billy Boy's "mnemonic monolog" (*Tournament* xxx) with other sources. First, there is the chronology of the events of Bart's life, the factual bare bones of his existence; then comes the thesis, the insight that "these stages along Bart's road were punctuated by experiences which made him what he was and were explained by his trying to be what he was never meant to be" (*Tournament* xxx); lastly, Asa confesses that having emerged with "the complete figure" (*Tournament* xxx), composed after sifting through all the facts and opinions which mattered, he has come back, full circle, to his starting point, revealed at the conclusion as his sole firm memory of Bart, that "each man, even when pressed closest by other men in their scramble for the things they offer one another with so little grace, is profoundly alone" (*Tournament* xxx). In effect, Asa acknowledges that his presentation of the past, while containing many facts, is finally a reflection of his own sense of the present, his own perspective on the orphaned and alienated condition of man. "The historian," Lowenthal remarks, "reaches an understanding distinctively of his own time. Such biases have creative as well as limiting implications. . . . Just as we are products of the past, so is the known past an artifact of ours" (216). Foote underscores this exchange by having Bart's actual last words displaced by a phrase from Asa's memory—words that he deemed the most significant as a reflection of his grandfather.

Rereading the novel in the light of this assertion, one feels the figure of Bart recede and the consciousness of the narrator take on a greater prominence. This refocusing is as it should be, since any history is conditioned by the limiting, but at the same time enlarging, aspects of hindsight: "hindsight paradoxically limits our ability to understand the past by giving us greater knowledge than people of the time could have had" (Lowenthal 217). The knowledge of the results of actions necessarily conditions any thinking about the past and leads to the recognition that "bias does not merely reduce the historical past but also enlarges it" (Lowenthal 217). This dynamic of enlargement and reduction (in the form of the various tellers of his tale) surrounds the character of Hugh Bart. Through Billy Boy we are introduced to Bart as the figure of romance "cast in the heroic mold" (*Tournament* xxx), the tragic hero whose life is recounted in terms of a rise, decline, and fall and whose story is told as an oral history in an "oracular" voice (*Tournament* xxix)—Billy Boy's "mnemonic monolog" (*Tournament* xxx), which resists interruptions that might "break the continuity" (*Tournament* xxviii). Set against this adulation are the recounted snippets of memory, opinion, and gossip that constitute the collective voice of Jordan County society. All of these versions are subsumed into the framework of the story itself: the implications of a tragic progression in the movement from rise to fall; the introduction of the staples of the Delta world (Solitaire, lake, river, hunt, sale—incorporating not just the natural rhythms of the place but the economic and cultural determinants as well); and the biblical resonances ascribed to individual anecdotes, which provide a mythical cast and a moral agenda to the tale. The controlling element behind the juxtaposition of these informing visions is Asa in his role as narrator; it is his sensibility that introduces the tension between the rhetoric of these conventional

78

structures of meaning—the generation of order implied by the patterns of romance, tragedy, and myth—and the insights of his own twentieth-century existential perspective. C. Hugh Holman, in his series of lectures entitled *The Immoderate Past: The Southern Writer and History* (1977), traces a similar tension in other southern novelists in relation to the contrast between Hegelian and Nietzschean approaches to history:

> In the dichotomy of historical theory divided into broadly Hegelian and Nietzschean, we found the dominant American mode Nietzschean, concerned with individual experience and distrustful of the lessons of the past, and the South, in contrast, Hegelian, interested in process, in time, in what the past meant and means. We have seen representative southern writers in every period utilizing the various novelistic modes to say what they have to say, but consistently concerned with history as event and process and distrustful of the individual outside the context of time and society. Such findings should not really be surprising, for they are in harmony with other qualities of southern writing, with its concreteness, its specificity, its Aristotelian rather than Platonic quality, its urgent sense of time and its deep respect for tradition. The past has been and still is an inescapable element of the southern mind, not as a myth, not as a retreat, not as a mask, but as a mystery to be understood, as a burden to be borne, as a guilt to be expiated, and as a pattern which can—if anything can—point us to the future. (100)

Bart's story, and the frame narrative in which the tale is placed, are representative of an elemental tension between the received aesthetic structures tied to Christian morality or historical romance and Asa's skeptical perspective and self-conscious modernism.

Tournament can be understood, on one level, as a parable of Foote's modernist conception of the relationship between present and past: his assertion of both an imaginative intimacy and a distancing, ironic perspective. As Rubin points out, Foote's first novel demonstrates the connection between Bart's view of the past and its ultimate failure. Drawing on the Proustian ideal of a past regained through the exercise of the imaginative and transcendent power of art, Rubin suggests that Bart's failure can be understood through his adherence to material existence represented by activity in time (and a corresponding inability to construct the story of his own life in any fitting or coherent manner). When, near the end of his life, Bart attempts to understand his present situation by telling his story to a passing stranger (a poor substitute for the immortality he sought through his dynastic ambitions), he is frustrated by his failure to shape language to the desired ends: "It was clear in his mind, if not shaped for his tongue, because that was the way he had lived it, clearly, openly, Spartanly, somewhat blindly" (*Tournament* 213). Bart subscribes to the fallacy that, in order to posit any kind of satisfying completeness, narrative time and material time must be one and the same—that to tell a life would require a lifetime: "how could he tell all that? Every [anecdote or incident] omitted, however, would be a space left blank on a canvas larger than life. So finally there was no question of trying to tell it. All he could do was what he had done in the past: continue to live it, cut off and alone" (*Tournament* 223). Bart recognizes his failure as a narrator: "[t]he truth lay in implications, not in facts. Facts were only individual beads; the hidden string was what made them into a necklace" (*Tournament* 223). Lacking the tools to fashion a narrative, Bart is unable to understand the meaning of his actions, to see past the present moment, or to transcend his material existence. Robert L. Phillips would extend this further, arguing that Bart's failure of imagination, his lack of a Proustian artistic vision, corresponds to the absence of the religious and historical dimensions naturally available to what Allen Tate called the "traditional man" (66–67). Asa, as a figure of the Proustian artist intent on reclaiming and reactivating the past, succeeds in providing a shape and a meaning to Bart's experience (albeit as a qualified truth).

The teleology of the biblical and romance structures in the novel is countered by Asa's assertion of a new kind of metaphor for human experience. In the chapter "The Lake," Asa introduces the image of a whirlpool or vortex to represent the limitations of a purely material existence. Bart, having achieved his vision of the planter aristocrat, his attempt to reproduce the "gone splendor" (*Tournament* 28) evoked by the Jameson name, pauses to take stock and finds, instead of fruition, emptiness: "He had made this life-way the goal of his early years; yet when he first reached it he was like a man who, overcome by a desire to leap into a whirlpool, thrashes about inside it, too busy to analyze his present sensations, let alone the nature of the impulse that prompted the leap" (*Tournament* 66). Bart's pause for reflection reveals that his attempt to re-create the lifestyle of the planter-aristocrat does not automatically imbue life with meaning. In a telling incident earlier in the novel, Major Dubose and his manuscript history of the Civil War sink into the flood tide of the Mississippi. His history, which by its very length and incompleteness suggests an approach to narrative akin to Bart's, disappears into an appropriately watery grave— Ararat displaced by its mirror image, the negative cone of the whirlpool— the ordered existence of the Old South subsumed into the vortex of the modern world. The subversive power of this image of meaninglessness indicates Asa's emerging perspective on the real relation of the past to the present.

The revelation of the connection between the vortex image and Asa's concept of modernity sends a revisionist ripple back through our understanding of the text. Asa's voice is the one that characterizes Bart's activities as sheriff in terms of a hopeless determinism: "being hired to protect a buzz saw from men who insisted on putting their hands against it" (*Tournament* 4). Asa's sensibility is the one that poses the unresolvable moral question raised by Bart's violent suppression of the renegade tenant farmer. While the past lives again in Asa's depiction of his grandfather's life, Foote takes pains to establish how clearly this version of the past is informed by the vision of the narrator. In the following five novels, Foote eschews this device of an identified artist-narrator (a sort of Stephen Daedalus figure) and highlights rather than blurs the artifice of the novels' forms. He is not suppressing the issue of bias in depictions of the past; instead, he indicates that the limitations of the present perspective must be reflected in the narratives themselves and in the self-conscious ironic stance of narrator. Asa's acknowledgment of the "hearsay" in his reconstruction does not invalidate his insights; it simply reinforces what was always the case, that the historian or novelist necessarily creates fictions to explain the truth of the present to himself.

Follow Me Down: *The Interplay of Story and Silence*

Foote's next novel, in order of composition, is the piece of historical fiction *Shiloh*. Written after Foote's service in World War II, when *Tournament* had failed initially to secure publication, *Shiloh* itself was not published until 1952—in the interim *Tournament* (1949), *Follow Me Down* (1950) and *Love in a Dry Season* (1951) had appeared. In this respect, Foote's narrative strategies for *Shiloh* suggest a development of his ideas in relation to history and fiction, with the framework of the novel playing an increasingly central role. While the complexity of the narrative structure of *Shiloh* reflects a considerable advance in technical mastery, it retains intriguing traces of the first novel—evident most notably through a comparison of the figure of Asa and that of young Lieutenant Palmer Metcalfe. In both novels, the sensibilities of the two young men frame the main action and suggest a parallel between Asa's imaginative odyssey and Palmer's experience under fire. The significant distinction between the two rests in the fact that Palmer has no artistic ambitions and that Asa's self-conscious artistry has been subsumed into the structure of the novel as a whole, and reappears only in various artist manqué figures. Since a close reading of *Shiloh* opens the discussion of Foote's moral vision and the operation of his aesthetics of limitation in *The Civil War* (chapters 4 and 5), and the broad cultural sweep of the reversed chronology of *Jordan County* (1954) forms the backbone of chapter 2, at this point let us consider how the three later novels (*Follow Me Down, Love in a Dry Season,* and *September September*) illustrate Foote's mature approach to the issues of narrative and the past raised in his first book.

The pivotal point of *Follow Me Down*—the keystone in the narrative arch or the still point of "The Vortex" (the novel's original title) (*Correspondence* 12)—is the section devoted to the final moments of Beulah Ross as she drowns at the hands of her lover, Luther Eustis. Beulah, as a result, is trapped in an eternal present: "For me it's not remembering—it is. I watch the bubbles trailing upward, pearls on a string unwinding from my inwards in slow motion, reeling lazy toward the crinkled surface moonlight cant get through" (*Follow* 125). At the very moment when she would tell Eustis of their unborn child, the message—like the breath from her body—escapes her. Beulah's story assumes an ironically concrete—if temporary—form as the bubbles move upward toward dissolution and silence. This image of the missing piece (the tale that escapes telling, accessible to the reader, but available to none of the characters), lies at the heart of the novel—a point that the lawyer Nowell recognizes when constructing his argument for Luther's defense: "I began to think . . . what a thing it would be if I could call up the ghost of Beulah and put her on the stand tomorrow morning. However, it wouldnt do—for more reasons than one. The trouble with the dead is not that you cant ask them questions. You can. You can ask them hundreds of questions. The trouble is they wont answer"

(*Follow* 242–43). Content with acknowledging this impossibility, Nowell draws strength from his imaginative grasp of this gap in his understanding. Whereas Nowell's argument is restricted to the provable facts and influenced by his bias against women (he consciously creates a caricature of Beulah as evil in order to make his argument), Foote the novelist is free to complete the narrative, to provide the missing link (a portrayal of the essential goodness and innocence of Beulah herself). By doing so, he emphasizes the difference between the limited perspectives of the characters and the shaping vision of the author. As White and Sugg note: "[Beulah's] innocent tone plays against the ways she is seen by other characters variously as merely a sex object, a victim, or an embodiment of evil" (34). Since it recounts a memory at the very point when memory is extinguished, Beulah's monologue makes us conscious of the malleability of time and the relativity of truth in the context of narrative art.

This authorial consciousness of form (and its ironic comment on truth) is mirrored by the multiple ironies found within Beulah's story. Her monologue in *Follow Me Down* is, understandably, the most completely closed section; it comes full circle, beginning with the "Now" of her immersion and ending with the exhaustion of the bubbles, tale and life complete. Yet it too is lacking the art that gives shape to experience. Like the child in her womb that will never come to term, Beulah's story has closure but finds life only when it is brought into relation with the other parts of the narrative, when it becomes a part of the interplay of memory and the past in the novel. "The reader thus possesses," White and Sugg suggest, "more of the truth of it than any of the characters—including the principals" (28). Just as the "little death" of her orgasm with Eustis on the floor of the cotton shed ("All there was was Now: the swoon and surge and swoon and surge" [*Follow* 129]) engenders her recitation to him of the story of her first life (the one before she met him), so too the timeless moment of her impending death provides the rationale for the narration of her life experience. The beginning and the end are brought together in Beulah; this closure supports Asa Bart's observation that no story is in itself complete until translated out of the world of experience and into the world of art.

The structure of *Follow Me Down* illustrates the complexities humans face when they generate narrative in order to reflect the nature of reality and to understand the past. The multiple points of view demonstrate the vexed process of writing history. The themes and structure of the novel reflect how distorting and limited such contextualizing can be. The image of the pearl is just one example—related to the voice and the personality of Beulah, the archetypal prostitute with a heart of gold. Her inner beauty and integrity—misread even by Eustis—is glimpsed in this section, accessible only to the reader, surrounded by the various assumptions and prejudices of the other characters' points of view and effectively enclosed in the hard shells of their distorting perspectives. Ironically, these layers give the pearl its luster and the story its art. The pearls of truth that escape toward the surface as Beulah drowns, an image of transcendence, are enclosed in the throttling hands of Luther Eustis, hands whose thumbnails are described by the reporter Russell Stevenson as being "thick as little oyster shells" (*Follow* 51).

This image of enclosure finds a parallel in the worldview of Eustis (a figure described by Walter Sullivan as "a man of God in the old sense—a monstrous sinner, like David or Jacob, bound by some terrible and mystic affection to the Almighty" [379]). In his biblical literal-mindedness, Eustis initiates his relationship with Beulah as an act of salvation, seeing her as a pearl of great price to be redeemed from the fallen world by removing her to the new Eden of the island. When Eustis, within the limited compass of his morality, begins to see Beulah as the whore of Babylon and the vehicle of his own corruption—"Depraved. . . . She's all the way depraved" (*Follow* 115)—salvation turns to enclosure and murder at his hands. Beulah is presented in many ways in the text: in a series of literal images (Beulah being strangled; her body being wrapped in wires and weighted by Eustis; her corpse being photographed and then lifted "into the basket" [*Follow* 36] by the undertaker); in various figurative representations of her by the reporter Stevenson (most notably his ironic description of her body in the style of the society page); in the lawyer Nowell's presentation of her story (as seductress, as fallen woman) in his opening argument for the defense; and, finally, in the framing of her section in the structure of the novel. She comes to represent the way reality, however defined, is shaped by the arbitrary contexts generated by the human need for narrative explanation.

The opening section of the novel raises this idea by presenting a summary of the case and a series of vignettes of the major figures and then suspending the action as the jury retires to deliberate its verdict. The reader's situation is analogous to Judge Holiman's when he asserts: "I am retired. I'm clean away from this world and sitting in judgment on it" (*Follow* 4). By this means, Foote supplies an author's instruction to the "greater" jury of his audience (a warning or an invitation regarding judgment?). He also sets in motion the two contrary elements of the narrative structure: the forward impetus toward a verdict (a final judgment vis-à-vis the facts of the case) and, in contrast, the nature of the individual stories (replete with their singular biases) as they circle around Beulah's unknowable thoughts. The structure is meant to confound judgment, paradoxically by increasing the depth of our understanding. Supplementing the speakers' progressively more intimate involvement with the murder is Foote's presentation of their connections, first, to issues of the nature of language and literalness; and second, as a means of developing how fact and hearsay are related to the idea of truth. The structure of the novel functions as an illustration of a journey into the heart of darkness and also as a paradigm for the way that "facts" are contextualized and brought into relation to form a cogent story—how the unfathomable is rendered comprehensible, with an ironic undercurrent that acknowledges just how much is sacrificed in the process.

The first sections of *Follow Me Down* are an education in questioning the context and assumptions of the various storytellers. At the start is the chronological overview offered by Ben Rand, the circuit clerk, while waiting for the verdict; here, Foote juxtaposes two kinds of knowledge: one is the abstraction of the "Law" (*Follow* 10), and the other is the gossip and hearsay provided by the clerk. The next stage is presented through the perspective of Russell Stevenson, the local reporter—the most narrowly focused of the points of view in the novel. He pursues the story from the discovery of Beulah's body on a Friday in June 1949 to his composition of a "follow up" piece on the Monday afternoon after his interview with the imprisoned Eustis. Stevenson, described later by Parker Nowell as "hard-faced already from living off the misdeeds of people" (*Follow* 221), demonstrates a limited imaginative and empathetic capacity and lives almost exclusively for the present moment. (The Eustis story pushes any memory of the recent Lundy murder, Bristol's last newsworthy crime, out of Stevenson's mind.) This superficiality is underscored by Stevenson's two comments on writing and narrative. The first is offered as he reads Eustis's confession in the jailhouse: "I was into the confession by then. It was as if I could see them the whole time I was reading; the thing came alive in my hands. If I could write like that, I told myself, I'd be at the top of the ladder by now. The trouble is, you have to have lived it first. No thanks: it isnt worth it" (*Follow* 47). Like Hugh Bart, trying to frame the story of his life, Stevenson is limited to a continual present. His own outline for the Eustis piece that he hopes to submit to *True Detective* underscores this bent.

Sketching out his chronological model for the story, Stevenson recites his credo: "The main thing was to keep the story simple, pour on action action action so fast the reader wouldnt have time to look up for a sip of coffee, and keep it short, short, short" (*Follow* 55). Stevenson possesses a debased literary sensibility (his first encounter with Eustis, for instance, stimulates a distant memory of Satan in John Milton's *Paradise Lost*, although he cannot call to mind the pivotal words "obdurate pride" and so misses the point) and prefers the more sensational, and hence more profitable, clichéd expressions. With Ben Rand and Stevenson, Foote begins a dialogue between concepts such as truth and hearsay, art and reportage, that form the philosophical base for the novel.

The last of these initial points of view belongs to James Elmo Pitts (Dummy), the deaf-mute adolescent son of Miz Pitts. The account of Dummy, one of the characters closest to the events, is also two-dimensional, but in a more complex fashion than Stevenson's; here, Foote moves the issue of language to its most elemental level, that of the word, and at the same time introduces questions about the nature of human self-awareness. Locked in his silence, Dummy explores the correspondence between the dictionary definitions of terms and the "real" world around him; he arrives at the conclusion that "The trouble with the dictionary is it tries to explain with words, and there is a limit to what can be said with words: No one can know what a word means till he feels it. I knew that, now" (*Follow* 61). For Dummy, words are visually shaped by the lips of the speaker or reverently shaped in concrete terms by the pen on the page, and he assiduously reads this world, seeking answers about how to understand the Other—whether the Other is the mystery of sexuality embodied by Beulah; the morality of Luke (Eustis), whose Bible exists as a visible contradiction to his situation and identity; or the way the dream world informs our conscious actions.

The disruptive impact of Eustis and Beulah contributes to Dummy's sense of disorientation when he leaves to reveal Eustis's real identity to the sheriff in Bristol: "I knew where East was, I knew where West was. But where was I?" (*Follow* 69). Emerging into adolescence and sexual awareness within the confines of the island retreat, Dummy is propelled by Beulah's murder into a consciousness of the existence of evil. Dummy's unsuccessful attempt to use a lamp to light his way across the levee, an act that brings, instead of illumination, legions of stinging gnats and mosquitoes, symbolizes his fall. Thwarted, he decides to rest in darkness and, upon extinguishing the flame, finds that "the dark walls rushed together like pressure into an abolished vacuum (I almost believed I heard the resulting clap) and I was nowhere" (*Follow* 70). Forced to spend the pre-dawn hours in the limbo of the levee wilderness, Dummy finds the time filled with fitful dreams (a situation that anticipates Eustis's own confusion in moral and experiential terms) and raises similar questions about the nature of desire. His conclusions on this score, that "I had not brought the pain out of my dream: It had seeped into my dream from the conscious world" (*Follow* 72), anticipates the nature of Eustis's spiritual crisis, while ironically reversing his conclusion. In microcosm, then, Dummy's section stresses the limitations and the disjunctures evident in the linguistic moral systems by which humanity orders experience. The nexus, fittingly, is the compromised worlds of memory and the written word. The impossibility of viable absolutes (in the Word, in law, in a true story of the past) is reinforced in the figure of an isolated boy, locked in a silent world.

Having been prepared by the preceding sections to question the context and assumptions of the storyteller, we approach Luther Eustis's version of his life, as "one long straight road" (*Follow* 88–89), with a certain skepticism. As the sections spiral in toward the center of the vortex, through what Eustis calls "all the swirl" (*Follow* 77) of events, his initial monologues suggest an increasing conflation of the past (the act of memory and retrieval) with the present (comprehension). In a long backward glance, Eustis suggests the tale of his infatuation is based on a fundamental misreading of the message from God: "A thing like that begins. Then something grows out of it and you look back. Chances are, you tell yourself it was all foretold in the seeds of that first beginning, if you could only have read them. But that was not the way it was with us. . . . We were caught up in events concerning others, like a man out for a holiday swim that paddles full tilt into a whirlpool, never suspecting it was there until he begins to spin and hears it gurgle" (*Follow* 86–87). The notion of Eustis's unreliability was introduced earlier by Stevenson's observation that his speech and thought seemed "disconnected" (*Follow* 52). The lawyer's observations reinforce this impression, suggesting that when Eustis talked it was about motives, and in his "Faust story," "Beulah . . . changed roles with each telling. One day she was the devil's emissary—the next she was his victim" (*Follow* 232). The religious cast of Eustis's tale, as a "two-way pull" (*Follow* 92) between God and Satan, reflects the deterministic bent of his vision and the limitation of his imagination. The whole is a cautionary reminder about the relativity of truth.

Foote's narrative creates an ongoing dialogue about the vexed relationship between fact and truth. This reciprocity is mirrored by Eustis's suggestion of a Manichaean contest between good and evil in the world ("every inch I pulled her away from evil, I slid an inch closer myself" [*Follow* 99]). As the novel moves forward toward its center (Beulah's section), the narrowing perspective of the speaker evokes greater caution in the reader. At the climactic moment in Eustis's narrative, just after he decides to remove the evil he feels Beulah represents (the "snake" in paradise), he interrupts the story with a sense of déjà vu: "I lived through this before!" (*Follow* 116). The exclamation clearly serves as a reminder that this intimate confession is not reality in any absolute sense, but simply one more story refashioned in memory and therefore subject to Eustis's conditioning and rationalizing. Indeed, his sections of the novel are permeated with indications of his limited imaginative and interpretive capacity. These personal limitations lead to the conjunction of his dangerously literal biblical interpretation and the act of strangulation: "Whatever I read, I'd ask as soon as I finished: Was that some kind of a message meant for me? Was that meant for a guide on what to do? It seemed to me, out of all I'd read and thought, there had to be a message. Maybe all of it together was a message, it all tied in" (*Follow* 123). Multifold are the ironies in the self-serving "message from God" that Luther finally deciphers as "I'll leave it to you, Luther Eustis" (*Follow* 123).

Individual impulses toward erasure and denial, Foote suggests, are intimately tied to the process of recovering the past. Eustis's literalism and limited imaginative abilities are in no way altered after Beulah's murder. In a scene reminiscent of Dummy's dream-visions, Eustis experiences a conflation of the waking and the dreaming worlds, except that in his case the ache he brings with him out of the dream is considered "a sign from God" (*Follow* 147). Beulah is subsumed into the "daylight world of memory" (*Follow* 148), into the reality that Eustis wishes to see, finding as he does that it is untenable to "stand between" the two worlds of dream and daylight, "groping in both directions" (*Follow* 148). Eustis lacks the perspective the author possesses, which is to exist imaginatively on more than one level—to see reality as a myriad of incompletenesses. Eustis, instead, must reduce Beulah to something two-dimensional—"all straight lines and flattened planes" (*Follow* 148)—in a figurative attempt to erase her memory, having already ended her physical existence. What results is a kind of living death, an eternal present (ironically echoing Beulah's experience of dying), as Eustis stands in Ithaca on his way home: "I stood alone in the silence, looking up the street and down. It might have been two weeks ago; I might never have left, might never have been on an island at all. There might never have been a Beulah. I've heard of people aching to turn back the clock, but for me there wasn't any clock to ache to turn back: all there was was Now, and nothing that was past had ever been. Or so I thought. Or so I told myself" (*Follow* 185–86). The irony of this position is compounded when Eustis is sentenced to life imprisonment in Parchman, Mississippi's infamous prison farm. The sentence provides him with a future, but, as Roscoe the jailer outlines it, this future is really a regression into the past, back to a world before the Fall (whether one understands that to be before Beulah, before his parents' tragedy, before the Civil War, or even before the Fall of Adam and Eve): "'I'll tell you true,' [Roscoe] said. It ain so bad considering. . . . They dont have cells like this, for one thing. No walls, no bob wire. Nothing like that. . . . It's a farm . . . a plantation like back in Slavery days—eighteen thousand acres, mostly cotton. They give you your own mule and everything. . . . Stay in line, you'll be all right. Otherwise the sergeant's got a strap. . . . It's better than solitary. (They dont have solitary like most prisons. Solitary's inhuman, the warden says)" (*Follow* 268). In a wry ironic turn, Foote's conclusion for the novel suggests that the erasure Eustis strove to effect in his memory will instead be accomplished by judicial fiat. A faux version of the past is the equivalent of Eustis's individual act of revision. Foote's novel is asserting an imaginative and cumulative vision for engaging history and truth.

In the sections following Eustis's monologues, Foote signals an engagement with the idea of historical consciousness. The section entitled "Wife," told as a straightforward chronological recounting of Kate Eustis's knowledge of Luther and his family history, serves as a counterpoint to both Luther's and Dummy's accounts. Just as Dummy's story provides a means to engage the themes of language and the unconscious, Kate's section demonstrates the process of historical conceptualization. The focus rests primarily on the relationship of fact and fiction, memory and "hearsay" (*Follow* 202). The distinction that Asa withholds until the last lines of *Tournament* is now placed near the center of the narrative and forms an active element in the novel instead of an enlightening afterthought. Foote balances the earlier public, immediate, and superficial accounts (the circuit clerk's and the reporter's) with a more private and contemplative perspective (beginning with the "Wife" chapter).

Significantly, Kate's monologue begins with a warning that "sometimes it's only after you know the answers that you understand the questions" (*Follow* 198)—a statement in keeping with Asa's sense that the patterns of a man's life can only be established after his death or that written accounts are always incomplete histories. Kate suggests that the pursuit of meaning will always lead to distortion or embellishment. Warning against the presence of hearsay in stories about Eustis's parents and his father's origins, she remarks, "likely someone made it up to keep from admitting there was something they didn't know; people will do such things" (*Follow* 197). This is particularly telling after the complex rehearsal and rationalization of events we have observed in Eustis's section. In fact, Kate's recounting of the adultery and murder in her husband's "double heritage" (*Follow* 204), when combined with her commonsense explanations of Eustis's activities before his departure—an ironic counterpoint to his own cosmic explanations—inaugurates the contemplative tone adopted throughout the latter part of the book. Having finished her tale of the adultery of Eustis's mother, the sense of failure in his father (bested in farming by the grandfather and defeated in bed by the insatiable desire of his wife), and the resulting apocalyptic murder and fire, Kate pauses to signal a primary shift in her, and in the reader's, focus: "So much for hearsay, invention. The rest is fact" (*Follow* 202). As with Asa, fact here refers to immediate personal experience—memory, in a word—and as such is distanced from a validation as truth. The comment serves as a reminder that the epistemological odyssey of the novel (toward history) involves a complex mélange of facts, suppositions, biases, and imaginative insights.

The guiding spirit for this examination of history and narrative is Parker Nowell, the lawyer for the defense. Paired with the monologue of the reporter in the forward progression of the action, Nowell's section develops an interpretation of Eustis's story in contradistinction to the rather facile approach of Stevenson. Whereas Stevenson caters to the lurid public tastes, developing the sensationalistic aspects of the case (sex, murder, voodoo, etc.) with an eye to material rewards, Nowell constructs his version of events in accordance with the pursuit of justice (although here too it should be noted that there is a private agenda—Nowell's personal crusade on behalf of those men "wronged" by women). While drawing on the quite different materials of personal biography and psychological speculation, Nowell, in fact, also plays to an audience and in doing so simplifies and reduces the reality:

They thought me evil. That was a result of their new Liberalism, by which nothing is really bad provided they can understand it—a tolerant attitude, you think: except it also follows that everything they cannot understand is evil. So they feared and hated me. Likewise, as incapable of comprehending him, they feared and hated Eustis. That was my problem: to make the jurors think they understood him. But I had to do it in simple terms, which was only doubtfully possible because the facts were far from simple. Once they saw how truly complicated it was, the case was lost. So I had decided to do it the easy way. Make them believe he was insane and the scales would fall from their eyes; they would "understand"; the fear, the hate would be gone, evaporated. "So that is it," they would say; "he's crazy. I knew it all along." They might even begin to pity and sympathize. Good old Hollywood Christianity: God's gift to the Defense. (*Follow* 237)

The cynicism of Nowell's assessment, while a winning legal strategy, prevents complete acceptance of his argument as truth. Harking back to the position ascribed to the reader at the outset of the novel (as being like that of the judge, "clean away from this world and sitting in judgment on it" [*Follow* 4]), Foote carefully interposes an ironic distance in relation to this most cogent, persuasive, and artistic of the monologues.

Casting himself as a secular "father confessor" to the inhabitants of the modern world of "mechanistic materialism" (*Follow* 220), Nowell turns a baleful eye on the human condition, extending and deepening the cynicism introduced by his counterpart, Stevenson. To illustrate this progression Foote introduces a set of parallel images—the two men's views of the remodeled county jail. Stevenson, while acknowledging the "hard uncompromising . . . strictly utilitarian" lines of the modern exterior, nevertheless retains a memory of the old brick building underneath, with its "beauty only Time can bring," glossing the image, rather superficially, as "the Old South under the garish facade of the New" (*Follow* 45). Ironically, it is within these walls that Stevenson, in a comparable "priestly" role yet with no thought of questions of sin or absolution, scans Eustis's confession for material to pander to the public tastes. Nowell's reaction to the courthouse building indicates an even more extreme disillusionment. For Nowell, the courthouse (representing a paternal legacy, as well as the abstract ideal of justice) and the jail ("a two-storied concrete abortion" [*Follow* 220]) are equally ugly—

symbols of debased ideals. With his interest in time, and with the historical, almost artistic, consciousness he manifests in framing his case, Nowell is a "Mephistophelean" (*Follow* 226) presence in the novel, beguiling and tempting the reader with his nihilistic vision of the Delta world and the human condition: "Love has failed us. We are essentially, irrevocably alone" (*Follow* 233).

It has been commonly accepted that Nowell exists in the novel as a surrogate for the author, a figure of the artist. As Robert L. Phillips remarks: "He has the skills in language and music to recognize and understand but also to use and explain. His knowledge of language and art makes him an artist, or at least an artificer, even though the purposes to which he puts his skills do not necessarily qualify him as a man exercising his talent in a living tradition" (97). Foote, though, indicates quite clearly by the parallel images and personal context that Nowell's vision of truth, while more cogently presented than any other, is subsumed into the larger framework of fact and hearsay in the novel. At the heart of the book is Beulah's avowal of faith and the unshakable belief in her connection to Eustis, while at the other extreme lies the cynicism and the nihilism of Stevenson and Nowell respectively, tied to the vision of the failure of love and the reality of isolation. The reporter and the lawyer are both capable of building the material into a story, but neither can bridge the divide outlined by Nowell when he muses on calling up "the ghost of Beulah" in order to elicit her story (*Follow* 243). What Nowell must test against the rigors of evidence in formulating his argument, the narrative of the novel supplies in full. Foote suggests that the novelist's vision is in service to nothing but truth, whereas Nowell's is not. Nowell's professional and intellectual interest, for example, is exhausted with the composition and delivery of his formal closing argument; the completion of his strategy is his central concern, regardless of the verdict the jury will render.

It is left to the comic figure of the turnkey, Roscoe Jeffcoat (a Delta equivalent to Macbeth's gatekeeper), to complete the temporal and narrative structure. The last of the monologues in the book, Roscoe's section traces the events after the trial is completed and the verdict brought down: "'Life. . . . They gave him life'" (*Follow* 260). As White and Sugg note, commenting on Roscoe's special function: "[he] ponders justice, human relationships, and the order of things. He supplies data and arrives at insights that would surprise the elegant Nowell, for example, and the reader is accordingly alerted to the circumstance that there is more to Jordan County than can be wrapped up in sonata form" (35). Indeed, the whole of this last section is a return to the present of current events and a reminder of the unquenchable human capacity to hope for the future. Nowell's high-flown ruminations on justice and time are deflated some-what by Roscoe's observations on the seeming inequities created by Nowell's personal biases—suggestions of which were also raised by his counterpart, the circuit clerk. Comparing Eustis's fate to that of old man Lundy (life imprisonment as opposed to death by electrocution), Roscoe suggests: "It dont seem fair. One gets the chair, another gets life—all because Nowell's wife ten years ago . . . picked up her skirts and skipped off with a so-called friend of his, soured him on the world and all it had to offer, and now he hits back this way. No wonder they say Justice is blind. No wonder they put a bandage round her eyes" (*Follow* 261). Echoing an analogy Eustis remembers from Brother Jimson's preaching as he con-templates the moral dangers of his involvement with Beulah ("There had to be a balance in the world, so much corruption to so much sanctity, or everything would come undone" [*Follow* 99]), the unreligious Roscoe meditates about the implications of the whole tale: perhaps the world "is in a balance: so much sin and evil, so much good. Maybe we ought to be thankful to the ones that get in trouble. Maybe they draw the evil like a billy goat in a barnlot draws the fleas" (*Follow* 263). The ironic reso-nances of Roscoe's metaphor extend past the scope of his own compre-hension and return us to the floor of the cotton shed, where sexual desire and the urge for salvation—Pan and Christ—are conflated in Beulah's observation that Eustis smelled "like a billy goat" (*Follow* 94, 129). The sacrificial lamb and the Judas goat, good and evil, faith and doubt, all the unresolved oppositions around which the book is constructed, continue to press against the impulse for completion—the energy of the vortex at odds with the closure Roscoe would supply. Similarly, in the temporal sphere, the last section introduces the possibility of the future—Eustis's "life" at Parchman—as a sort of eternal return of the desire for a mythic paradise, Parchman being a "plantation like back in Slavery days" (*Follow* 268). The legacy of modern Solitaire gives way, ironically, to Roscoe's vision of prison "utopia," re-creating for Eustis the sharecropping "paradise" he left for Beulah. Judgment (at least for the reader—remembering Judge Holiman) is completely confounded. Foote's narrative is designed

THE AESTHETICS OF LIMITATION

to frustrate the idea of objectivity (in law, in history). What's left? The view of the artist: imaginative bridges, contingent wholes, histories with gaps, an unresolvable dialogue—paradox and irony.

Love in a Dry Season: *Dissolution, Desire, and Narrative*

Follow Me Down reflects from the outset a tension between the forward imperative to judgment (closure) and the gradual immersion in the "vertical" complexities of the story. *Love in a Dry Season* adopts a different strategy, emphasizing a satirical distance, situating the reader in the role of voyeur, at one with the other "watchers" (*Love* 143) who make up the Bristol public. A social "comedy of errors" (*Love* 158), *Love in a Dry Season* foregrounds the reader's detachment using a third-person omniscient perspective. The ironic distance associated with this omniscience delivers, White and Sugg suggest, "a mordant judgement" (37). The authorial presence in this book is more pronounced and intrusive than in any other Foote novel. His presence is embodied by an incidental figure—the bookkeeper in Major Barcroft's office. A minor functionary whose appearances bracket much of the main action, the bookkeeper sits (apparently unaltered throughout the dozen years of Harley Drew's residency in Bristol) "hunched above his ledger" with an "old-time dip pen" in hand (Foote's own preferred writing implement), resembling "a figure in an allegorical painting, indicating a name in the doomsday book" (*Love* 191–92). "[Q]uizzical and amused, faintly risible" (*Love* 62), this figure reflects, in microcosm, the detached perspective enforced by the design of the novel as a whole, with its various episodes constituting a long tally sheet of "pride and fear and guarded hope, breathing the close atmosphere of death" (*Love* 146) that makes up the raw material of this dark comedy. As Robert L. Phillips notes when he identifies Amanda Barcroft as an "allegorical modern Everywoman": "The failure to discover some humanizing spark of life, together with the necessity of the narrative to suggest what they do not see, gives the narrator a crucial role and, at the same time, gives the novel traces of allegory" (115). Foote's "allegory," though, is without a stable foundation of values—hence, modernist and ironic.

The mock allegorical dimension of the text is captured in Foote's depiction of the social ritual surrounding Florence Barcroft's death. The normally aloof neighborhood women stand witness to the tragedy, examining the usually inaccessible interior of the Barcroft house with "the feverish eyes of archeologists breaking into an Egyptian tomb" (*Love* 147). They gather in the parlor to converse in "low tones out of respect for the dead . . . at once compassionate and prying, officious and perverse" (*Love* 148). Having outlined the mixed motivations of the women, the narrator then offers, in a direct address to the reader, a comment indicative of the paradox at the heart of the novel: "Here human cruelty was displayed at its worst, you say, until you considered the reverse of the medal and saw the possibility of a worse cruelty still: an absence of concern, that is, or even curiosity" (*Love* 148). Foote's characteristically ironic stance considers the issue in terms of the lesser of two "cruelties," yet the positive element of this curiosity, the communal concern, is clearly underscored. The narrative structure of the novel reinforces this paradox of objectifying voyeuristic impulse combined with genuine human connection.

By continually distancing the reader from the events, and by deliberately refusing to evoke a sympathetic engagement with any of the characters, Foote concentrates the novel on the interplay between individual isolation and the impulse toward community. Indeed, at the two climactic points in Harley Drew's pursuit of erotic and material gratification, the narrator emphasizes the often incompatible nature of individual and communal desires. In the first instance, at the moment when Drew and Amy consummate their relationship in a seedy roadside cabin, the paradoxical aspect of this shared pursuit of satisfaction and connection is stressed:

> Thus his prayers had been answered after the flesh, after the week-long comedy of errors. He feared it might be an end as well as a beginning. . . . He feared it was probable that he had failed the test, for time after time—while, eyes rolling, she moaned "Not yet! Not yet!" writhing and panting like a swimmer in high surf—he had been unable to restrain himself. . . . he had been infected with Amy's frenzy: except that whereas in her case it had meant a prolongation, with him it had precipitated matters. (*Love* 158–59)

This sexual discordance stands, in microcosm, for a host of other equally incompatible agendas in the novel, a plethora of oppositions that simultaneously draw the characters together and push them apart. To remain with the sexual metaphor for just one more example, we can move to the last time Amy and Harley are together, when the pursuit of climax involves not just sexual satisfaction, but also the culmination of the jealousy and desire experienced by Amy's cuckolded husband. While the lovers are busily engaged, Jeff silently enters the room. Though he is blind, he succeeds in taking advantage of their preoccupation to exact his revenge:

> He moved quickly, silently. Halting alongside the bed he placed his left hand in the small of Drew's back, palm down, rested the base of his other fist upon it, gripping the pistol, and walked the left hand up Drew's backbone like a tarantula. This was all according to plan; the backbone guided the pistol to the brain; this time he would not miss. Drew, if he felt the hand at all, must have thought it was Amy's. However, it is unlikely that he felt it, for he was approaching that brief ecstasy which is characterized—as is no other sensation, except perhaps extreme pain (and maybe nausea)—by a profound indifference to the world around him; whatever feelings of warmth and tenderness may lap the shores of these tiny timeless islands in the time-stream, no man is ever more alone than in this moment of closest possible contact. Amy, though, feeling something brush her knee, opened her eyes and saw Jeff with the pistol. She gave a yelp and a start of surprise. But here again Drew, if he noticed at all, must have taken her cry of alarm and her sudden writhing as evidence of a gratification similar to his own. Yet it was no matter—he had so little time anyhow; for then Jeff pulled the trigger. (*Love* 222)

In each case, the image invoked is of the conjunction between a desire for communion (however debased or ironical) and the ultimate isolation of the individual (it might be pointed out, as well, that the scene also confirms Harley's worst fears: that is, that Amy is not completely engaged enough to dismiss that brush on her knee). In true comic fashion, the only temporarily chastened Harley Drew survives the assault. The novel continually invokes the juxtaposition of such opposites: motion and inertia, honor and self-interest, guilt and desire, fact and fiction—reinforcing this elemental human comedy through the distancing, but not indifferent, narrative perspective.

Foote implicates the reader in this ongoing construction of a communal heritage. He develops the narrative tension between the isolated individuals moving inexorably into closer proximity, while underscoring how their stories are reduced to stereotype genres within the communal context. Indeed, the individual dramas of the "secret triangular lives of people" (*Love* 241) are deliberately set against the backdrop of the collective consciousness of the community. Referred to a number of times as the "enormous Bristol eye" (*Love* 146), this web of individual stories constitutes the collective past (a mixture of fact and fiction, reality and hearsay); it leaves the outlander Harley Drew thinking that it was "as if God, an enormous Eye in the sky, were telling secrets" (*Love* 104). As White and Sugg remark, in considering one of the rhythmic patterns of the novel: "'Bristol's view' punctuates the narrative from time to time. Gossip, the 'speculation' of the enormous Bristol eye, is constant. Bristol has peaks of excitement but tires quickly and creates myths" (45). Foote employs the elements of his narrative to make his readers conscious of their participation in this process.

The process of a modulation from individual to stereotype, from unique narrative to the generic, is most clearly manifest through the figure of Amanda—Phillips's "allegorical modern Everywoman" (115). When she is introduced in the first section of the novel, Amanda, like her sister and father, lives apart from the world, one of the "family group . . . reflected in the huge fuliginous pupil of the enormous Bristol eye" (*Love* 146). Enmeshed in the web of Drew's plans to seize the "main chance" (*Love* 59), Amanda experiences the awakening of a possibility for freedom. After years of waiting for her release through Florence's death (which Drew likens to a "monstrous horserace, in reverse" [*Love* 90]), Amanda is abandoned by her lover and enters a "sort of posthumous existence" (*Love* 175) reserved for spinster daughters. Her existence as an object of public scrutiny is diminished: "She was no longer on the public tongue save in rare instances when strangers, seeing her pass, would ask about her . . . for her face was not only vacant now; it was dazed, distrait, like a person just recovering from an unexpected blow. The new versions were more prosaic than the old, without the eager surmises, the improbable conjectures. 'Who? That? That Amanda Barcroft, old Major Barcroft's daughter; she got jilted. Remind me to tell you about her some time.' It was as if a shadow were moving across the family portrait reflected in the enormous Bristol eye" (*Love* 175). Amanda's story, her allegory, moves from romance to comedy to tragedy (or its twentieth-century equivalent, pathos).

Her ironic final release comes after the Major's death. Amanda is absorbed into the community at large—she becomes one with the watchers:

"It was as if, brooding there like a gargoyle, her image had been imprinted on the public retina so long that now, at last, she had been absorbed by it, had now herself become a part of the enormous eye, and was looking out as all those others had done" (*Love* 248). This transformation is related to Amanda's identification as a reader, albeit one who reads "her own story without recognition" (*Love* 241), and provides an important clue to interpreting the novel. This "epilogue" (White and Sugg 38) serves to draw deliberate "attention to the art of fiction" (Phillips 132). The absorption of Amanda into the communal consciousness completes her odyssey from isolation to "normalcy" and serves notice to readers of their own problematic role, guided by the ironic voice of the narrator, as voyeuristic participants in the continual negotiation between fact and hearsay, between individual and stereotype, and between various genre-related expectations. As Phillips points out: "The narrator of *Love in a Dry Season* is conscious, too, that the reader of his work is in a position analogous to Amanda's but in the very act of writing, he seems to hope that the reader/observer is perhaps less benumbed than the other watchers" (133). Amanda's story constitutes, in fact, a challenge to each reader's awareness about the nature of narrative and story; it is, like Foote's other work, a parable about how narrative invariably constructs and distorts.

The intrusions of the authorial voice in *Love in a Dry Season* draw attention to the way that the reader (like the Bristol public) manufactures a version of reality. Time and again Foote fractures the polished surface of the story to indicate his role as guide, magus, or manipulator. All are ironically related to the voice of the narrator, who from the outset of the novel signals the artifice of its construction and stage-manages the action. Consider two almost random examples: the first from the conclusion of the first section—"There was a suitor on the way" (*Love* 25)—and the later injunction, "Observe her, then . . ." (*Love* 129), as a signal to mark the implications of Amy's sense of an "alienation of attention" (*Love* 128). Seen in this light, the main male characters become comic versions, or debased representations, of the artistic impulse: Harley Drew is the quintessential campaigner, plotting his grandiose strategies (yet failing on a tactical level); Major Barcroft, the armchair general and despot, devolves into a stereotype of a panderer attempting to smooth the way in his rearguard action to protect the family honor; and, finally, there is Jeff Carruthers, whose carefully orchestrated plan for revenge—the one that "would not miss" (*Love* 222)—goes so badly awry. Failed artists, faux creators, these characters remain locked in forms of impotence and blindness: Drew's pursuit of the good life—never to learn that "his desires were merely steps on an endless staircase leading nowhere" (*Love* 200); Amy's restless desire for stimulation—her "essential promiscuity" (*Love* 211); the Major's quest for military distinction—"the dream of pomp and glory" (*Love* 5); Jeff's frustrated desire—"For what could be more pitiful than a voyeur in the dark?" (*Love* 45); and the Bristol public's yearning after legend and myth—"Romance wasnt dead, they told themselves" (*Love* 128). All the while, Foote directs his reader's line of vision past the characters toward the process of narration itself.

To create a self-conscious narrative, Foote introduces his own voice as the point of triangulation, underscoring the act of reading itself as a form of voyeurism. Early in the story, Amy guides her blind husband around the Tarfeller mansion and responds to Jeff's queries of "'Whats it like?'" (*Love* 31) with a spoken description (ironically, to the "uninformed observer" [*Love* 32], all the while seeming to be guided by him). The implication is that the blind are truly leading the blind. This sort of aside leads White and Sugg to call the novel "a multiple play upon voyeurism" (43). The authorial voice also directs the reader's attention to the integral role that form and structure play in the book, where the widest possible vision produces the fundamental ingredient of ironic distance. As Phillips points out: "One can infer from the narrator's consciousness of his relationship with the reader that . . . the novel itself, can be an art form observed. Perhaps, for this observer and participant, there is at least some scrap of hope" (133). In a later example, as Jeff addresses this same issue of hope, the narrator steps in to supply an answer; significantly, it reproduces an immigrant's perspective of the New World (with its ironic echoes of Fitzgerald's "green breast" of America), a stark confrontation of the old dream and the jaded modern reality:

> Ambrose Light was a disappointing bell buoy. Then off to the right lay Coney Island, its ferris wheels and scenic railway distributed in spidery silhouette. The ship's wake described a milky curve, pale on the limitless green, and leaving the no-man's land of sea they entered the harbor where Liberty, gigantic and bland, held up her torch. Ahead the city waited, shining white and vertical, with dissolving and renewing plumes of steam announcing noon; a long gray smear fed by stacks was banked above it like an error

on a student's watercolor; this was America, clean as slabs of marble newly quarried and set on end. The ship mooed and the tugs came out and suckled. (*Love* 121)

Amy's "almost mystical elation" (*Love* 121) upon disembarking has been expertly contextualized by the narrator's appropriation of her role as seer. Similarly, throughout the novel, we are invited to participate consciously in the process of seeing, watching, and observing and to move past the limited purview of the participants—in short, to capitalize on the insights possible through the gift of omniscience and to see ourselves, in our reading, as (and this is crucial) a self-conscious part of the enormous eye.

September September: *Fact, Fiction, and a Generative Double Vision*

Foote's fascination with this communal perspective and its application to the reader is amplified in *September September*. As White and Sugg suggest: "Everything he learned about writing novels in the first phase [of his career] proved transferable to writing history. It appears that the discipline of research, consideration of all aspects of a large public event, and increased appreciation of human capacities are carrying over from the experience of producing *The Civil War* into the fiction Foote now writes" (127). *September September* signals—in keeping with the national scope of *The Civil War*—an end to the parochial concentration on the world of Jordan County that dominates the earlier novels. Foote's most recent novel provides a new perspective on the idea of the communal by acknowledging the impact of the advent of Marshall MacLuhan's "global village" on the denizens of Memphis, Bristol, and backwater Mississippi, in the month of September 1957. Where the gossip and collective memories of the Bristol populace form the backdrop of *Love in a Dry Season* and implicate the reader in the process of generating myths, *September September* stresses the paradoxical nature of the sense of connection and alienation represented by the world of television (described by Martha Kinship—with ironic exactitude in a novel charged with racial tension—as a world in "flickering black and white" [*September* 148]). The shaping influence of world and national events, and the immediate impact of the political climate of America at the outset of the Civil Rights movement, is central to the vision

of the novel. The technological changes in the world of 1957, Foote suggests, have forever altered the insular culture of the South. It is hardly
accidental, then, that this novel begins with the image of Rufus, Reeny,
and Podjo emerging out of the Delta, cresting the Chickasaw Bluff, and
heading for Memphis (the reverse of Drew Harley's journey and an echo of
Foote's own move in 1954). Scattered throughout the book are images,
such as the impending demolition of Memphis's railway station, "empty as
an abandoned barn—or better, the de-sanctified cathedral it resembled"
(*September* 109–10), that signal the displacement of the pre–World War II
dominants of the region in favor of the pervasive and homogeneous influences of television, the automobile, and big-city experience. The residues
of the Delta world give way to the burgeoning, borderless materialism of
the consumer culture and its universal urban sprawl.

The narrative structure Foote employs in *September September* suggests
a similar marshaling of resources, combining as it does aspects of all of
Foote's previous novels, the "Voices" chapters (2, 4, and 6) returning to the
interior monologues of *Shiloh* and *Follow Me Down,* and the four other chapters (1, 3, 5, and 7) re-creating the omniscient perspective of *Love in a Dry
Season* and the framing structures of *Tournament* and *Jordan County.* Foote
employs these narrative approaches to reproduce, in the framework of the
novel, the tension between an empathetic descent into questions of individual motivation and emotional experience (the spiraling inward of *Follow Me
Down*) and the ironic detachment, with its self-reflexive possibilities, of the
guiding omniscience of *Love in a Dry Season.* The conjunction of these two
strategies, and the wider spectrum of political and historical interests suggested above, introduces another concern of the narrative procedure (one
perhaps more pronounced in this novel because of its situation as the first
after Foote's immersion in historical narrative): that is, the blend of historical data and imaginative events, not unlike Foote's procedure in *Shiloh,* in
which a similar concern for temporal and spatial veracity in the movements
of fictional characters within the historical field is evident. As Podjo
remarks toward the close of the novel, albeit in a somewhat different, more
personal, context: "I couldnt get over it; having things come full circle like
that" (*September* 253)—an apt observation, particularly from the one character who ironically paraphrases the words of former slave trader and
Confederate general Nathan Bedford Forrest when discussing the tactics of
their own campaign of exploitation: "We've gotten all we want out of [the
Little Rock unrest] by now. Whatever those troopers do tomorrow wont

change what was done yesterday and today, before they got there. We stand pat and *keep up the scare*" (*September* 143, italics added). The novel takes Foote's oeuvre back full circle, with the ironic juxtaposition of this kidnapping and Governor Faubus's political exploitation of events to the campaigns fought for heartfelt—if misguided—principles almost one hundred years before. The book marks a completion of Foote's engagement with the theme of racial exploitation and injustice—the germinal point of the conflict he chronicles in *The Civil War*. The novel acts as a coda both for his narrative history and also for the fictional Delta sequence. In a sense, *September September* signals a closure to the preoccupations of the modernist writer emerging from the era of the Southern Renaissance, an acknowledgment that the themes and agenda have shifted toward those defined by Eben Kinship as emergent activist, in a world both broadened and diminished by that "clouded crystal ball" (*September* 19), the television—the late-twentieth-century equivalent of Bristol's enormous eye.

The nature of this communal consciousness has changed significantly, however, from *Love in a Dry Season* to *September September*. In the earlier book, Foote can still insist on the paradox that the seeming cruelty of the community's curiosity can be mitigated by the compassion that accompanies it. The point is established by Amanda's story and also earlier, in the first section of the novel, when the narrator summarizes the community's judgment on Major Barcroft: "They could forgive him his reverses, the sorrows that crowded his life, but they could not forgive him his reported million dollars and his high-born insularity. They, or others like them, had watched him all his life, and when trouble came they resented that he did not call for help. They would have preferred it so; they would have enjoyed watching him run shrieking into the street with his hands in the air: 'Help me! Help me! My affliction is more than I can bear.' In that case they might even have gone to help and comfort him. But as it was, their eyes were hostile as they watched him pass" (*Love* 25). While certainly a hard-nosed assessment of the vagaries of human nature, this resignation of the possibility of compassion tempers the tone of callous indifference and resentment. In *Love in a Dry Season*, though, this communal consciousness retains a measure of compassion and connection—contact still exists on a human scale. The intimacy of the Bristol context finds no correlative in *September September;* the small town has been replaced by an urban world wholly composed of "outlanders," past and present, famous and infamous—Andrew Jackson, Davy Crockett, Bedford Forrest, Casey Jones, Machine

Gun Kelly, or Ed Crump—"none of them born here, yet all of them Memphis-connected, like Eben himself and his father-in-law" (*September* 195). To this list one might add Rufus Hutton, Podjo Harris, and Reeny Perdew, the three Jordan County expatriates.

Gone, as well, are the intimate oral histories and gossip of Bristol; they are replaced by radio, television, and newspaper—alienating and impersonal media. The new forms of connection, Robert L. Phillips suggests, "form a unifying thread through the text of the novel, creating the effect of a chorus" (215). The characters on both sides of the racial divide in *September September* watch the same television programs, read the same headlines, share to a great extent the same culture, yet never actually meet—a point strikingly conveyed in the image of the ransom drop, as Podjo stands watching behind a board fence while Eben leaves the money (*September* 224), with the two figures in dangerous and intimate proximity, yet never connecting. Foote reinforces this opposition of connection and division by suspending this pivotal moment between sectional divisions in the chapter; the meeting that is not a meeting is highlighted by a shift from Eben's desperate perspective as he confronts his moment of decision to Rufus's exultant celebration of the successful completion of the kidnappers' plan. The motif of contact, in both its debased and transforming aspects, frames the whole of the abduction. Reeny's first gesture upon initially confronting Teddy in the street is to reach "out and [lay] one hand on the boy's shoulder" (*September* 85), while her last action is a tender gesture of farewell: "'Goodbye,' she said, hand on his shoulder, the way it had been that other time just before she snatched him up" (*September* 259).

The structure of the novel corresponds with this image of phantom contact. As Foote suggests, "I think that wisdom, if there is any, is going to have to proceed from a recognition of the basic loneliness of man. And all you can do is combat it. You can never be not alone. Never. But you can, working from a basis of recognizing the basic loneliness, achieve contact. But you can't achieve contact and be surprised at the loneliness that goes along with the contact, or the contact will be shattered" (*Conversations* 101). Foote employs parallels between the characters' sensibilities, ironic inversions of the black and white symbolism, and juxtaposed frames of reference to establish the shared cultural milieu, all the while continually stressing the social reality of racial division and segregation. The temporal framework plays an important role here, as each day's activity in the two separate spheres is recounted in detail. The strict schedule of events, for instance, is determined first by the plans of the kidnappers (from arrival to departure—the month of September in the title) and then marked by the daily chronicling (in newspapers or on radio and television) of the racial conflict unfolding in Little Rock and the political maneuvering of Governor Faubus and President Eisenhower. The time sequence in *September September* (as rigid as that in *Shiloh*) pays close attention to incidental details (the weather, television programs) that mark the passage of time and contribute to its classification, by a French critic, as a "thriller au ralenti," or "slow-moving thriller" (*Conversations* 260). Besides using these events as a form of internal clock for the novel, Foote also employs them for humorous effect (Reeny and Podjo make love on the couch as Robert Young is on the television, playing the epitome of middle-class virtue in *Father Knows Best* [*September* 175–76]) or as ironic backdrop to events (Eben's tirade against the activities of the civil-rights advocates in Arkansas reflects his own complacency and privilege, soon to be shattered by the very inequities in the system he so vehemently supports [*September* 19]). The unfolding of the racial unrest in Little Rock, in fact, functions as a direct counterpoint to the building suspense of the unfolding plans of the kidnappers. In the larger public sphere, the action begins with the "Little Rock explosion" (*September* 95), which then tapers off under smaller headlines and diminishing coverage. The private trauma of Teddy's seizure, however, works in the opposite direction, building toward the pivotal moment of the exchange and his release—concurrent with the falling-out among thieves that ends in Rufus's immolation (*September* 297). In a fitting irony, like a moral coda in Aesop's fables, Rufus's corpse burns like "a grasshopper caught in the flame of a blowtorch" (*September* 297), while Eben Kinship, phoenixlike, rises transformed from his trial by fire.

Foote's attention to the spatial framework of *September September* reinforces this paradox of connection and disconnection. From the moment of the kidnappers' arrival from Bristol and Jordan County in "Three Came Riding" to the westward departure of Podjo and Reeny in the last section, "Some You Lose," Foote assiduously charts their movements through the city, devoting whole paragraphs to the street names and directions. Similar attention is paid to Eben's movements (to and from his workplace on Beale Street, at the trial drop in Handy Park, and later at the actual drop opposite Clayborn Temple on Pontotoc Street), as well as to his children's progression to and from the school. The ritualized nature of these passages emphasizes the spatial proximity of the players and forms a counterpoint for the shared temporal framework. Such careful attention to patterns serves, as well, to indicate points at which the characters diverge from their intended routes and undergo alterations in consciousness. For example, Eben arrives at his moment of truth, his confrontation with the rage he feels at his impotence as a black man within the white system, when he rejects the kidnappers' injunction and looks back—literally, when he returns to the drop point, but also figuratively, when he reassesses his situation in relation to his people's history as blacks in the society of the South. This rejection of the plan marks Eben's difference from the other characters. Rufus fulfills his destiny, sticking to the pattern of his life, the "ache for failure" (*September* 275), when he succumbs to the urge to change his relationship with Podjo and Reeny "from rivalry to revenge" (*September* 231) and in doing so destroys their carefully laid plans, their main chance at escape, and sends them all down the long, straight road to oblivion. Podjo and Reeny, while escaping westward, are left at the conclusion of the novel where they began: scrounging for a grubstake, living on the hope that their luck will change.

The paradox of connection and disconnection also determines the structure of the novel. While Foote's attention to temporal progression and spatial movement establishes the perimeter of the action (the limiting frame within which the "plot" unfolds), the divisions within the book reinforce the idea of enclosure and separation. Each chapter of the novel, whether consisting of omniscient narration or interior monologue, involves an interplay between black and white perspectives. For instance, the middle sections of the first and last triadic chapters are devoted to the Kinship family—a reflection of their vulnerability to the encompassing world of the whites. This pattern is repeated in the two chapters ("Voices" 2 and 6) that consist of the monologues of the male characters. In each case, Eben's reflections, memories, and experiences are contained within the framing monologues of Podjo and Rufus, with Rufus's voice occupying the interior position, closest to the central three chapters of the book (these, chapters 3, 4, and 5, begin with the actual kidnapping and end with Eben's payment of the ransom). Up to this point—the three central chapters—the symmetry of the novel creates a perfect mirror image, front and back, displaying a progression not unlike that of *Follow Me Down* or *Shiloh*. This pattern corresponds to the social context that Foote has developed through the temporal and spatial frames—a representation of the curtailed existence of the black members of an endemically racist society.

Chapters 3 and 5, while offering the first deviation from this pattern, have their own particular symmetry. Chapter 3 is largely devoted to the action of the kidnapping itself. Its first and last sections recount the activities of Podjo, Reeny, and Rufus; the middle section reflects Eben's situation as passive victim (acted upon instead of acting). Here, the closed circles of the white and black communities overlap when Teddy is abducted—a point Foote neatly underscores by the kidnappers' bungling attempt to "absorb" him into their midst during the abduction by the application of "clown white" (*September* 109) paste: "the boy had the look of a death's head, of a dwarf made up hurriedly by amateurs to play the role of Death in a morality play or pageant. . . . what Teddy in fact resembled was a blurred photo negative of a diminutive minstrel end man" (*September* 110–11). Moving from one sphere to the other in this segregated world engenders a recourse to stereotypes—an indication that even at this moment of literal connection the distance remains in place; Teddy is not assimilated but instead is enclosed under a false veneer of "porcelain" (*September* 110) whiteness. Chapter 5 reverses the pattern of sections established earlier in chapter 3, with the first and last sections devoted to Eben and his increasing awareness of the reality of his own victimization and helplessness. In effect, another transformation takes place here, as Eben sheds his complacency and the "porcelain" veneer of white middle-class existence in favor of an identification with his own rage and his rejection of the tacit support for segregation adopted from his father-in-law and the teachings of Booker T. Washington. Where chapter 3 delineates action (the traditional exploitation of the secondary status of blacks by whites), chapter 5 outlines an equally powerful reaction in Eben's raging self-analysis (an alteration in Eben's consciousness that foreshadows the transformation of the past into the impetus for change).

The epicenter of the novel is contained in chapter 4, the three pivotal interior monologues devoted to the two female characters; the first and last are Reeny Perdew's, and the central voice—"the still point of the turning world"—belongs to Martha Kinship. These sections provide Foote's most intimate portrayal of the distorting impact of racism on an individual and the real cost of the corresponding black philosophy of accommodation. The inequities of this balance are illustrated by Reeny's account of the kidnap note Rufus composes: "'You dont get the drift.' Rufus explains to Podjo, 'I tried for a balance; something that would scare and reassure them, both at once'" (*September* 131). Reeny's sardonic observation that "it seemed to me if I was Teddy's mother I'd go running out in the street, hair on end, and yell for help from anyone around, cops or whatnot" (*September* 131), anticipates her identification with the maternal role and the main point of contact between the two characters. Indeed, Teddy intu-itively recognizes this connection when he later, quite innocently, asks Reeny: "Are you my mamma now?" (*September* 166). Martha and Reeny are two halves of a whole. The structure of the novel supports this by link-ing the three sections through the device of the impending, and then real-ized, telephone conversation between the two women. Reeny's strong empathetic response is in sharp contrast to prevailing tendencies toward brutal objectification: "I felt strange from having talked with her after all we'd done and were doing to her. She seemed a lot realer, now that I had talked with her, and somehow I seemed less real" (*September* 162). Teddy's comic-ironic transformation by greasepaint heralds more lasting ones. The clown paste is an attempt to shift him into a white context; Reeny, on the other hand, is shifted toward an identification with the victim, the black context. Her empathy with Martha caps a section largely devoted to re-counting her exploitation at the hands of various men—from her father, the Reverend Jimson, who values her only insofar as she conforms to his ideal of virgin purity; through husbands and lovers who manifest inadequacies in forms central to Foote's diagnosis of the perennial Delta spiritual ills (loins and heart); leading finally to Rufus Hutton, who values Reeny for their sexual relationship, which provides his only sense of achievement and self-completion. That the relationship between Reeny and Rufus finally ends in a rather extreme, if comic-absurd, form of coitus interruptus (when Teddy accidentally walks in on their frenzied love-making) suggests the retrograde nature of this particular form of self-realization. In keeping with the motif of connection and disconnection, the pair ironically mistake orgasm (the ultimate isolation) for connection (and completion).

Later, Reeny continues to pursue fulfilment through sexuality (Podjo's promise as a lover providing her main hope for their future): "All there was for me was men, and I kept trying" (*September* 139). Martha Kinship, on the other hand, attempts to realize herself through accommodation and denial. In this central section of the book, encompassed as it is by Reeny's crisis of conscience regarding the exploitation of the black family's vulner-ability ("Those poor damn people" [*September* 164], Reeny says to an un-comprehending Rufus, ironically echoing Eben's insensitive reaction to the initial news of the unrest in Little Rock), Foote develops Martha's character in terms of her internalization of the role of victim. On a familial level, Martha's self-loathing is engendered by her accommodation to the dictates of her father's emulation of the white middle-class society. She attempts to refashion herself in keeping with the formulas supplied by popular women's magazines and represses her sexual desires ("jungle doings" [*September* 157]) because of her uncritical absorption of racial stereotypes. The conjunction of her history of self-denial with her father's articulation of his philosophy of the mutual benefits of segregation provides the central irony of the novel. Indeed, the very real possibility of Teddy's death at the hands of these "faceless" (*September* 146) representatives of white society propels Martha to new levels of self-awareness; significantly, her awakening involves a consciousness of form that encompasses the narrative as a whole. Anguishing over her sense of loss and the jarring impact of Teddy's absence, Martha articulates the primary distinction between the white and the black characters in the story and anticipates the motivation behind Eben's transformation: "At times like that, with everything still and empty-feeling all around you, you see things you never saw before: the way sunlight falls on a rug, say, and shows you colors you didn't know were in it until then. So it is with people, sometimes, in the lives they lead. What you have been makes you what you are, and in times of strain you see things in the pattern you never saw before" (*September* 150). Martha might remain unconscious of the Jamesian echoes in her "figure in the carpet" analogy, but the author does not. Foote highlights his most affirmative vision by endowing this unlikely individual with the sensibility of the artist. What Hugh Bart lacked and his artist-grandson supplied (through the empathetic exercise of creative hindsight), Martha discovers at her moment of greatest trauma—the key to the pattern. The statement is an avowal of the importance of a consciousness of the past; it is also an affirmation—whether fashioned out of "times of strain" or an artist's imaginative power—that the identification of new patterns (specifically narrative patterns) informs the impetus for understanding and the possibility of change.

The last of the framing motifs speaks directly to the audience and addresses the implications of this fundamental change in social perspective. At two brief points, bracketing the main action of the novel, Foote draws attention to the present time of the book's composition. The first direct address to the reader occurs in the second sentence of the novel (following a clearly Dickensian opening to mark the "revolution" in consciousness the Civil Rights movement portended). Foote explicitly connects the events of September 1957—"twenty years ago" (*September* 3)—with the America of 1977: "It was a bad time in many ways, some of them comprehensible, others not. We had a great big kewpie doll in the White House, commander-in-chief of all the cold-war warriors on our side, and the Russians were up to something they would fling skyward from the dusty steppes of Kazakhstan just one month later" (*September* 3). This nod toward futurity, uncharacteristic of Foote's fiction, harkens back to the framing device he employs in *Tournament* as Asa outlines the vantage from which he explores Hugh Bart's life. Asa also defines the period between the New and the Modern South that is the frame of reference for Foote's fiction. Speaking of the limit of this time frame, Foote remarks: "The world practically stopped for me along about 1960 or so" (*Conversations* 129). Indeed, *September September* can be seen very much as an end and a beginning, an alpha and omega, for the author's central concerns. It marks the end of the South's long emergence from the period of retrenchment inaugurated by Reconstruction (source of Faulkner's subject matter) and casts a forward glance to the world of the postmodern South, where the themes and focus of the writer reflect not just a regional but a national or global perspective—the war, in effect, has moved elsewhere.

The second authorial address to the reader in *September September* acts as an epilogue or coda to Foote's oeuvre, a passing of the torch. It is tied to Theo Wiggins's endorsement of Eben's declaration of the necessity for change. Supporting Eben's request, Theo remarks: "You wont have the edge I had, using their own system to beat them with. Or maybe you will. Maybe you will. Maybe you will find a way to do that too. Anyhow, what you do you'll have to do it your own way, not in mine. Mine's gone by, or it's going, going fast. I know that now. But knowing's one thing. Doings another. I wont change." Immediately, the authorial voice interjects: "He was wrong. He changed. We all did" (*September* 289). Sputnik is launched, and Foote pauses to hear the music of the brave new world, the "beeping in A-flat around and around a world that would never be the same" (*September* 289). The elegiac tone is tempered by a note of hope—adaptability to circumstances being a reignition of the "spark" (*Tournament* 67) that Hugh Bart extinguished when he turned his back on the past. Indeed, Kinship's declaration of the need for change stands in marked and ironic contrast to the "proleptic" (*September* 301) anticipations of the future that are introduced in relation to Reeny and Podjo's hopes for a windfall in Nevada contained in the last section of the novel. What hope Foote endorses lies with those who, like Eben, embrace the challenge of change in the world around them, rather than those, like Podjo and Reeny, who pursue the ephemeral dreams of the gaming table (Bart's curse) or the chimera of the western frontier (never, apparently, having read Frederick Jackson Turner's pronouncement of its closing). At the beginning of his "Bibliographical Note" to the third volume of *The Civil War*, Foote quotes from the prologue of Geoffrey Chaucer's *The Legend of Good Women* (circa 1386): "Farwel my book and my devocion" (*CW* III.1063)—a quite fitting closure to the work of twenty years. Yet, in many ways, *September September* offers a more appropriate farewell: a fictional completion that envelops and magnifies the insights of the historical narrative and brings the two facets of this writer into proper symmetrical equipoise.

This idea of balance extends to the tension Foote establishes in all his mature fiction between the formal attributes of the narrative and the presentation of individual perspectives found within them. His aesthetic of limitations, operating on a thematic level with respect to the situation of the individual characters and on a self-conscious aesthetic level in the mind of the reader, invokes a continual recognition of the central role of narrative in negotiating between "fact" and "hearsay." As David Lowenthal suggests, in speaking about the significance of narrative to history:

> Understanding the past demands some awareness of the temporal location of people and things; a chronological framework clarifies, places things in context, underscores the essential uniqueness of past events. The way history is now taught, with "glittering pearls of Romans, cavemen, the battles of the First World War, medieval monks, and Stonehenge, suspended in temporal, non-causative isolation, hardly enhances appreciation of the necklace of time." The pearls of history take their value not merely from being many and lustrous, but from being arranged in a causal narrative sequence; the narrative lends the necklace meaning as well as beauty. (224)

Foote, I think, would agree wholeheartedly. In *Tournament*, Hugh Bart tries to offset his sense of the modern world as a "snarl of causation" (*Tournament* 212) by attempting, unsuccessfully, to translate his life into narrative, only to recognize that the "truth lay in implications, not in facts. Facts were only individual beads; the hidden string was what made them into a necklace" (*Tournament* 223). As Appleby, Hunt, and Jacob eloquently suggest: "The human intellect demands accuracy while the soul craves meaning" (262). By drawing the reader's attention to the existence of this "hidden string," by accentuating the role of narrative as a site for mediating between fact and hearsay, Foote asserts the essential capacity of the imaginative vision (even when conscious of its limitations) to wrest meaning from the seeming waste of indifferent determinism or individual existential despair.

Chapter 4

Writing the American *Iliad*

Character in *The Civil War*

As for method, it may explain much for me to state that my favorite historian is Tacitus, who dealt mainly with high-placed scoundrels, but that the finest compliment I ever heard paid a historian was tendered by Thomas Hobbes in the foreword to his translation of The Peloponnesian War, *in which he referred to Thucydides as "one who, though he never digress to read a Lecture, Moral or Political, upon his own Text, nor enter into men's hearts, further than the Actions themselves evidently guide him . . . filleth his Narrations with that choice of matter, and ordereth them with that Judgement, and with such perspicuity and efficacy expresseth himself that (as Plutarch saith) he maketh his Auditor a Spectator. For he setteth his Reader in the Assemblies of the People, and in their Senates, at their debating; in the Streets, at their Seditions; and in the Field at their Battels." There indeed is something worth aiming at, however far short of attainment we fall.*

> —Shelby Foote, *The Civil War: A Narrative*, 1963

I demonstrate, demonstrate, demonstrate!—both with action and description.

> —Shelby Foote, letter to Walker Percy, October 17, 1950

oote, in a letter written while composing his treatment of the Atlanta campaign, talks about William T. Sherman's advocacy of total war and the general's bewilderment over his postwar reputation in the South. "After the war," Foote writes, "he was hard put to understand why former Southern friends wouldnt speak to him on the street. He claimed he wanted to reduce bloodshed by shortening the war; and did. Red-headed Sherman. I have a scene of him taking a bath in the Chattahoochee, talking with a teamster on [the] bank; beard bristly and grizzled, face freckled, liver spots on backs of hands, pubic hair pink in sunlight. Cant use any of it; I made it up. Wait, sweet Christ, till I get back to novels!" (January 19, 1970; *Correspondence* 139). In fact, Foote does include this incident in *The Civil War*, and the form it takes is instructive about the way he disciplines his novelist's imaginative license and creates a style that, to employ Peter Gay's phrase, "opens windows on both truth and beauty—a bewildering double vista" (6). The episode follows Foote's description of the latest retrograde movement by the Confederate forces across the Chattahoochee River, a shift that brings General Joseph E. Johnston and his troops to within a scant five miles of Atlanta. The relentless tempo of the "red clay minuet" in which the two armies were engaged, from Dalton to Atlanta, is suspended briefly as Sherman contemplates his next move. Utilizing the homespun detail of Sherman's bath, Foote seizes this moment in his narrative to re-create the lived quality of this lull in the action—a moment for summation, reflection, and return to commonplace activities.

> While the red-haired general pondered and pored over maps and reports, his troops moved up to the unguarded Chattahoochee, anticipating their first leisurely bath in ten weeks. Admiration for their commander had grown with every tactical leap or sidestep, and now it reached a climax in which almost anything seemed possible. "Charley," one dusty infantry man told a comrade as they approached this last natural barrier and saw smoke rising from the buildings along its banks, "I believe Sherman has set the river on fire." Nor was the wonder limited to wearers of the blue. A butternut prisoner, conducted rearward past exuberant Federals in their tens of thousands, was so impressed by their multitude that he said to his captors: "Sherman ought to get on a high hill and command,

'Attention! Kingdoms by the right wheel!'" The general, in point of fact, was squatting naked in the Chattahoochee at the time, discussing the temperature of the water with a teamster who admired him from the bank, while all around them other soldiers lolled neck deep in the river, soaking away the grime of more than a hundred red-clay miles of marching and fighting and the caked sweat of seventy days of exertion and fear, or else whooped and splashed in pure delight at having nothing else to do. (*CW* III.406–7)

In this fashion, Foote's imaginative visualization of Sherman, with its descriptive exactitude, finds a place in the historical narrative.

The fact of Sherman's "dip in the Chattahoochee" (*CW* III.407) is Foote's vehicle for establishing some of the less tangible and "human" elements in the conflict. The anonymous soldiers are a means of indicating the sense of esprit de corps that Sherman, as a "winning" general, created. As well, by placing the increasingly legendary leader in close, "stripped," proximity to the men he commanded, Foote provides an implicit corrective to the opening hyperbole of the two foot soldiers and includes a reminder that an army is not just its commander—that, finally, they are all simply men. The scene also conveys an impression of the physical discomforts endured during the campaign and places these details in the concrete terms of time elapsed and distance traveled. Sherman's bath, while trivial in itself, shows the great strengths of Foote's approach to history. By devoting such attention to this brief moment of relief after a long, dangerous campaign, by developing the contrast between the brutality of the fighting and the simple, almost innocent, pleasures, Foote gives credence in an understated way to the intensity of the "exertion and fear" both generals and soldiers experienced—travails that occupy almost one hundred pages preceding this passage. The texture of the writing in *The Civil War*, the quality that makes it more than academic military history, is Foote's sensitivity to the totality of the experience; the richness of his presentation of the war lies in an master craftsman's attention to style, characterization, and plot.

Robert L. Phillips, in *Shelby Foote: Novelist and Historian* (1992), suggests that *The Civil War* "developed from the form that had given shape to [Foote's] fiction. The history develops from and subsumes the earlier efforts" (179). This symbiotic relationship between the novelist and the historian is embraced by Foote himself when he suggests that "[b]oth are seeking the same thing: the truth—not a different truth: the same truth—

only they reach it, or try to reach it, by different routes" ("Novelist's" 219). On August 9, 1954, writing to Walker Percy in a letter that contains the first preserved mention of Foote's Civil War project, the author summarizes his narrative strategy for the whole. "I built a frame," Foote says, "that will take all the strain I can place upon it. It is revolutionary in its simplicity." He then elaborates:

> I adopt strict point-of-view; that is, the reader always has a definite standing-place from which he looks out. His point of view (3d person, of course) is that of Lincoln, Davis, Grant, Lee, etc.—whoever happens to be at the storm-center of the current subject. This gives it a validity and a vitality that will be cumulative and intense.
>
> It is strictly chronological; there is no anticipation of events— so that, in a sense, a person might read it to find out "how it comes out." There is no anticipating the fall of Vicksburg, no pointing out along the way what the consequences of an action will be, unless the planner takes into account what they might be.
>
> I make no wise over-all comments except as they were made by people who were there; the events, whether battles or political maneuvers, are presented for their own sakes. Whether or not (for example) Grant was surprised at Shiloh is better shown than told; all the evidence is there.
>
> It sounds terribly simple, and it is. But the resulting heightening of the drama, the narrative drive, is really wonderful. The story has its climaxes and denouements, and they fell marvelously into place. Outlining it on the above basis, I was in a continuous state of wonder and excitement. It will be an American Iliad—I mean that. In another sense, it will be like reading wartime newspaper accounts, if the reporter had full knowledge of what went on behind closed doors—and (I hope) style.
>
> You can see the kinship to Shiloh. I want that same immediacy, achieved not through the fictional narrators but through a straightforward third-person account. (Letters, August 9, 1954)

The nature of this kinship between Foote's fiction and history is the focus of the next two chapters. The present chapter considers how Foote's history is an extension of his vision of the human condition first articulated in his explorations of Jordan County. Chapter 5 looks at the contribution that

Foote's artistic sensibility and novelistic techniques—his aesthetic of limitations—makes to the composition of his historical narrative. In each case, the discussion begins by exploring the "kinship" of his novel *Shiloh* to the matter and method of *The Civil War*. While the length and depth of the tale that Foote presents in *The Civil War* could supply material for a dozen books, the following discussion of selective aspects of the narrative helps to establish—but in no way exhausts—the impressive nature of Foote's accomplishment.

War, Courage, and Authenticity in Shiloh

In commenting on Stephen Crane's *The Red Badge of Courage* (1895), Foote asserts that one of the marks of greatness in Crane's novel is the sympathetic (if ironic) depiction of Henry Fleming's humanity—his metamorphosis through a variety of attitudes as he struggles to define what it is to be "a man." The question, posed by Crane at the beginning of the twentieth century, in a context drawn from near the middle of the nineteenth, defined a central issue for the modernist writers who followed him. The Naturalist school—with whom Crane is sometimes erroneously linked—offered a grim vision of man as a hapless victim of determinate forces, economic or atavistic. F. Scott Fitzgerald looked out on the modern world and saw an intractable progression of materialism corrupting the last vestiges of American idealism. William Faulkner explored the issue in relation to the troubling legacy of the southern past (race, defeat, lost innocence) and defined the central modernist theme as "the human heart in conflict with itself," with humanity's only consolation as a stoical capacity to endure. Ernest Hemingway—perhaps the most knowledgeable of any of these writers about the grisly realities of twentieth-century warfare—diagnosed civilization as suffering from an enervating existential malaise, a collapse of traditional verities; and, having delineated the problem, he found a solution by re-creating the idea of honor on his own terms, in the form of a code of individual conduct. This bedrock modernist issue of what it means to be human, in the face of technological change and copious evidence of man's inhumanity, is an important part, as well, of Shelby Foote's writing.

In the second volume of *The Civil War*, during Foote's development of the conditions that lead up to the Battle of Chancellorsville (the historical setting, incidentally, for Crane's depiction of Henry Fleming's baptism by

fire), the narrative is suspended to enable the writer to include an anecdote—a short parable—on the nature of fear. What makes this aside significant is that nowhere else, to my knowledge, does Foote fracture the
present time of his story to include such a vignette or acknowledge by name
a debt to a twentieth-century writer—one who had no immediate connection to the events of the war. Such an exception on Foote's part demands
careful examination. I reproduce the reference here in its entirety; the paragraph picks up at the point when General "Fighting Joe" Hooker has suc-
cessfully moved his forces around the flank of Lee's army and then inex-
plicably declines to press his advantage. He has just received intelligence
information about Confederate movements.

[The information about Confederate dispositions] also explained—all too clearly—the sudden clatter of musketry and the
boom of guns, first down the turnpike, then down the plank road,
not long after the two columns set out eastward through the forest.
In part, as well, it accounted for Hooker's reaction, which in effect
was a surrendering of the initiative to Jackson, who plunged deeper
into the Wilderness in pursuit. But there was a good deal more to
it than this: a good deal more that was no less valid for being less
specific. Perhaps Hooker at last had recalled Lincoln's admonition,
"Beware of rashness." Perhaps at this critical juncture he missed
the artificial stimulus of whiskey, which formerly had been part of
his daily ration but which he had abjured on taking command.
Perhaps he mistrusted his already considerable accomplishment in
putting more than 70,000 soldiers in Lee's immediate rear, with
practically no losses because he had met practically no resistance.
It had been altogether too easy; Lee must have wanted him where
he was, or at any rate where he had been headed before he called
a halt and ordered a pull-back. Or perhaps it was even simpler than
that. Perhaps he was badly frightened (not physically frightened:
Hooker was never that: but morally frightened) after the manner of
the bullfighter Gallo, who, according to Hemingway, "was the
inventor of refusing to kill the bull if the bull looked at him in a certain way." This Gallo had a long career, featuring many farewell
performances, and at the first of these having fought the animal
bravely and well, when the time came for killing he faced the
stands and made three eloquent speeches of dedication to three

distinguished aficionados; after which he turned, sword in hand, and approached the bull, which was standing there, head down, looking at him. Gallo returned to the barrera. "You take him, Paco," he told a fellow matador; "I don't like the way he looks at me." So it was with Hooker, perhaps, when he heard that Lee had turned in his direction and was, so to speak, looking at him. Lowe had signaled at noon that the rebels were "considerably diminished" on the heights behind Fredericksburg. Consequently, at 2 o'clock, Fighting Joe wired Butterfield: "From character of information have suspended attack. The enemy may attack me—I will try it. Tell Sedgwick to keep a sharp lookout, and attack if can succeed." In effect, now that Lee had turned his attention westward, Hooker was telling Sedgwick: "You take him, Paco. I don't like the way he looks at me." (*CW* II.280)

After noting the myriad of possible influences on Hooker at this juncture, Foote arrives at a central distinction—that between physical and moral fear (and their opposites: physical and moral courage). By following this point with the wry, comic anecdote drawn from Hemingway's seminal treatise on the art of bullfighting, *Death in the Afternoon* (1932), Foote provides us with an important reference for his own philosophical (and stylistic) allegiance. Everywhere in his fiction, and his history, Foote confronts the decline of the South (in lifestyle, in morals, in terms of family and tradition and honor). The South as an entity is already past. What replaces it, in Foote's view, is the modern world of accident (the "snarl of causation") and the isolation of the individual. With this reference to Hemingway's work, one that touches on the central metaphor—the bullfight—through which he explored a way of countering the meaninglessness of the modern condition for isolated man, Foote indicates the criteria for value in his own work. Foote identifies the point of contact between the chivalric and the existential systems when answering a question about his own military experience: "Growing up in Mississippi, [Confederate veterans] were the embodiment of gallantry and chivalry. . . . You were expected to measure up to those standards, most of all with regard to physical and moral courage" (Horwitz 149). Honor in the southern chivalric sense operated in terms of a set of fixed and conventional values dictated by the community; honor in the new context of the modern world is closer to a Hemingwayesque distinction between authentic and inauthentic responses of an individual in a violent, chaotic arena. A distinguishing aspect of Foote's work is the displacement of the southern code in favor of this existential one.

It is along these lines that *Shiloh* and *The Civil War* can be read as investigations into the nature of being (in twentieth-century terms). Certainly, Foote's characters in either genre provide depictions of both physical and moral fear, as well as the possession, or not, of "grace under pressure." Foote is fascinated by individual reactions to the paradox that is the Civil War—a conflict "Churchill called . . . the last of the old-fashioned romantic wars and the first of the modern wars" (*Conversations* 138), where the outdated tactics of the eighteenth century met the weaponry of the mid–nineteenth century. In an interview, Foote acknowledges the foreignness of the men's conception of their role:

> It [the country before 1860] had a simplicity that we are not able to comprehend. Many people spent their entire lives not being over fifty or a hundred miles from home. But they gained things. They weren't torn on the bias the way we are. They weren't pulled at from so many different directions. Lincoln said human nature doesn't change, and human nature hasn't changed, but men's belief had a startling simplicity to it. . . . they fought for four years, which is a long time, and the simplicity was severely tested, but they never lost it. Duty, bravery under adversity, very simple virtues, and they had them. (Ward 264)

Foote's interest in the war is also an examination of the way this simplicity (those basic verities that Victorianism so tenaciously asserted) gives way to the moral ambiguities of the modern world.

Shiloh

In *Shiloh,* the monologues of Luther Dade, private in the Sixth Mississippi regiment, and Otto Flickner, a Union cannoneer, form the heart of Foote's novel—much as the Gallo and Hooker analogue constitutes a criteria of values in *The Civil War.* These two central monologues carry the action from dawn until almost midnight of the first day of the battle. Dade and Flickner represent the ultimate goal of a battle narrative: to depict the impact of the experience of combat on the individual sensibility and to explore the nature of courage. Although quite different in character, Dade and Flickner act as complementary aspects of every soldier's experience. The two also provide an apt demonstration of the narcissistic dimension of civil war. On one level, Foote is revisiting a seminal modernist text, as well as one of the earliest and best examples of Civil War fiction—*The Red Badge of Courage.* By giving the wound, the "red badge of courage," to the rebel Dade and the crisis of conscience to the Union man Flickner, Foote opens up the experience (and perspective) Crane condensed into the single figure of Henry Fleming. Foote's novel can be understood as a re-engagement with Crane's material (informed by the aesthetic and historical vantage of mid-century). Dade's and Flickner's monologues recapitulate and complete each other in a series of ironic correspondences. Typically, Foote's empathy is even-handed; bravery without self-consciousness is not aggrandized, and cowardice faced and consciously overcome gains dignity and is treated with wry and compassionate understanding. Dade and Flickner, for this reason, are limited vehicles for presenting historical context. Foote narrows the focus of the narrative to an imaginative exploration of the "incommunicable" experience of those anonymous thousands who fought.

Dade's and Flickner's sections re-create the larger movements of the battlefield—the vigorous Confederate advance in the early hours and the grudging Union retreat. The monologues themselves reflect this larger rhythm. For instance, we follow Dade's thoughts in the present from before dawn until he witnesses General Johnston's death at about 2:30 that afternoon. The one significant deviation from Dade's immediate experience occurs near the conclusion of the chapter when he is marked as a survivor of the conflict by providing incidental information about Johnston's use of a tin cup to direct the battle—information that could only be available to him through hindsight. The directness and simplicity of the narrative structure fit Dade's character and attributes, but also afford an unfiltered glimpse into a novice's first encounter with combat. In contrast, the structure of Private Flickner's monologue reinforces the nature of the day's numerous retreats. After an initial depiction of his arrival to join the other skulkers under the bluff, the events of the day are recounted in a long flashback punctuated by his brief recollection of setting out to war and culminating in his self-analysis about the nature of his fear.

The parallels between these two soldiers—the Johnny Reb and Billy Yank of the novel—are established in other ways as well. Dade's experience is full of forward momentum, mirroring the chronology of the day:

reveille, preparation, forming ranks, advance, charge, and engagement. Emphasis on time is kept to a minimum—not surfacing until Dade is clear of the fight, wounded and in search of medical aid. The absence of temporal notation enables Foote to introduce the time theme—in this case, the relativity of time: by noon, when he falls out, Dade has "aged a lifetime since the sun came up" (*Shiloh* 84). Dade's monologue, from the nightmare of battle through his feverish wanderings, is characterized by a fluidity of time and space. The conjunction of Dade's final exhausted collapse and General Johnston's death scene (a meeting of relativity and fixity, mortality and immortality) signals the end of one era and the beginning of another.

The corollary to Dade's experience of relativity is found in the structure of Flickner's section. Here, the present time of the narrative begins at about 4:30 P.M. (as Flickner emerges from the fighting around the Hornet's Nest to join the skulkers under the bluff) and extends to the conclusion of his quest to rejoin his battery at about midnight. In the interim, Flickner reflects on the day as a whole, beginning with the pre-dawn rumblings of picket fire, through withdrawals and retreats and ending with his crisis of spirit during the engagement at the sunken road. Flickner's experience is marked by a series of dislodgements, each precisely noted in terms of time and conveying a sense of combat akin to Dade's. Both men experience engagements and retreats, the noise and horror, and the personal exposure to gunfire (Dade's response—"*Lord to God, theyre shooting; theyre shooting at me!*" [*Shiloh* 74]—matching Flickner's "Thats coming *my* way. . . . That one's for *me*" [*Shiloh* 107]) and end up searching for aid—physical or spiritual. In these two characters, Foote highlights a phenomenon important to Faulkner and Proust: the malleability of time, the existence in experience and memory of a sort of Bergsonian *durée* (as a counter to the way time is depicted in histories). For each man, a sense of futurity is implied by the character's ability to draw on materials outside the immediate time frame. Dade will survive his physical wound, as Flickner survives his psychological one. The true casualty lies, apparently, in the loss of a stable set of values or worldview (Cavalier or Victorian) represented by the figure of General Johnston.

The Dade and Flickner sections of *Shiloh* are a meditation on humanity's capacity to endure violence and destruction. While Dade moves forward during the advance, various incidents related to language chart his process of descent in symbolic terms. One of the first episodes is Dade's response to the high-flown rhetoric of Johnston's address to the troops: he hears only fragments of the polished words and remarks, "I hadnt hardly heard a word he said" (*Shiloh* 67). In this wry, ironic fashion, Foote under-cuts the significance of the romantic vision of war associated with the other young Confederate, Lieutenant Metcalfe. The outline of the battle plan, as explained in progressively simpler terms by the Colonel, the Captain, and the Sergeant, also reinforces a skepticism about such reductive abstractions (whether in plans or in language). As Dade remarks: "It sounded fine, the way he told it; it sounded simple and easy. Maybe it was too simple, or something" (*Shiloh* 68). Just as the soldiers are reduced to the most fundamental aspects of their characters when contemplating the battle ("All the put-on had gone out of their face—they were left with what God gave them at the beginning" [*Shiloh* 65]), so too the rhetoric and posturing prior to combat are rendered ironically in Dade's section.

Dade's initiation into combat progresses from the comic to the absurd to the horrific. The motif of distorted language is carried like a banner into the battle by the indefatigable Captain Plummer, a marvelous cameo character whose speech impediment results in his comic rallying cry of "Wally here! 6th Mississippi, wally here!" (*Shiloh* 83). Next comes General P. R. Cleburne's farcical episode in the bog—blind to what his men could plainly see, he rides straight in and is promptly thrown from his horse, emerging red-faced and covered in mud. This broad comic touch (no less so for being true) is followed by Dade's identification of what he initially thinks is a wounded man; instead, he is greeted by the sight of overweight Burt Tapley, who has collapsed with a stitch in his side brought down by his own glut-tony—"all that fine food, canned peaches and suchlike" (*Shiloh* 74). The tenor of the narrative begins to change quickly when Dade encounters op-posing fire, and the pace shifts to reflect the rapidity of his breath and heartbeat—underscored by Foote's use of clipped phrases and breathless syntax. The comic modulates into the surreal. Dade's bewildered moment of frozen terror when first fired upon is ended by an accidental collision, making his return to forward motion more unwilled necessity than deliber-ate bravery. Neither does he remember the sound of his first rebel yell. This fabled battle cry—according to Foote the germinal point of the tale itself (*Conversations* 200)—remains an enigma throughout; much described by the various characters' homespun analogies, the yell is, finally, silent and unreal, lost in the past and representative of the ultimately incommunica-ble nature of the experience.

Dade's account then shifts from the absurd to the horrific and puts the rhetoric of war into proper relation to unimaginable reality. When he sees a dead but still-running soldier, Dade says, "That scared me worse than anything up to then. . . . it was just that he'd been running when they shot him and his drive kept him going down the slope. But it seemed so wrong, so scandalous, somehow so unreligious for a dead man to have to keep on fighting—or running, anyhow—" (*Shiloh* 80). Bitterly recalling the comforting euphemism used to describe the Confederate strategy ("[t]hey had told us we would push them back to the river. Push, they said; that was the word they used"), Dade suggests such language is a betrayal of the experience: "But it wasnt the way they said. It wasnt that way at all. Because even the dead and dying didnt have any decency about them" (*Shiloh* 80). Dade carries this clearsightedness to the end of the novel when, in contrast to Lieutenant Metcalfe, he recognizes the reality of the Confederate defeat. The obscene nature of the debased language and the horrible indecency of war is brought together by Foote in an image found at the climax of Dade's combat experience. During hand-to-hand fighting with a Yankee soldier, Dade receives his own wound and kills his opponent. In delivering the deathblow, again ironically more by accident than design, Dade's bayonet goes "in under [the Yankee's] jaw, the handguard tight against the bottom of his chin, and the point must have stuck in his head bone" (*Shiloh* 82). This series of analogies suggests the nature of war does violence to more than flesh—it changes one's conception of speech, language, and the world they represent.

Dade's section is a descent into the inferno, and Foote leaves him at the end suspended between life and death, time and eternity, consciousness and unconsciousness. The focus then shifts to Flickner to begin the ascent. With the change in perspective from rebel to Union soldier, we move into the purgatory of the "demoralized" (*Shiloh* 97)—with a corresponding change to the reflective and contemplative mode. Here, under the protection of the bluffs at Pittsburg Landing, each man arrives alone and silent from the battle, intent on getting "away from the fighting . . . [and also] trying to walk right out of the human race" (*Shiloh* 114). Abstractions such as duty and patriotism are meaningless. Flickner's path out of this hell involves a confrontation with himself, a reflection on his actions, and an acceptance of his all-too-human failure: "I looked at myself in my mind, watching myself as if I was another person—God maybe—looking down and seeing Otto Flickner fighting the rebels on Shiloh battlefield. He did all right, considering. He was scared from time to time, no different from the others, but he did all right until word came down to retreat from the sunken road" (*Shiloh* 120). Flickner's distancing strategy (on a personal level) corresponds to an historical overview. The quest for objectivity is different in degree but not in kind from the historian's voice in the framing sections. Such distance enables Flickner to reestablish a link between his experience (of physical fear) and his humanity (his moral capacity): "I wasnt demoralized back there at the sunken road: I hadnt even lost confidence. I was just plain scared, as scared as a man can be, and that was why I walked away from the fight" (*Shiloh* 120). Having reunited the word with the thing in the most elemental act of naming, Flickner returns to the field, ending his own wanderings by rejoining his battery. Flickner wins this battle with the self and demonstrates a sense of moral courage. Individual experience and the larger historical perspective meet in Flickner's adaptation of this "God's-eye" view of his own actions; and at this point Foote brings us back to the forward flow of the time frame of the battle.

The Battle of Shiloh as Narrative History

The panoramic view created by the narrative frame in *The Civil War* stresses the abstract process inherent in the strategic aims and tactical movements (military and political). It also creates within the framework a space for imaginative, empathic expression. Whereas the fictional surround in *Shiloh* carries embedded in the monologues the requisite factual background, in the history the reverse is true—the temporal and factual framework shoulders the burden of background and historical context, thus affording Foote opportunities to introduce a lyrical tone and an emotional texture. The selection and placement of such details contribute to conveying Foote's own historical perspective, that "the Civil War defined us as we are and it opened us to being what we have become, good and bad things. And it is very necessary, if you're going to understand the American character in the twentieth century, to learn about this enormous catastrophe of the nineteenth century. It was the crossroads of our being, and it was a hell of a crossroads" (Ward 264).

The key to Foote's balanced perspective is his treatment of character (his recognition of the myriad permutations of physical and moral courage). Even in this brief section of the larger volume, the range of characterization extends from brief descriptive epithets that establish a perspective on individuals to a larger cumulative process that extends character development over the time frame of the war. Henry Halleck's characteristic

situations or gestures ("deskbound . . . scratching his elbows and addressing his goggle-eyed stare . . ." [*CW* I.314]) are a good example of the former
method, employed to suggest the anxious nature of the general's personality and his distant, somewhat theoretical, perspective on events. Similarly,
repetitive diction, in Halleck's case a stress on his "reaction" as events
unfold (*CW* I.315), helps to establish Foote's presentation of the character
of the man in relation to evidence of his political machinations. An alternative method is to cross-reference characters in terms of similar traits,
which helps to highlight and foreshadow the larger cultural shifts—themes
such as the change in conceptions of warfare from the chivalric to the
"modern" (total war). Foote's description of General Earl Van Dorn during
the Pea Ridge campaign, which opens this middle chapter of the volume,
anticipates both the defeat at Shiloh (another failure of overly complex
strategies coupled with inexperienced troops) and the motif of the southern
Cavalier carried forward in P. G. T. Beauregard and Johnston. About Van
Dorn, Foote remarks: "Except for his size (he was five feet five: two inches
taller than Napoleon) he was in fact the very beau sabreur of Southern fable,
the Bayard-Lochinvar of maiden dreams" (*CW* I.277). Foote balances this
sketch of the public persona with the man's real accomplishments but nevertheless establishes a paradigm for the attitudes set of the Southern generals at this early juncture in the war. The next sentence continues: "Not
that his distinction was based solely on his looks. He was a man of action,
too—one who knew how to grasp the nettle, danger, and had done so many
times" (*CW* I.277). The cumulative effect of these correspondences in individual characters, unobtrusive to a large degree, confirms, over the course
of the narrative, broad changes in cultural values as a result of the continuing pressure of the conflict.

   With respect to the characterization of the major historical figures,
Foote's narrative approach, stressing the individual placed in the immediate present of the action, helps establish the interplay between the "God's-
eye" and the subjective perceptions. Foote continually develops our impressions of the characters over the course of the narrative by chronicling
their reactions to immediate concerns. Consider, for example, his depiction
of General Beauregard throughout the Shiloh section. Prior to the engagement, as Beauregard is collecting the scattered Confederate forces in
Corinth and contemplating his strategic options, Foote introduces a number
of significant details. First, we are given an excerpt from Beauregard's
address to the troops, invoking the defense of the homeland, the expecta-

tions of the southern womenfolk, the justice of the cause, and the "protection of the Almighty" (*CW* I.319). This seemingly empty rhetorical flourish is buttressed by the very real accumulation of troops under his command, substantiating his claims and rendering his highflown hopes and aspirations more legitimate. Indeed, Foote's procedure establishes a curious tension, pulling the reader in two directions: a distrust of the language, yet also a recognition of the factual realities that prompted the speech. This balance militates against any cursory judgment or trivialization of the man—it speaks to our twenty-first-century distrust of such rhetoric and then subverts the anticipated reaction (just as Asa's existential vision, found in the narrative frame bracketing Bart's story in *Tournament*, conditions our response to the ostensible hero of the tale).

Over the course of the next four paragraphs outlining Beauregard's preparations, Foote gently tips the balance by including other details that register the general's thirst for glory. Introducing an anecdote about the elite New Orleans regiment in which Beauregard is an honorary private, Foote begins to shade in the general's character: "'Pierre Gustave Toutant Beauregard!' rang out daily at roll call, like the sudden unfurling of a silken banner; 'Absent on duty!' the color-sergeant proudly answered for him" (*CW* I.319). The flourish here matches the rhetoric above and is then tied immediately to Beauregard's anticipation of "combinations and maneuvers that would be nothing less than Napoleonic in concept and execution" (*CW* I.319). After providing information about the numerical strength of the troops, Foote then includes a reflection that the size of this force would "be almost twice as large as the combined force that had covered itself and its generals—particularly Beauregard—with glory at Manassas" (*CW* I.320). This association with past glory and reputation (First Manassas being a decidedly unmodern battle), while factually true, also suggests a man working in the shadow of his reputation and perhaps overly concerned with the public eye. Two other details round out this impression in the paragraphs that follow.

The first concludes a summation of Beauregard's strategies and reinforces the imaginative nature of the general's plans to pounce on Ulysses S. Grant's divided command: "Beauregard saw and rehearsed it thus in his mind, complete no doubt with the final surrender ceremonies at the point of deepest penetration" (*CW* I.320). The last example concerns his response to General Johnston's gesture of appreciation (offering Beauregard nominal command of the army in the field, while Johnston retained only his designation as department commander): "Beauregard's heart gave a leap at this, touching his fiery ambition as it did, but he recognized a gesture when he saw one, and declined" (*CW* I.321). The cumulative effect of these details, with the most explicit statement of character at the end, provides both insight into the personality and a subtext to the outline of the Confederate strategy—anticipating, to some extent, the reasons for its flaws. The remaining descriptive elements associated with Beauregard over the course of the battle build upon the images found in these four paragraphs outlining the Confederate preparations. Twice—once at the start of the battle in reference to the red cap he wore, and again at the end of the first day with regard to lessons unlearned—Foote links the general to the Battle of Manassas, the site of his greatest triumph and really the last point of "innocent" military romanticism in the American Civil War. By this means, he carries forward the implication that Beauregard's military vision has not developed past the now outdated concepts of the Napoleonic era and his personal idea of glory. The judgment is a telling one but does not finally detract from the virtues of the man himself. It is, after all, Beauregard who warns of possible disaster with the loss of the element of surprise. As well, on two separate occasions—the first during the defensive action of Monday's fighting, the second during the retreat to Corinth—Beauregard's personal courage and sterling example as an inspiration to his troops are emphasized. The staggered nature of this depiction of character, and its balance in terms of vices and virtues, forestalls any quick or dismissive judgment on the part of the reader and leaves open the narrative potentials for surprise. Beauregard is allowed to exist, in Foote's narrative, in the lived present, protected, at least until the story is complete, from the judgments of history.

An interesting contrast can be seen when we turn to the depiction of General Grant, at this juncture fresh from his triumph at Fort Donelson. After a brief introduction devoted to the resurrection of General Sherman's reputation (from prescient "insanity" to competent rationality—an alteration of public perspective and not military reality), Foote traces a similar superficial transformation in the public persona of "Unconditional Surrender" Grant. The more obvious alterations brought on by the "aura of fame" (*CW* I.322), cigars, trimmed beard, and so forth, are then balanced by details designed to convey that Grant's pragmatic nature was untouched by the public adulation. For instance, after the reports of his direction of the Donelson battle, cigar in hand, "readers had sent him boxes of them to express their admiration, and since Grant had never been one to waste things, least of all good tobacco, the long-stemmed meerschaum that had given him so much satisfaction in the past was put away while he concentrated on smoking up those crates of gift cigars" (*CW* I.322). (That Grant eventually died of throat cancer, largely the result of those cigars, is an unspoken irony Foote evokes in those already knowledgeable in Civil War lore.) Two other details serve to undercut the public changes and take us closer to Foote's assessment of the dominant characteristics of the man— really, it is a form of "symbolic interpretation" akin to that done by the troops themselves, looking for insights into the motives and decisions of their superiors. First, he trims his beard—an insignificant event by anyone's measure, except for the reading of it Foote provides: "It seemed to the soldiers, observing him now, a gesture not unlike that of a man rolling up his sleeves in preparation for hard work" (*CW* I.322). The second hint at his character introduces the following paragraph, which deals with the strategic thinking behind Grant's choice of Pittsburg Landing and reflects his tradesman's approach to labor: "For him, work meant fighting; that was his trade, the only one he had ever been any good at or able to earn a living by, and he wanted to be at it right away" (*CW* I.322). This important juxtaposition illustrates both the contrast in motivations between the two commanders and, more importantly, the unqualified and hard-nosed frankness of Grant's approach to the task—what some might call brutality, and others realism. Foote leaves the issue undecided, as before, laying the groundwork for his reading of the man suspended between the existential moment and the building impact of history's inexorable process through time.

Even in the relatively short section devoted to the Battle of Shiloh, Foote takes care to avoid caricature and to balance his presentation of Grant. He offers ample evidence about a quality that was Grant's major strength and also partly responsible for the degree of unpreparedness of the Union troops—his concentration on the future at the expense of the present. Foote's description of the lack of fortifications in the Union encampment and the generally complacent attitude among the officers is directly linked to the perspective of the commander. Grant's central trait, mentioned just prior to the outset of Sunday's fighting, is that "[m]ostly, though, he kept his mind on the future" (*CW* I.330), and later, after the cost of the battle is made apparent: "Grant tightened his security regulations, as instructed, but he did not seem greatly perturbed by the criticism. Now, as always, he was a good deal more concerned with what he would do to the enemy than what the enemy might try to do to him . . ." (*CW* I.351). Foote's unattributed appropriation, at this early juncture in the war, of a remark Grant was to make two years later after the Battle of the Wilderness, highlights, in contradistinction to his usual procedure, a fixed aspect of Grant's personality. To temper the impact of this assertion, however, Foote balances this ironic forward glance with Grant's own statement that, "from Shiloh on, '[he] gave up all idea of saving the Union except by complete conquest'" (*CW* I.351). Just as Foote offsets the depiction of Shiloh as arrant bungling on both sides by introducing the subsequent judgment of its modernity, so too, in the case of Grant, he offsets the charge of indifference by violating the strict chronology of events.

The definitiveness of this portrayal of Grant is tempered in other ways. For example, Foote introduces into his description of the costly first day of the battle, when the troops had suffered considerable losses in part from their vulnerability, a couple of humanizing incidents, as if to modify the reader's inclination toward harsh criticism of the general. In the last paragraph devoted to the renewed Union hopes for the next day and fallout from the first—namely the arrival of Don Carlos Buell's and Lewis Wallace's troops and the presence of thousands of skulkers under the bluff—Foote portrays Grant's solitary and sleepless night on the field. Here he remarks that the dispirited men play no part in Grant's plans for Monday, "[fear being] a highly contagious emotion" (*CW* I.344), and then goes on to suggest that "[p]erhaps, too, he saw them as a reproach, a sign that his army had been surprised and routed, at least to this extent, because its commander had left it unintrenched, green men to the front, and had taken so few precautions against an enemy who, according to him, was 'heartily tired' of fighting" (*CW* I.344). In conjunction with the implications of guilt, Foote suggests Grant's actions of that night become a kind of penance when, after a final inspection, he is driven from a sheltered point by the screams of the wounded being treated nearby and "returned to his oak and got to sleep at last, despite the rain and whatever twinges he was feeling in his ankle and his conscience" (*CW* I.344). The speculative nature of these assertions suggests that Foote is moving again to give his characters the benefit of the doubt, to set into play his sense of the man and the facts of the case. In this respect, Foote walks a fine line between the demands of the history and the sympathetic imagination of the writer of fiction. As he pointedly remarks when assessing the final import of the battle, all of these men react "as always, according to their natures" (*CW* I.351). This recognition of human limitations is coupled with Foote's acknowledgment of man's capacity to transcend those limitations occasionally—a paradox that becomes a central theme developed over his entire treatment of the war: the capacity of historical figures to surprise us.

The organizational frame for the narrative, with its primary focus on the superstructure of command and troop movements, enables Foote to deepen the portraits of recurring characters over a long period. This expansiveness, while helpful for Grant, Lincoln, or Lee, is not available for those figures who emerge only momentarily or are lost during the fighting. In this respect, the narrative treatment of Shiloh affords a number of examples indicative of how Foote adjusts the balance of the tale to highlight partic- ular individuals. The depiction of Albert Sidney Johnston offers a case in point. Foote creates an interesting parallel between this officer and Beauregard, providing an address to the troops by each and examples of their personal valor, although one cannot help but feel that Beauregard loses by the comparison. Johnston's portrait, as an example of the chivalric gentleman, "tall and handsome on his tall, handsome horse" (*CW* I.337), is substantiated by his conduct in the battle (he personally leads the charge that breaks Stephen A. Hurlbut's resistance in the peach orchard and actively encourages the men in the field). Foote completes this picture by assigning Johnston's death a privileged place in the narrative; the episode stands at the center of the section covering the first day's battle and effec- tively provides a climax for his description of the Confederate perspective.

In his treatment of Johnston, Foote both anticipates the humanity of General Lee and signals the end of an era. Quoting Jefferson Davis's words regarding the loss of Johnston ("When he fell . . . I realized that our strongest pillar had been broken" [*CW* I.351]), Foote suggests an echo for his own apocalyptic imagery, last noted in the pillar of fire and smoke marking a shift in fortunes during the Battle of Pea Ridge (*CW* I.288), the first of a string of Confederate reverses dominating this middle section of volume 1. Perhaps written more broadly than the other characterizations, Foote's depiction of Johnston emphasizes a fundamental alteration in the kind of war following this "first great modern battle" (*CW* I.338). Indeed, the inclusion of this phrase, placed in the middle of his description of the unraveling of the grandiose Confederate battle plan approved by Johnston, makes the same point in less poetic terms. Another correlative to Johnston's role as old-world figurehead is found on the Union side when Foote recog- nizes the contribution of General Benjamin M. Prentiss and his men to victory. A general who figures mainly in this one battle, Prentiss is given due acknowledgment for his central role during the fight around the Hornet's Nest on the first day. From roughly 11:00 in the morning until 5:30 in the evening, Prentiss's division held on to the sunken road, and Foote notes both the valor and the tactical importance of this action. Eventually surrounded by the Confederate forces in the late afternoon, Prentiss is captured; yet Foote, as narrator, awards him the battle:

> He could hear [the Confederates] yelling back there, triumphant, but he fought on, obedient to his strict instructions to "maintain that position at all hazards." The dead lay thick. Every minute they lay thicker. Still he fought. By 5.30—two long hours after Ruggles' guns began their furious cannonade—further resistance became futile, and Prentiss knew it. He had the cease-fire sounded and surrendered his 2200 survivors, well under half the number he had started with that morning. Sherman and McClernand on the right, and Hurlbut to a lesser degree on the left, had saved their divisions by falling back each time the pressure reached a certain intensity. Prentiss had lost his by standing fast: lost all, in fact, but honor. Yet he had saved far more in saving that. Sherman and McClernand had saved their divisions by retreating, but Prentiss had saved Grant by standing fast. (*CW* I.341)

Coming so close after the scene of Johnston's death (precipitated by his honorably sending his personal physician to tend wounded prisoners), Prentiss's actions, and the rhetoric in which they are couched, echo the traits that made the Confederate general so admired; yet Prentiss also represents the nature of the new warfare—total and unrelenting. His last appearance in the chapter is also intriguing; as he plays the role of a prophetic voice in the Confederate camp Sunday night, predicting rebel defeat on Monday. By employing clipped and understated sentences to encapsulate the action, and the forthright language of praise that echoes the ideals of the participants themselves, Foote allows Prentiss's actions and depiction to dominate the reading of the battle that he and his troops, more than anyone else, had won. Yet, the crucial word is "honor," and the nature of the battle itself has begun its redefinition.

Existential Man and "That Fate Business"

Concluding his discussion of Foote's *The Civil War* as "humanistic history," Wirt Williams remarks that the overriding theme of these volumes is "that this war like other wars was at once a collision of huge impersonal forces and of highly individuated human beings, that fate and personality co-exist in an indivisible equation" (436). Robert L. Phillips identifies these themes with Foote's use of form in *The Civil War*, employing a slightly different context: "Through its form the book brings the reader who participates in the text with an active imagination into proximity with the determinants of his own being and, at the same time, with the experience of others, of mankind. These concerns for the shape and rhythms of time do not, however, seem to imply that we are observers of a linear progress in time toward some utopia; that history involves progress does not seem to be his conviction" (182). Phillips's assertion that Foote eschews a sense of humanity's evolution toward utopia is well founded (one only has to consider the long backward gaze that forms the essence of *Jordan County*, with its subversion of the idea of "Progress"). Humanity's existence in time, whether the natural rhythms of the seasonal changes and the ordinary march of days or the reality of life in times of war, represents Foote's conception of fate and supplies the armature upon which the narrative is constructed.

Immediately following the end of the fighting, Foote moves to sum up in abstract terms the experience of reading the preceding 2,815 pages. He writes: "All things end, and by ending not only find continuance in the whole, but also assure continuance by contributing their droplets, clear or murky, to the stream of history. Anaximander said it best, some 2500 years ago: 'It is necessary that things should pass away into that from which they are born. For things must pay one another the penalty and compensation for their injustice according to the ordinance of time.' So it was with the Confederacy, and so one day will it be for the other nations of earth, if not for earth itself" (*CW* III.1040). The quotation from Anaximander reflects ideas central to Foote's narrative. First, history is presented as a continuum akin to the processes of the natural world—birth, life, and death, as parts of a cyclical return. Second, the continuum is enhanced by the moral vision Anaximander posits, the idea that "things must pay one another the penalty and compensation for their injustice according to the ordinance of time" (*CW* III.1040). Foote's adoption of this credo suggests a natural and moral equilibrium within which the fallibility and inconstancy of human experience exists.

In such a context, the role of the artist is twofold. On the one hand, he discovers a symmetry and pattern in the events representative of these natural and moral balances; on the other, he depicts individuals making decisions and taking actions in accordance with their limited perspectives. Thus, Foote's narrative constitutes a series of balances, North and South (in political orientation), East and West (with respect to the two fronts of the war), and common soldier and general (in relation to the experience of combat). The greater the reader's awareness of symmetries or correspondences within the whole narrative, the finer the texture of the ironic vision Foote conveys. He places his trust in the generative power of the plot, in the ironies that only emerge when specific events and actions are related to his moral framework, to the ordinance of time. Describing his intention to Walker Percy, Foote declares his aim is to be "analytical in a new sense; not explanation but demonstration—the problems are not so much analyzed as just shown, together with their effect on the men who tried to solve them" (August 8, 1956; *Correspondence* 109). Plot frees Foote from an obligation to write conventional historical analysis; instead he concentrates on the subtleties of descriptive exactitude.

Understanding history, in Foote's view, will always involve writing about events "from a human point of view . . . as problems impinging on a man" (*Conversations* 171). *The Civil War* is constructed to reflect the relationship between the man at the center of the storm and the large impersonal forces that surround him. The draft title for Foote's novel *Follow Me Down* was "The Vortex"; the image applies equally well to his history, not only in terms of themes (war as a national crucible), but also in terms of structure (the descent and emergence motif centered around the Battle of Gettysburg). Foote's narrative method in the novel, where the reader's judgment is suspended through the telling and retelling of the events, foreshadows his strategy in *The Civil War*. The architectonics of *The Civil War* produce a similar tension between centrifugal force and chronological imperative found in the novel. Following Phillips's lead, one can see all three volumes as organized around the description of the Gettysburg campaign, the "highwater mark" of the Confederacy, the symbol of the national crisis of identity, and the epicenter of the narrative (181). One has only to think of the brooding silence that descended over the field on the third day just prior to George E. Pickett's charge: "By now it was noon, and a great stillness came down over the field and the two armies on their ridges. Between them, the burning house and barn loosed a long plume of smoke that stood upright in the hot and windless air. From time to time some itchy-fingered picket would fire a shot, distinct as a single handclap, but for the most part the silence was profound" (*CW* III.538–39). If this still point constitutes the eye of the maelstrom, then the outermost frame extends to the formative experiences of Jefferson Davis and Abraham Lincoln and their ghostly presences at the end—disembodied voices intoning a requiem for the whole.

Responding to an interviewer's comment about the sense of determinism that pervades his fiction, Foote acquiesced by saying, "Yes, a lot of that fate business . . ." (*Conversations* 101). In this respect, the narrative enshrines a sense of destiny, of design, of belief in a divine order, native to the sensibilities of the nineteenth century. Fate, or the ordinance of time, can be understood to exist on a number of levels in the text. On a basic level, Foot employs natural elements to suggest processes beyond the human struggle: mud, for instance, and the role it plays in George McClellan's slow movement up the peninsula or Ambrose Burnside's disastrous "Mud March" following Fredericksburg. Natural phenomena, geographic characteristics of the land, and the alteration of the seasons constantly reaffirm this larger world. Time is measured largely by hours elapsed, days, weeks, and months past, or in terms of anniversaries of past battles and campaigns—in other words, living memory. In one sense, components such as seasons and geography are indifferent and valueless, existing as a stage to be refashioned or exploited by the vision of the commanders depending on their skill or good fortune. In another sense, though, natural elements are presented as they are observed by the participants, invested with value and indicative of the shaping hand of God or Fate. One might recall the appearance of the aurora borealis in the night sky after the Battle of Fredericksburg (*CW* II.42–43) or the sunlight streaming through the clouds to grace the podium as Lincoln begins his second inaugural address (*CW* III.812). Foote's association of the stars with destiny extends to the commanders themselves. General Lee, seemingly blessed by fortune, only to have it desert him at Gettysburg, is described thus: "Coincidents refused to mesh for the general who, six weeks ago in Richmond, had cast his vote for the long chance. Fortuity itself, as the deadly game unfolded move by move, appeared to conform to a pattern of hard luck; so much so, indeed, that in time men would say of Lee, as Jael had said of Sisera after she drove the tent peg into his temple, that the stars in their courses had fought against him" (*CW* II.461).* Indeed, the association of Lee and starlight that figures prominently in the Gettysburg campaign is carried forward even to the night before his surrender at Appomattox, when "Lee prepared to take his last sleep under the stars" (*CW* III.935), his reserves of skill and good fortune exhausted. Foote's employment of such tropes helps to maintain a balance and to generate ironic commentary, by juxtaposing the limited perspectives of the characters with the moral and temporal framework—the ordinances of time.

These symbols of fate are not exclusive—fate, after all, is indiscriminate in its influence and can be understood to be capricious. Playing on such conventions is part of the subtlety of Foote's ironic approach. For example, when describing the day of Lincoln's second inauguration, Foote draws on the image to highlight the occasion—a cosmic foreshadowing of the sense of divine purpose Lincoln alludes to in his speech (and a neat contrast between Venus and "Mars Robert" [*CW* I.586]): "The rain let up before midmorning, though the sun did not break through the scud of clouds, and around 11 o'clock a small, sharp-pointed, blue-white diamond of a star—later identified as the planet Venus—appeared at the zenith, directly over the Capitol dome, bright in the murky daylight sky" (*CW* III.810). The meteorological portents continue, following the farcical interlude of Andrew Johnson's swearing in as vice-president, when Lincoln rises to deliver his address: "Just as he did so, the sun broke through and flooded the platform with its golden light. 'Every heart beat quicker at the unexpected omen,' the reporter declared. Certainly Lincoln's own did. 'Did you notice that sunburst?' he later asked. 'It made my heart jump'" (*CW* III.812). Even Jefferson Davis is not neglected in this respect, with the last chapter of the narrative, "Lucifer by Starlight," focusing on his final years as the living embodiment of Confederate history. The balance achieved by this inclusive and cumulative

---

* Foote's use of this phrase is another possible link to Hemingway. The biblical quotation and the title, "The Stars in Their Courses," both appear in a story about Gettysburg written by Colonel John W. Thomason Jr. and originally published in *Lone Star Preacher* (Scribners, 1941). Thomason's story was reproduced in a 1942 anthology, *Men at War: The Best War Stories of All Time* (Crown), edited by Hemingway. It is intriguing that the volume contains work by many of the authors Foote refers to as his own models and that Hemingway's introduction constitutes a summation of the credo from *Death in the Afternoon* reproduced by Foote in *The Civil War*.

approach to images associated with fate helps to reinforce the impression of design (moral and narrative) in Foote's presentation.

Foote's representation of fate in the narrative is an acknowledgment of the participants' sense—somewhat alien to the twentieth century—that they all, from the lowliest soldier to the commanders of armies, were part of a larger destiny. The desire in the nineteenth-century mind to reconcile the enormous, inhuman cost of the war with a sense of divine purpose, made evident in Foote's narrative, translates the war into a trial of the belief in certain immutable eternal verities—a crisis with repercussions that appeared in Foote's earlier fictional depictions of the postwar South. "As we lay there watching the bright stars," one Confederate lieutenant remarks during the siege of Petersburg, ". . . many a soldier asked himself the question: What is this all about? Why is it that 200,000 men of one blood and one tongue, believing as one man in the fatherhood of God and the universal brotherhood of man, should in the nineteenth century of the Christian era be thus armed with all the improved appliances of modern warfare and seeking one another's lives? We could settle our differences by compromising, and all be at home in ten days" (*CW* III.640). Man's relation to the larger framework of historical process is a point Lincoln himself ponders in a letter to a Kentucky friend, just prior to the beginning of Grant's campaign in the east, as Foote presents some of the vital "lessons" Lincoln had learned through hard experience. "It was as if, having tried interference to the limit of his [Lincoln's] ability, he now was determined to try abstention to the same extent. He had learned patience, and something more; he had learned submission. 'I attempt no compliment to my own sagacity. . . . I claim not to have controlled events, but confess plainly that events have controlled me'" (*CW* III.138). Whether this implies a conception of ultimate design or of ultimate contingency, Foote's history does not answer. One is left, rather, with an aesthetic order, a self-consciously limited narrative wholeness.

The narrative works on the premise of a continuum of civilizations— the rise and fall in cyclical progression of different worldviews that C. Hugh Holman identifies with the Hegelian (and southern) perspective on the past. Employing a technique reminiscent of his use of the four "dominants" to chart the changes in Jordan County society from the Old South to the New, Foote signals the larger cultural shifts brought about by the war through two narrative "digressions' that encapsulate the changing "Ages." In the first volume, Foote underscores the divergent views, North and

South, of the direction of American development. In the second volume, with the war well under way, Foote chronicles the widening gap between ways and means in the North and the South with a brief overview of "The Age of Shoddy." With respect to the northern society, Foote writes: "much of the undoubted ugliness of the era—the Age of Shoddy, if you will—was little more than the manifest awkwardness of national adolescence, and unquestionably, too—despite the prevalent gaucherie, the scarcity of grace and graciousness, the apparent concern with money and money alone, getting and spending—much of the growth was solid and even permanent" (*CW* II.149). Meanwhile, in the South, Foote notes what was "perhaps the greatest paradox of all: that the Confederacy, in launching a revolution against change, should experience under pressure of the war which then ensued an even greater transformation . . . than did the nation it accused of trying to foist upon it an unwanted metamorphosis, not only of its cherished institutions, but also of its very way of life" (*CW* II.158). After the conclusion of the war, this "Age of Shoddy" gives way to the "raucous era whose inheritors were Daniel Drew, Jay Gould, Jim Fisk, and others of that stripe" (*CW* III.1042), in "what Mark Twain . . . dubbed the 'Gilded Age'" (*CW* III.1047) when "*Laissez faire* meant *laissez nous faire*" (*CW* III.1043). The primary focus of the narrative remains the action on the battlefields, yet as these interludes make clear, the effects of the war cannot be understood outside the context of these moral and societal changes.

The world that is left behind at the outset of the war is presented more by implication and selected details than by means of a summary of societal assumptions. For example, as Davis rises in the Senate to say his farewell in the opening scene of volume 1, Foote remarks: "He had never doubted the right of secession. What he doubted was its wisdom. Yet now it was no longer a question even of wisdom; it was a question of necessity—meaning Honor" (*CW* I.4). Through the biographical sketches of Davis and Lincoln that constitute most of the first section, and his outlining of the assumptions and actions of men involved in the first conflicts of the war, Foote suggests—as he did in *Shiloh*—how the concept of honor, and the political idealism that is its corollary, conditioned the reactions and decisions of the antebellum nation in its final days. The distinction between conceptions of honor is a regional one, as Ritchie Watson notes: "Bertram Wyatt-Brown [in *Yankee Saints and Southern Sinners*, 1985] has explained that the concept of honor, as opposed to the inner-directed notion of conscience, tightly binds an individual's sense of personal worth to the acceptance of his self-definition by the community at large. To possess honor, therefore one must possess the respect of others" (118). In the matter of secession, the southern conception of honor as individual adherence to communal consensus often overrode personal doubts. "Thus the Cavalier code did more than simply persuade southerners that they were members of a superior, aristocratic race," Watson writes. "The concept of honor, which was an integral part of this code, eventually made secession seem obligatory because it was perceived as the South's only honorable course of action" (119). There is also a more contemporary distinction at work in Foote's narrative; the "Cavalier code," with its stress on conventional societal verities that forms the basis for the ideal in Faulkner's work, is being displaced by a shift to a more individualistic and existentialist perspective, a code defined in terms of authenticity or competence that is closer to the Hemingwayesque. The dialogue in the narrative in this respect is part of Foote's shift away from the matter of the South. The account of the first year of the war in volume 1 is largely devoted to the story of the disintegration of conventional values in the face of the Realpolitik inaugurated by the war period. By presenting the histories of the two presidents, westerners both, who share a frontier heritage yet come to embody the two opposing visions of American society—the conservative and aristocratic planter's view in Davis's case and northern egalitarianism and pragmatism in Lincoln's—Foote presents the subtle change in perspective from the world ruled by divine destiny to a world made up of "linking accidents and crises" (*CW* I.19), of individual actions that shape and create the process of historical change.

The corollary to this nineteenth-century conception of fate is Foote's twentieth-century conviction about "[t]he basic loneliness of man":

> I find him alone in orgasm, alone in nausea, utterly alone—not to mention at his death. And it absolutely fascinates me. At the time when you're closest to God, dying, you're the most alone. . . . And I think wisdom, if there is any, is going to have to proceed from a recognition of the basic loneliness of man. And all you can do is combat it. You can never be not alone. Never. (*Conversations* 101).

In this conception of the human condition, Foote shares much with William Percy, who found "daily life [to be] isolated and lonely" and without meaning, whereas the experience of war "moved *sub specie aeternitatis*" and was "the only great thing [he] was a part of . . . the only heroic thing we all did together" (223). *Shiloh* and *The Civil War* are enriched by

Foote's exploration of such paradoxical conjunctions: contact and isolation, speech and silence, courage and fear.

Consider, for example, his description of the fighting that took place in "The Bloody Angle" at Spotsylvania:

> Tamped back into the toe of the Mule Shoe, Hancock's troops found cover by recrossing the log parapet and taking shelter behind it. There they stayed and there they fought, sometimes at arm's length much as Wright's men were doing on their right, down the western face of the salient, where the region of Upton's abortive penetration acquired a new name: The Bloody Angle. The term had been used before, in other battles elsewhere in the war, but there was no doubt forever after, at least on the part of those who fought there, that here was where the appellation best applied. It soon became apparent to both sides that what they were involved in now was not only fiercer than what had gone before today, but was in fact more horrendous than what had gone before, ever. This was grimmer than the Wilderness—a way of saying that it was worse than anything at all—not so much in bloodshed, although blood was shed in plenty, as in concentrated terror. These were the red hours of the conflict, hours no man who survived them would forget, even in his sleep, forever after. . . . Neither victory nor defeat was any longer a factor in the struggle. Men simply fought to keep on fighting, and not so much on instinct as on pure adrenalin. Slaughter became an end in itself, unrelated to issues or objectives, as if it had nothing whatever to do with the war. (*CW* III.221)

This description, building as it does on the other "angles" of the war (those past at Chickamauga and Gettysburg, and those still to come at Cold Harbor or the fighting outside Franklin) resonates backward and forward in the text. Here, at the angle, Foote combines an image of intimacy and connection (the fighting in close proximity) with the idea of individual isolation. In the following passage, Lee has just sent in reinforcements to bolster the Confederate line.

> It was noon by then and men were falling there from nervous exhaustion as well as from wounds. Veterans who had survived the worst this war afforded, up to now, went through the motions of

combat after the manner of blank-faced automatons, as if what they were involved in had driven them beyond madness into imbecility; they fought by the numbers, unrecognizant of comrades in the ultimate loneliness of a horror as profoundly isolating in its effect as bone pain, nausea, or prolonged orgasm, their vacant eyes unlighted by anger or even dulled by fear. (*CW* III.222)

Foote's portrayal of this particular moment represents the nadir of his vision of elemental human isolation. Close-packed by the thousands into a brutal killing field, each man is alone. The unfathomable nature of this paradox, and the ironies that arise from its contemplation, are central to Foote's conception of the effects his narrative must achieve.

Foote's interest in juxtaposing existential moments and impersonal fates extends to his rendering of the experiences of recognized historical characters. One example is his treatment of the reactions of Ulysses S. Grant at two pivotal moments in his military career: 1) the end of the first day's fighting at Shiloh, when the brutal character of the war becomes starkly evident, and 2) his first test as commander of the Army of the Potomac, after the Battle of the Wilderness. During his description of the night that follows that first day's fighting, Foote recounts Grant's restless search for a peaceful place to sleep and his settling, finally, for the discomfort of the out-of-doors, away from the "screams of the wounded and the singing of the bone-saws . . . despite the rain and whatever twinges he was feeling in his ankle and his conscience" (*CW* I.344). The text suggests solitary reflection, a coming to terms with the terrible reality of the battle. Half a dozen pages later, contemplating the aftermath of the three-day contest, Foote paraphrases a remark Grant was to make two years later: "Now as always, he was a good deal more concerned with what he would do to the enemy than he was with what the enemy might try to do to him" (*CW* I.351). Foote violates the chronology of the war—something he rarely does—in order to link the present experience with the general's next personal trial.

The connection becomes clearer when Foote concludes, in volume 3, the description of the Army of the Potomac when it is attacked in the Wilderness: "[it] had been Grant's hardest [day] since the opening day at Shiloh" (*CW* III.184). Confronted by a panicked officer, Grant reacts: "[He] was not a curser, but his patience had run out. He got up from the stump, took the cigar out of his mouth, and turned on this latest in the series of prophets of doom and idolators of his opponent. 'Oh, I am heartily tired of hearing about what Lee is going to do,' he said testily. 'Some of you always seem to think he is suddenly going to turn a double somersault and land in our rear and on both our flanks at the same time. Go back to your command and try to think what we are going to do ourselves, instead of what Lee is going to do'" (*CW* III.185). Foote follows this Wilderness demonstration of the general's tenacity with evidence of his human frailty. After Grant arranges for the strengthening and protection of his flanks, fulfilling his duties to the army, Foote announces, simply and directly: "He broke."

> Yet even this was done with a degree of circumspection and detachment highly characteristic of the man. Not only was his personal collapse resisted until after the damage to both flanks had been repaired and the tactical danger had passed; it also occurred in the privacy of his quarters, rather than in the presence of his staff or gossip-hungry visitors. "When all proper measures had been taken," Rawlins confided, "Grant went into his tent, threw himself downward on his cot, and gave way to the greatest emotion." He wept, and though the chief of staff, who followed him into the tent declared that he had "never before seen him so deeply moved" and that "nothing could be more certain than that he was stirred to the very depths of his soul," he also observed that Grant gave way to the strain "without uttering any word of doubt or discouragement." Another witness, a captain attached to General George Gordon Meade's headquarters—Charles F. Adams Jr., son and namesake of the ambassador—put it stronger. "I never saw a man so agitated in my life," he said. (*CW* III.185–86)

Foote's depiction of Grant's private hell provides a psychological correlative to the images of man's ultimate isolation. Indeed, the portrait gains further dimensions when Foote's compares Grant in the Wilderness to General Hooker at Chancellorsville; Hooker also fought Lee near this ground, and when he was put to the test, he "broke inside as a result of similar frustrations" (*CW* III.186). Grant, conversely, "broke outside, and then only in the privacy of his tent. He cracked, but the crack healed so quickly that it had no effect whatever on the military situation, then or later" (*CW* III.186). Foote's comparison of these two reactions turns on the Hemingwayesque distinction between those who possess not only physical, but also moral, courage. In the conception of the human condition outlined by Foote (ultimate aloneness in the face of impersonal forces), the focus on individual mental fortitude—authentic action in the face of existential crisis—is used as an essential measure of character.

Foote's interest in the moral dimension of individual experience is presented succinctly in his account of the impact, political and personal, of the Emancipation Proclamation in 1863. Having recounted the immediate history of its formulation—Lincoln's long wait for a Union victory, or something that at least resembled one—Foote traces the reactions, northern, southern, and European, to the document. Concluding his discussion of Europe's recognition that the proclamation had, despite its equivocal nature, redefined the war, Foote suggests: "With this one blow—though few could see it yet: least of all the leader most concerned—Lincoln had shattered the main pillar of what had been the southern President's chief hope from the start. Europe would not be coming into this war" (*CW* I.709). Although this seems sufficient for the narrative, Foote presses the point further by closing the section with a reflection on "[a]nother change the document had wrought, though this one was uncalculated, occurring within the man himself" (*CW* I.709). Of equal importance to the political gains is the emergence, in Lincoln, of a sense of a personal relationship with God. Having been carried along in the stream of events, and professing no specific religious affiliation, Lincoln now experiences a spiritual awakening. "[O]ut of the midnight trials of his spirit, out of his concern for a race in bondage, out of his knowledge of the death of men in battle," Foote writes, "something new had come to birth in Lincoln, and through him into the war" (*CW* I.710). In a curious juxtaposition, and a paradox typical of Foote, his Lincoln combines a profoundly traditional view of the divine order with a demonstrably modern view of the isolated condition of man.

Foote's skillful depiction of the war as a nexus of the old and new worldviews helps create the ironic web and the "thickened" texture in his narrative. It is these attributes that lead Wirt Williams to praise the work as "humanistic history" (429). Foote's foregrounding of the actions and reactions of individual men, caught up as they were in the immediate reality of war but also operating in a moral framework and subject to the ordinances of time, is what gives the work its persuasive sense of lived experience. As James M. Cox suggests, speaking of the "particular perspective" of Foote's whole narrative:

If one puts the war not only in the foreground but as foreground, it no longer seems the result of political forces but is itself the very means of political force. It is the violent action to which politics and history have surrendered; by being narratively true to its dominance, Foote implicitly reveals a superior political vision of those four years. The war was, in all its intensity and bloodiness, the superior reality of that long moment to those who fought it and to Lincoln, who ultimately presided over it. (196)

By creating an intricate counterpoint between man and fate, Foote protects the essential humanity of the participants caught up in "that long moment." His work achieves a goal articulated by his most notable successor in the field of Civil War narrative, James M. McPherson, who in his preface to *Battle Cry of Freedom: The Civil War Era* (1988) advocates a "narrative framework" as best suited to reflect "this dynamism, this complex relationship of cause and effect, this intensity of experience" (ix).

"Now gods, stand up for bastards": An Ironic Historian's Approach to Characterization

In November 1949, years before the conception of *The Civil War*, Foote considered writing a trilogy of three novels devoted to Civil War battles important to Mississippi—of which Shiloh was one, Vicksburg and Brice's Crossroads the others. To prepare for the undertaking, Foote tells Walker Percy, he is reading Proust and various military histories. After quoting Proust on style, Foote goes on to outline his own method for absorbing historical data and translating discrete elements into narrative. First, he reads the primary sources and then works through the action by drawing a series of maps. "[F]or the first time," he remarks, "I really understood Jackson's Valley campaign; and as a result, I really began to understand Jackson himself" (November 19, 1949; *Correspondence* 19). Like his choice of reading materials (Proust's masterpiece on the minutiae of consciousness combined with "objective" military histories), the account of Foote's method of study is intriguing; it reminds one of the narrative process in *Shiloh*, where the map, the "God's eye" view, subverts the usual expectations of a battlefield map in order to focus on human character.

Remarking on how he understood great novels to be conceived, Foote suggests that they begin with this delineation of character: "All good novels are kin to each other because they're concerned about relationships between people. I've often thought . . . that [when] a good writer starts . . . his conception of a story is: 'how about a man who in a situation does so and so?' A bad writer starts: 'how about a situation in which a man does so and so?'" "[T]he [G]reeks," Foote says, "know that better than anybody. A man's own character is his demon. Not what society is trying to do to him. . . . His own character, his inner workings are what made his tragedy" (*Conversations* 24). In a sense, Foote asserts as much in the first volume of *The Civil War* when, about two-thirds of the way through, he makes a comparison between General George McClellan, "Little Mac," and General William T. Sherman. The narrator suggests: "Above all, in their different ways, they had a flair for the dramatic. McClellan's men would turn from their first hot meal in days for a chance to cheer him riding past, and Sherman could make a soldier proud for weeks by asking him for a light for his cigar. It was personal, a matter of personality" (*CW* I.563). Foote's approach to characterization is built around the intersection of the "matter of personality" and the matter of history and is intimately involved with plot. He creates what James M. Cox calls an impression of "lived experience" (198); this "quality of vision" relies on the reader's gradual comprehension of the historical characters, of their essential merits and demerits, as revealed by immediate events. At the heart of *The Civil War*, Cox remarks, is "[t]he humanity of Foote's vision of men at war. They are never so much wrong or right as they are human" (205).

One would expect that Foote, as a novelist writing history, might experience a certain limitation in the delineation of character—one imposed by the "given" nature of the factual materials associated with historical characters. This, apparently, was not the case. Meticulous research into the appearance, bearing, and actions of the individual in question was a substitute for the similar decision-making process experienced by the wholly created fictional character. Before beginning his history, Foote suggests to Percy the centrality of character to his fiction: on December 31, 1950 he remarks that "the main interest, as in all [his] work, is based on Character" (*Correspondence* 39), and in a second comment, from January 10, 1953, Foote maintains that "[p]lot should always be an outgrowth of character" (Letters). He touches on much the same thing in interviews: "The man has to come first, for a good writer. It seems to me his concern is not with the idea for a novel, not the confrontation, but the two people confronting each other. And I hope that the people always come first with me. I think it's very important that they do. And I have never conceived a story as a situation.

It has always been a man's character creating the situation" (*Conversations* 94). In *The Civil War* Foote holds true to his aesthetic principles. History, when all is said and done, is comprised of the actions of men, and its fascination is largely based on how individuals respond to pressures of all kinds. The opening of volume 1 immediately signals the importance of character with Foote's portraits of Jefferson Davis and Abraham Lincoln. The present moment of Davis's receipt of his acclamation as president of the Provisional Government of the Confederate States matches Lincoln's last full day in Springfield before departing for Washington and his inauguration as president of the United States. Each man is placed in the context of a shaping past, a pressure-filled present, and an unknown (in the context of the narrative) future. As George Garrett observes, Foote's "approach to the presentation of character . . . may be described, with obvious oversimplification, as a method of continuing development rather than characterization by discovery" (87). And in this respect, characterization in *The Civil War* becomes "dramatic and dynamic . . . a source of narrative suspense, thus of forward motion in the whole narrative" (Garrett 88).

The centrality of character to Foote's conception of history—character, that is, developed in time, in response to the dictates of plot—is a point he stresses in "The Novelist's View of History." Having emphasized the importance of style, of a writer's acquisition of a "command of language" and his development of a "way of looking at the world" ("Novelist's" 220), Foote turns to the question of character.

> In an address some years ago to the Southern Historical Society of which he then was president, Francis Butler Simkins advised the historian to mix "sympathy, understanding, and a bit of kindness with his history." Nowhere, I think, does this better apply than to the treatment of character; and yet historians, who claim above all to be impartial, are at their worst—or at any rate their most partial—within this province. In the case of any controversial figure (such as Aaron Burr or Huey Long) the historian apparently first examines the record to determine what he thinks of this particular person; then, having decided, he marshals every document he can lay hands on, so long as it shores up the decision already reached. The rest are only included to be refuted. There appears to be no room for straightforward presentation; it is as if such a thing would necessarily be boring—devoid of interest—without "opinion" overhanging every word.

It is here that the historian most gravely violates the novelist's canon. And it is here, too, I think, that he most sorely departs from truth. There must be sympathy, or there will be nothing— as Shakespeare demonstrated superbly in his handling of the villains in his later plays. It lies at the heart of Macbeth's great power to draw us outside ourselves. It is the bedrock reason for Edmund's speech in *Lear:* "Now, gods, stand up for bastards!" ("Novelist's" 221)

"Sympathy," historian Barbara Tuchman agrees, "is essential to the understanding of motive" (49). In Foote's case, sympathy translates into the development of the historical character in direct relation to immediate events; as he suggests elsewhere, it depends on the gradual presentation of material, on "information . . . released over the pages instead of in a clump" (*Conversations* 70). It is a process that conveys information in the fashion of lived experience, an intimation of memory in the lives of historical characters, and the creation of a textual memory for the reader. And the effect, as George Garrett remarks, "is that these figures are seemingly in constant motion" (88).

In this matter of sympathy, Foote emphasizes how it achieves a balance in the presentation of both attractive and unappealing characters, rejecting the idolizing of the former (Lee or Lincoln) and the wholesale denigration of the latter (Edwin Stanton or Braxton Bragg). "Even if," Foote suggests, the purpose "is destruction. . . . the historian does wrong to go about it in this way; as any novelist could tell him. The proper and effective way to accomplish the destruction of a man is to show him sympathy, and in the course of showing that sympathy, permit the man himself to show that it is undeserved" ("Novelist's" 221). Foote then provides an illustration, drawn from K. P. Williams's *Lincoln Finds a General* (1949), of the method he is arguing against ("that of intermittent or constant condemnation and malicious speculation" ["Novelist's" 222]).

The general Lincoln found, of course, was Grant. Now at this late date I think we will all allow that Grant was in many ways an attractive person and a great general. (As a matter of fact, I happen to think that he was more attractive than he was great, but that's beside the point.) In the course of tracing Grant's career, Dr. Williams praises every step Grant took along the way. Grant was not surprised at Shiloh, for example; or if he was somewhat surprised, the surprise could be explained away; he expected to be surprised, it seems—which makes him even more of a butcher than the one I was taught to recognize in the public schools of Mississippi. At any rate, Grant could do no wrong in Dr. Williams' eyes.

McClellan, on the other hand, could do no right; Dr. Williams is merciless to him. Every time McClellan gets his head up, the professor knocks it down again. I think, here too we will all agree that McClellan had serious faults and certain unattractive characteristics—plus the fact he has since been cast as playing Judas to Lincoln's Christ, an unrewarding role. And yet by the time we are a couple of hundred pages into the book, we find ourselves pulling for McClellan, seeking out those virtues which the writer will not allow him, and finding streaks at least of gray beneath the surface which the author painted black. . . . Conversely, we discern flaws beneath Grant's surface, which the author has rendered in pure and dazzling white. ("Novelist's" 222)

Having set out his own preferences on the issue of characterization, Foote goes on to praise Williams's more balanced renderings of generals such as Henry Halleck or John Pope. His observations in this essay, however, provide a point of reference and a particular example (from among the myriad of possibilities in the narrative) for a consideration of his own treatment of character in *The Civil War*. Let us turn now to his presentation of General McClellan (a character who poses some challenges, as Foote has acknowledged) to illustrate his approach to characterization and to test his narrative against his stated claim to "stand up for bastards."

In the case of McClellan, his personality is linked to the conception, current at the time, of "the man of destiny." Having figured in a brief and successful campaign in the mountainous regions of West Virginia, McClellan is identified as a general of promise; indeed, as Foote suggests, "The North had found an answer to the southern Beauregard" (*CW* I.70), a comparison that at this early juncture seems entirely complimentary but is rendered increasingly ironic as aspects of Beauregard's character emerge in the narrative. The irony is deepened by our knowledge that Robert E. Lee's disastrous experience in West Virginia marks the low point in his reputation at the start of the war. After the Confederate victory at the First Battle of Bull Run, Lincoln swallowed his disappointment and looked around for a new commander for the Army of the Potomac, and believed he had "found his man of destiny" (*CW* I.86) in McClellan. It is a telling phrase. Earlier, Lincoln himself was introduced in similar terms when he delivered his "house divided" speech accepting the Republican nomination in a race for a Senate seat against incumbent Stephen Douglas. "It was at this point," Foote suggests, that the "Lincoln music" began to sound, and "Lincoln's political destiny and the destiny of the nation became one" (*CW* I.30). The phrase echoes an even earlier reference to Jefferson Davis who, arriving in Montgomery to accept the election as president of the Provisional Government of the Confederate States of America, is introduced to the crowd by William Lowndes Yancey in these terms: "The man and the hour have met" (*CW* I.17). This was the tenor of the times; and Foote is meticulous in depicting the context of crisis and heightened expectation into which McClellan was thrust. Indeed, after his initial success is noted, McClellan's reappearance to assume the command of the Army of the Potomac is delayed while Foote recounts the rise and fall of two other "men of destiny" (*CW* I.86), Robert Anderson and John Fremont. Foote tells of the qualified success of Anderson's passive resistance to the rebellious ferment in Kentucky, along with his subsequent personal exhaustion and retirement, and follows this with an examination of the outright failure of Fremont in Missouri (a story with elements of both hubris and farce). Before the first hundred pages are past, Foote establishes the genuine desire that lay behind the epithet McClellan inherited and also a cautionary or ironic perspective on the hyperbole.

Earlier in the narrative, before he acquires this potentially troublesome mantle of greatness, McClellan is presented as a man of energy and accomplishment. "At thirty-four, Major General George Brinton McClellan, commanding the Ohio volunteers, had earned both a military and a business reputation in the fifteen years since his graduation near the top of his Academy class, as a distinguished Mexican War soldier, official observer of the Crimean War, designer of the McClellan saddle, Superintendent of the Illinois Central, and president of the Ohio & Mississippi Railroad" (*CW* I.69). This first page-and-a-half recounts McClellan's early triumphs at Rich Mountain and Laurel Hill, the victories that brought him to Lincoln's attention, and establishes a triangulated relationship between the successful military action, the climate of public expectation, and the nature of McClellan himself. Each component is carefully counterpointed. For example, the theater of operations, the field of McClellan's triumph, is introduced in these terms (which manage to give and take at the same time): "From northwest Virginia the news was not only good, it was spectacular. Here the contest was between Ohio and Virginia, and the advantage was all with the former . . . 8000 loyal troops against 4000 rebels in an area where the people wanted no part of secession. It was an ideal setting for the emergence of a national hero, and such a hero soon appeared" (*CW* I.69).

McClellan's performance capitalizes on these advantages, and he is given due praise for the successful night attack against Philippi, West Virginia, as well as the subsequent combination of holding and flanking maneuvers that defeats the Confederate forces. Small details serve as checks and balances for the action. Foote's use of incidental details helps to temper adulation with reserve. For instance, the fact that McClellan carried a "portable printing press [as] part of his camp equipment" (*CW* I.69) and used it to produce somewhat self-aggrandizing statements such as "I have heard there was danger here. I have come to place myself at your head and share it with you. I fear now but one thing—that you will not find foeman worthy of your steel" (*CW* I.69) serves to raise certain questions with the reader. A similar qualification is inserted between the outlining of McClellan's tactics against the Confederates at Rich Mountain and Laurel Hill and their successful resolution. Prior to describing the Confederate defeat, Foote introduces McClellan's rationale for the complicated maneuver: "'No prospect of brilliant victory,' he explained, 'shall induce me to depart from my intention of gaining success by maneuvering rather than by fighting. I will not throw these raw men of mine into the teeth of artillery and entrenchments if it is possible to avoid it'" (*CW* I.69). "Either way," the narrator resumes, "it was brilliant" (*CW* I.70). The brilliance is not gainsaid, but its reiteration in the paragraph concluding Foote's description of McClellan's first campaign (once by the general himself in his report and again by the narrator) serves to introduce McClellan's own complicity in generating the climate of heightened public expectation that will haunt him throughout the war.

McClellan's next appearance in the text draws attention to the effect that this public adulation might have on the character of the man. After Foote's pointed reminders (via the Anderson and Fremont episodes) that destiny can hold failure as well as success, McClellan is reintroduced onto the scene as the "third [who] was rising, and he kept rising" (*CW* I.99). Appropriately, pride of place is given the general's accomplishments in transforming the post–Bull Run Union army from a demoralized mob into a "well-trained, spirited . . . superbly equipped" force of 168,000 men (*CW* I.99). His youthful energy and aura of confidence are reflected back in the public reaction to his elevation, when he describes himself as being "looked up to from all sides as the deliverer" and deferred to by "President, cabinet [and] Gen. Scott . . . [whereby through] some strange operation of magic I seem to have become the power of the land" (*CW* I.99). What follows is the reason for that public confidence, the sense of optimism and glamour that McClellan injected into the Union army, the discipline and order he brought to the process of transforming raw recruits, and the impact of his own charismatic presence: "He did not seem young; he was young, with all the vigor and clear-eyed forcefulness that went with being thirty-four. His eyes were blue, unclouded by suspicion, his glance direct. He wore his dark auburn hair parted far on the left and brushed straight across, adding a certain boyish charm to his air of forthright manliness" (*CW* I.100). As Foote points out: "Something new had come into the war; Little Mac, the soldiers called this man who had transformed them from a whipped mob into a hot-blooded army that seemed never to have known the taste of defeat. He brought out the best in them and restored their pride, and they hurrahed whenever he appeared on horseback" (*CW* I.100).

Describing each aspect of McClellan's accomplishment, Foote includes a balancing note, a fleeting shadow, to temper this aura of excitement. For example, the description of order and discipline restored and the inauguration of rigorous training on the parade grounds around Washington closes with McClellan's confident statement that "I shall carry this thing *en grand*" (*CW* I.100). His ability to engender a sense of pride in his men is followed by the description of his "glittering cavalcade" (*CW* I.100) of staff officers and visiting nobility—further evidence, presumably, of McClellan's "chivalric" sense of the proper style for warfare. Rounding out his sketch of the general's attractive physical appearance, Foote includes an allusion to his being lionized by the press and the absurdities of such public adulation (and, perhaps, McClellan's own sense of being trapped by the expectations): "The Young Napoleon, journalists had begun to call him, and photographers posed him standing with folded arms, frowning into the lens as if he were dictating terms for the camera's surrender" (*CW* I.100). Finally, Foote's portrait stresses the general's impact on his army, the "reciprocal" sense that "between them they felt that they were forging the finest army the world had ever seen" (*CW* I.101). Having outlined McClellan's public impact, Foote balances this with a glimpse at the inner man: "Yet all was not as confident in McClellan's mind as the soldiers judged from his manner on parade. In the small hours of the night, alone in his quarters, musing upon the example of McDowell, whose army had been wrecked on the very plains where the Confederates were still massing under the same victorious commanders, he took counsel of his fears" (*CW* I.101). Having fully described the effects of these expectations, Foote makes McClellan's isolation palpable—a sense that the private fear of failure keeps pace with the public perception of success. In keeping with Foote's ironic sense of equilibrium, McClellan's greatest gift to his troops is also potentially his most dangerous personal failing.

From this point on in the narrative, Foote's McClellan is a man divided between his public persona as savior of the nation and his private fears and reservations. As James M. Cox remarks: "Foote knows all of McClellan's weaknesses—every one—and exposes them, not, however, by argument but through narrative" (206). The cumulative nature of the evidence is indicative, but not prescriptive. Foote employs two thematic touchstones: 1) the question of pride or hubris and 2) its tragic correlative, a debilitating lack of awareness, a blindness to the political and personal responsibilities of his position. The first of these themes is emphasized through a comparison between McClellan and his superior, Lieutenant General Winfield Scott, the aging general-in-chief of the Union forces, "second only to the Father of his Country on the list of the nation's military heroes" (*CW* I.102). Scott's physical infirmities are matched by his "enormous pride" (*CW* I.102), a combination of incapacity and will the negative effects of which are offset in Scott's case by his awareness of his own limitations—a key qualification in that a similar division in McClellan is not mitigated by this vital aspect of self-consciousness. McClellan, convinced of his vocation (the "people call upon me to save the country. . . . I was called to it; my previous life seems to have been unwittingly directed to this great end" [*CW* I.103]), attacks Scott "where his adversary was weakest: in his pride" (*CW* I.103), and eventually forces Scott's retirement after the fiasco of Ball's Bluff. McClellan assumes supreme command of the armies, and Foote ends this section of his precipitous rise on a note that reinforces the dangerous isolation of the general's prideful nature. In response to Lincoln's cautions about the weight of the responsibility McClellan has assumed, the general answers, "I can do it all" (*CW* I.110). The declaration stands on its own, without commentary, as a challenge to fate.

As ever, pride cometh before a fall. Indeed, Foote begins the next section with a vignette that underscores the dangers of McClellan's self-satisfaction. After accompanying Scott to the railway station as he departs for a life of retirement in New York, McClellan writes to his wife, "The sight of this morning was a lesson to me which I hope not soon to forget. I saw there the end of a long, active, and industrious life, the end of the career of the first soldier of his nation; and it was a feeble old man scarce able to walk; hardly anyone there to see him off but his successor. Should I ever become vainglorious and ambitious, remind me of that spectacle" (*CW* I.111). McClellan's comment haunts the reader throughout the remainder of his tenure as commander of the Army of the Potomac and marks a shift in Foote's treatment from allusions to the dangers of pride to a concentration on the degrees and types of blindness by which pride is manifest in McClellan's actions. To highlight this idea, Foote pauses here to describe Scott's strategic legacy—his prescient "Anaconda" plan, blueprint "for total war" (*CW* I.111)—which McCellan shelved, yet which became the model for Grant's eventual victory.

Foote develops McClellan's character by implicit comparisons; one example is Scott, another is Beauregard, and yet another is Lincoln, who is also a "man of destiny." Beset by accusations of delay and incompetence leveled by members of the joint committee investigating the conduct of the war, McClellan's limitations as a politician are made apparent. As Foote suggests, "McClellan, who was a soldier, not a politician or a diplomat, could not or would not see that the context was political as well as military, that the two had merged, that men like Wade and Chandler were as much a part of it as men like Johnston and Beauregard—or McClellan himself, for that matter. Given the time, he believed he could get over or around the enemy entrenched across the Potomac; he could 'crush' them. He could never get over or around men like Wade and Chandler, let alone crush them, and he knew it. And knowing it he turned bitter. He turned peevish" (*CW* I.141). Eventually, this distrust extends to Lincoln himself. Increasingly isolated in his prideful certainty that the salvation of the nation rested on himself alone, McClellan first patronized (as unmilitary) and then came to resent (as politically motivated) the suggestions of the president. "If [Lincoln] noticed this at all," Foote muses, "[he] took it calmly. He was accustomed to being laughed at, and had even been known to encourage laughter at his own expense. Such friends as he cared about had a deep appreciation of humility, and he could afford to let the others go" (*CW* I.142–43). Continuing to develop McClellan's character, the narrative recounts the general's infamous snub of the president and Secretary of State William H. Seward as they waited in his parlor for an impromptu meeting, suggesting that Lincoln, in this instance, "drew the rebuke humility must always draw from pride" (*CW* I.143).

To highlight the general's self-destructive arrogance, Foote juxtaposes two reciprocal images. The first is Lincoln's remark, soon after being snubbed by McClellan, that he would "hold McClellan's horse if he will only bring us success" (*CW* I.143). And, after an intervening paragraph describing McClellan's new caution arising from reports of a Confederate army 90,000 strong, Foote picks up the motif from Lincoln's remark to illustrate the fruits of McClellan's pride:

> By now, though, more than the frock-coated congressmen were urging him forward against his will. While the clear bright days of autumn declined and the hard roads leading southward were about to dissolve into mud, the public was getting restless, too, wondering at the army's inaction. The soldiers loved and trusted him as much as ever; Our George, they called him still. But to the public he seemed overcautious, like a finicky dandy hesitating to blood a bright new sword, either because he did not want to spoil its glitter, or else because he did not trust its temper. Horace Greeley, the journalistic barometer, had recovered from his fright and recommenced his Forward-to-Richmond chant. Other voices swelled the chorus, while shriller cries came through its pulse to accuse the young commander of vacillation. McClellan was reduced to finding consolation in the approval of his horse, Dan Webster: writing, "He, at least, had full confidence in his master." (*CW* I.143–44)

Foote's narrative creates a context for understanding the self-pity and paranoia of the remark. By placing the words of the two men in such close proximity, without introducing conjecture or speculation, Foote's narrative builds a connection between the two isolated individuals. In this way, Foote's history incorporates a sense of contingency, missed opportunities, and other possibilities to set against the determinant force of events, of fate. This sense of balance, which is also reflected in the portraits of individuals, is generated by Foote's Proustian aesthetic of harmonization and the influence of a moral framework adhering to the ordinances of time.

As McClellan embarks on the peninsula campaign and later fights the Battle of Antietam, Foote returns to the themes of isolation and blindness introduced in these early scenes. For example, as the delays extend through the winter of 1861–62, political pressures for action and explanations increase in Washington: "By mid-January of this second calendar year of the war, however, so many congressmen had discovered the popular value of pointing a trembling finger at 'treason' in high places that their conglomerate, harping voice had grown into a force which had to be reckoned with as surely as the Confederates still entrenched around Manassas" (*CW* I.247). Once more the distinction between McClellan and Lincoln is made clear; here, with respect to the ideas of honor and gentlemanly conduct, the contrast is between McClellan's adherence to an antiquated chivalric code and Lincoln as a practitioner of Realpolitik. Facing the out-cries and accusations of the Washington politicians, Lincoln's and McClellan's reactions are described in the following way:

> Lincoln the politician understood this perfectly. They were men with power, who knew how to use it ruthlessly, and as such they would have to be dealt with. McClellan the soldier could never see it at all, partly because he operated under the disadvantage of considering himself a gentleman. For him they were willful, evil men, "unscrupulous and false," and as such they should be ignored as beneath contempt, at least by him. He counted on Lincoln to keep them off his back: which Lincoln in fact had promised to do. . . . Yet now he seemed to be breaking his promise to McClellan. . . .
>
> That was something else he never understood: Lincoln himself. Some might praise him for being flexible, while others called him slippery, when in truth they were both two words for just one thing. To argue the point was to insist on a distinction that did not exist. Lincoln was out to win the war; and that was all he was out to do, for the present. Unfettered by any need for being or not being a gentleman, he would keep his word to any man only so long as keeping it would help to win the war. If keeping it meant otherwise, he broke it. He kept no promise, anyhow, any longer than the conditions under which it was given obtained. And if any one thing was clear in this time when treason had become a household word, it was that the conditions of three months ago no longer obtained. (*CW* I.247–48)

Now, in addition to the idea of McClellan's prideful nature, Foote introduces this aspect of social distinction to explain some of McClellan's attitudes—the sort of limited middle-class conservative morality (what Daniel Singal called Victorianism) that created the Cavalier myth in the South. McClellan, for all his merits and accomplishments as an organizer, it seems clear, remains out of step with the reality of the war; his conception of warfare, built around the notion of gentlemanly contests, is an outdated one, a point made clear by another progressive comparison of McClellan and the grim realities of combat in the western theater at places such as Wilson Creek and Shiloh (and the "ungentlemanly" characteristics of Ulysses S. Grant).

Continuity between the early McClellan and the later man is established through details evoking constant aspects of the general's character. For example, one of the stellar accomplishments of McClellan's early triumph in western Virginia was the lightness of the casualties. His justifiable pride in this fact is reinforced by his own statement about his preferred strategy of "gaining success by maneuvering rather than by fighting" (*CW* I.69). Foote resurrects this idea when McClellan, in December 1861, introduces his strategy for circumventing the Confederate army and moving right up to Richmond—the stillborn Urbanna plan.

> McClellan had never enjoyed the notion of a head-on tangle with Johnston on those plains where McDowell had gone down. Someday, given the odds, he might chance it; that was what he was building toward. But to attempt it while outnumbered, as he believed his army was, seemed to him downright folly. Then Buell's refusal to advance against and through Knoxville, which would have placed his army on Johnston's flank, in a position to cooperate with the Army of the Potomac, caused McClellan to abandon all intentions of a due south attack, present or future. Poring over headquarters maps he had evolved "another plan of campaign," one moreover enlisting the assistance of the navy, flushed with its three recent victories. He would load his soldiers aboard transports, steam down the Potomac into Chesapeake Bay, then south along the coast to the mouth of the Rappahannock, and up that river a short distance to Urbanna, a landing on the southern bank, less than fifty airline miles from Richmond, his objective. Without the loss of a man, he would have cut his marching distance in half and he would be in the rear of Johnston—who then would be forced to retreat and fight on grounds of McClellan's choosing. The more he thought about it,

the better he liked it. It was not only beautifully simple. It was beautifully bloodless. (*CW* I.155)

However admirable McClellan's intention, and it had much to recommend it on strategic grounds, Foote's emphasis on its "bloodless" nature highlights the connection to the general's earlier statements.

McClellan, in a way, is hostage to his own inability to admit his fallibility. On the brink of shifting his army, he finds Johnston has decamped from the Manassas line: "Most of [Johnston's] army was already back on the banks of the Rappahannock, entrenching itself near the very spot McClellan had picked for a beachhead. To land at Urbanna now, he saw, would be to land not in Johnston's rear, but with Johnston in his own" (*CW* I.263). Chagrined by this "abrupt and, so to speak, ill-mannered joggling of the military chessboard after all the pains he had taken to dispose the pieces to his liking" (*CW* I.263), McClellan embarks on a sham invasion of North Virginia, "an opportunity to put the finishing touch to his army's rigorous eight-month course of training: a practice march, deep into enemy territory—under combat conditions, with full field equipment and carefully worked-out logistics—and then another march right back again, since there was nothing there that he should not gain, automatically and bloodlessly, by going ahead with his roundabout plan for a landing down the coast" (*CW* I.263–64). The bloody-mindedness of the public outcry at this humiliation is set against the feelings of the army (an antipathy toward casualties that actually weighs in McClellan's favor): "Civilians like their victories bloody: the bloodier the better, so long as the casualty lists did not touch home. Soldiers—except perhaps in retrospect, when they had become civilians, too—preferred them bloodless as in this case. The Centerville fortifications looked formidable enough to the men who would have had to assault them, peeled log guns or no" (*CW* I.264). But the end result, in the mind of the reader, is that McClellan's painstaking determination to avoid confrontation is akin to an egocentric chess player who forgets that his opponent can move as well. Foote's narrative develops McClellan's actions and statements into a pattern over time; and it is McClellan's inability to alter this pattern that finally confirms his character in the mind of the reader.

Foote also finds ironic resonances of McClellan's desire to "carry this thing *en grand*" (*CW* I.100) in his protracted advance up the peninsula. Confronting extensive Confederate entrenchments at Yorktown, McClellan

begins an elaborate siege operation, and Foote seizes the moment to con-
nect the present decisions with the earliest, and most fundamental, aspects
of the general's character to which we have been introduced.

> As April wore on and the rains continued, so did the siege prepa-
> rations; McClellan was hard at work. He had not wanted this kind
> of campaign, but now that he had it he was enjoying it immensely.
> Back in the West Virginia days he had said, "I will not throw these
> raw men of mine into the teeth of artillery and entrenchments if it
> is possible to avoid it." He still felt that way about it. "I am to
> watch over you as a parent over his children," he had told his army
> the month before, and that was what he was doing. If it was to be a
> siege, let it be one in the grand manner, with fascines and gabions,
> zigzag approaches, and much digging and shifting of earth, pre-
> paratory to blasting the rebel fortifications clean out of existence.
> (*CW* I.409–10)

That these extensive and time-consuming preparations are placed in a
mocking light by Johnston's abrupt departure, seems at this point simply
to confirm a pattern of behavior in keeping with what we understand
of McClellan's personality. Indeed, the general's propensity for self-
aggrandizement is underscored when his victory by default at Yorktown—
scene of Cornwallis's surrender to George Washington during the American Revolution—is placed in relation to McClellan's visit, just eight pages
later, to the home where Washington "had courted the Widow Custis"
(*CW* I.418). Honoring the request of Mrs. Washington's granddaughter,
Mrs. R. E. Lee, to preserve and protect the property, and "[g]lad of this
chance to show that the practice of chivalry was not restricted to soldiers
dressed in gray, [McClellan] then enjoyed a brief sojourn among the relics."

> Even though the house itself was a reconstruction, the sensation of
> being on the site where Washington had slept and eaten and taken
> his ease gave the youthful commander a feeling of being borne up
> and on by the stream of history; he hoped, he said, "that I might
> serve my country as well as he did." Riding toward the front on
> May 16, he came to old St Peter's Church, where Washington was
> married. Here too he stopped, dismounted, and went in. That night
> he wrote his wife: "As I happened to be there alone for a few

minutes, I could not help kneeling at the chancel and praying."
(*CW* I.418)

Given McClellan's track record to this point, Foote's inclusion of this incident serves as a reminder of a plethora of grandiose statements and postures, a sort of self-damning chivalric role-playing in the midst of the campaign. The pattern creates a perspective on McClellan without the necessity for overt invective on the part of the narrator. "Yet throughout the extended treatment of McClellan's command," James M. Cox observes, "Foote never finds himself defending or attacking McClellan. Instead, the narrative exposes his character at the same time that it comprehends it" (207).

A similar duality is operative in the way each encounter with another major character becomes a opportunity to develop the portrait of both men. We have seen how some of McClellan's limitations are developed through indirect comparison with other historical figures. Lincoln's forbearance and political acumen, for example, serve to set up McClellan's lack of political acumen about the Washington environment. Similarly, McClellan is, by inference, measured against his principal opponent, General Lee. Here the comparison is startling. McClellan, learning of Lee's assumption of command of the Army of Northern Virginia, is recorded as offering this assessment: "'I prefer Lee to Johnston,' McClellan declared when he heard of the shift—meaning that he preferred him as an opponent. 'The former is too cautious and weak under grave responsibility. Personally brave and energetic to a fault, he yet is wanting in moral firmness when pressed by heavy responsibility, and is likely to be timid and irresolute in action'" (*CW* I.465). Written, Foote carefully acknowledges, under "the influence of a new surge of confidence and elation" (*CW* I.465) occasioned by his pride in the army's performance at Fair Oaks, and followed by an example of his confidence-boosting oratory, the disastrously wrong assessment lies like a time bomb in the text, ready to explode in McClellan's face. Foote's appreciation of the irony of this misreading of Lee (who was, to give McClellan his due, misread by many others as well) is evident through his inclusion, three pages later, of Lee's assessment of McClellan. "[Lee] saw the problem posed for him by his fellow engineer: 'McClellan will make this a battle of posts. He will take position from position under cover of his heavy guns and we cannot get at him'" (*CW* I.468). That subsequent events reveal Lee to have taken completely the measure of the man, confirming what we already understand of his character, illustrates another aspect of McClellan's limitations. Indeed, by now McClellan is also being implicitly measured against Ulysses S. Grant; the former general is continually unmanned by incorrect numerical reports of Confederate strength, while his western counterpart begins to demonstrate, in battles such as Shiloh, his aptness for his subsequent role in the east as Lincoln's "killer-arithmetician" (*CW* II.828). Perhaps it is a question of moral courage, to pick up on Foote's use of Hemingway. In any case, it is interesting to read Hemingway's description in *Death in the Afternoon* of a matador who is a "truly great killer"— a description that would apply equally well to Stonewall Jackson or R. E. Lee: "A great killer must love to kill; unless he feels it is the best thing he can do, unless he is conscious of its dignity and feels that it is its own reward, he will be incapable of the abnegation that is necessary in real killing. The truly great killer must have a sense of honor and a sense of glory far beyond that of the ordinary bullfighter. In other words, he must be a simpler man" (232).

Near the close of Foote's treatment of the Seven Days, after McClellan orders the retreat of the Union forces from Savage Station in the direction of Harrison's Landing, the general's reactions take an aura of determinism, becoming predictable based on our knowledge of his personality as it has developed over the course of the narrative.

> It was well conceived, well thought out: McClellan took pride in the foresight and coolness which had enabled him to improvise the details under pressure. He did not consider the movement a retreat. It was a readjustment, a change of base required by a change in conditions. However, once the conference was over and the corps commanders had gone out into the night with their instructions for tomorrow, he began to consider the adverse reaction that might follow: not among his soldiers—they would understand—but among the members of the body politic, the public at large, and especially among the molders of popular opinion: the editors, and later the historians. The record would speak for itself in time. (*CW* I.492)

This, of course, this is exactly what the narrative has been doing. Yet history is more than one perspective—as the multiple viewpoints and implicit comparisons included in *The Civil War* demonstrate—and McClellan's assumption that his own view is the one truth, aside from the egotism already established, is damned for its limiting simplicity when set inside the complex web of Foote's history. The passage continues:

> He was confident that it would show how Lincoln and Stanton had thwarted him, diverting his troops when his back was turned and ignoring his pleas for reinforcements, in spite of documentary evidence that he was facing an army twice the size of his own. Meanwhile, though, he was not only in danger of being condemned and ridiculed; about to undertake one of the most difficult maneuvers in the art of war, the transfer of an army from one base to another across a fighting front, he was in danger of being physically destroyed. In that event, the record would indeed have to speak for itself, since he would not be there to supplement it before the bar of judgment. Therefore it had better be supplemented in advance, bolstered so as to present the strongest possible case in the strongest possible language. Shortly after midnight, before retiring to sleep for what he knew would be a grinding day tomorrow, he got off a wire to Stanton.
>
> "I now know the full history of the day," it began. After saying flatly, "I have lost this battle because my force was too small," he got down to cases: "I again repeat that I am not responsible for this, and I say it with the earnestness of a general who feels in his heart the loss of every brave man who has been needlessly sacrificed today. . . . If, at this instant, I could dispose of 10,000 fresh men, I could gain a victory tomorrow. I know that a few thousand more men would have changed this battle from a defeat to a victory. As it is, the Government must not and cannot hold me responsible for the result." The clincher came at the end: "I feel too earnestly tonight. I have seen too many dead and wounded comrades to feel otherwise than that the Government has not sustained this army. If you do not do so now the game is lost. If I save this army now, I tell you plainly that I owe no thanks to you or to any other persons in Washington. You have done your best to sacrifice this army."
>
> Having thus unburdened his troubled mind, and bolstered the record in the process, he took to his bed. "Of course they will never forgive me for that," he subsequently told his wife. "I knew it when I wrote it; but as I thought it possible that it might be the last I ever wrote, it seemed better to have it exactly true." (*CW* I.492–93)

Here, Foote returns to the themes of pride and blindness, finding in McClellan's concern for the record—"I now know the full history of the day"—a confirmation of an observation made earlier when Lincoln tried to warn the general of the real danger posed by his political adversaries in the capitol: "[McClellan] did not see, then or ever, that he had helped to bring all this trouble on himself by not taking Lincoln into his confidence sooner. And if he had seen it, the seeing would not have made the end result easier to abide; McClellan was never one to find ease in admission of blame" (*CW* I.254). And it is in this inability to see, in his refusal of blame, in his preemptive strike in the battle for the historical record, that McClellan stands in the worst possible light—as Lincoln stands in the best.

The final irony, after Antietam and McClellan's lack of initiative in pursuing the battered Confederate forces, is presented as his one moment of prescience. Over one month after the battle, and following a telegraphic exchange about McClellan's need for more men and new horses (his army being over 130,000 present for duty at this point) that culminates in Lincoln's exasperated inquiry: "Will you pardon me for asking what the horses of your army have done since the battle of Antietam that fatigues anything?" (*CW* I.752), McClellan finally sees "plainly what was coming. . . . 'I may not have command of the army much longer. Lincoln is down on me'" (*CW* I.752). When his removal has become fact, McClellan departs the narrative in a suitable mixture of pathos and dignity, in a scene reminiscent of General Scott's earlier departure upon McClellan's elevation to the command. McClellan's final self-assessment is an intriguing combination of insight and blindness: "I have done the best I could for my country; to the last I have done my duty as I understand it. That I must have made many mistakes I cannot deny. I do not see any great blunders; but no one can judge of himself. Our consolation must be that we have tried to do what was right" (*CW* I.756). In a sense, it is matched by Foote's presentation of the army's reaction to the news, which is suggested to be, in a similar way, self-serving:

> In their tears, in their passionate demonstrations of affection for this man who moved them in a way no other general ever had or ever would, it was as if the soldiers had sensed a larger meaning in the impending separation; it was as if they knew they were saying goodbye to something more than just one stocky brown-haired man astride a tall black horse. It was, indeed, as if they were say-

ing goodbye to their youth—which, in a sense, they were. Or it might also have been prescience, intimations of mortality, intimations of suffering down the years. There had been Pope, and now it appeared that there would be others more or less like him. Knowing what that meant, they might well have been weeping for their own lot, as well as for McClellan's. "My army," he had called them from the start, and it was true. He had made them into what they were, and whatever they accomplished he would accomplish too, in part, even though he would no longer be at their head. (*CW* I.757)

McClellan departs from the text on the wings of Lee's postwar compliment; it is a note seemingly at odds with the portrait developed over the course of the narrative, which might suggest that even Lee was not immune to a sort of wistful self-deception. Indeed, the ambiguities raised by Foote's balancing of event and individual perspectives suggests a tacit recognition of the limitations of his own narrative's ability to establish a definitive truth about the past.

In a letter to Percy of August 9, 1954, Foote outlined his procedure with respect to perspective in the narrative; he advocated a "strict point-of-view. . . . the reader always has a definite standing-place from which he looks out . . . (3d person, of course) . . . whoever happens to be at the storm-center of the current subject. This gives it a validity and a vitality that will be cumulative and intense." Foote's adherence to this dictum, like his employment of limited points of view in novels such as *Follow Me Down* and *Love in a Dry Season,* is an extension of a principle central to his artistic vision. For Foote, man exists as an isolated consciousness, striving to make sense of his place in the world on the basis of partial data and conditioned reactions and beliefs. The extent of his success in life is related to his ability to perceive the world around him; the artist's success is contingent on his ability to present a balanced view of this fallible condition, to string together the isolated consciousnesses into a whole greater than the sum of the parts. The completed story, the work of art, is equivalent to the narrative "string of pearls" that Asa achieves in *Tournament* or the inclusion of the "missing link" represented by Beulah's section in *Follow Me Down.* It is a truth that will, of necessity, be conditional. In a similar fashion, the individual historical characters in *The Civil War* are presented "in constant motion" as parts of a complex web of correspondences and juxtapositions; portraits that are compelling, marvelously balanced, and yet incomplete—necessary fictions.

When discussing the relationship between fiction and history in the essay "The Historian's Opportunity," Barbara Tuchman makes the following observation: "The more necessary use of imagination [in writing history] is in application to human behavior and to the action of circumstance on motive. It becomes a deliberate effort at empathy, essential if one is to understand and interpret the actions of historical figures. With antipathetic characters it is all the more necessary. . . . The effort to get inside is, obviously enough, a path to insight. It is the *Einfuhling* that Herder demanded of historians: the effort to 'feel oneself into everything'" (63). Foote's approach to characterization, through his method of "continuing development" and his avowed resolve to "stand up for bastards," is a mark of his essentially humanistic perspective on the past and a measure of his respect for all the participants—heroes and villains, successes and failures. Commenting on this aspect of Foote's narrative, Cox remarks: "Knowing both historically and imaginatively the full reality of the war, he does not have to be for or against it; instead, he believes in the war, believes in it enough to believe that the men who fought it were as real as its reality. His great task as a writer is to render their reality" (196). Foote's strategy of choosing to present his characters so fully in relation to the limitations of time, circumstance, and personality, as George Garrett notes, makes reading *The Civil War* an experience "analogous to [that] of a novel with a richly sensuous affective surface rather than a recapitulation of events" (91).

Chapter 5

Writing the American *Iliad*

Narrative Strategies in *The Civil War*

Dwight Macdonald, the journalist, once wrote that there were only three literary genres in the United States: fiction, non-fiction and Civil War studies, the last combining elements of the first two.

—Hugh Tulloch, *The Debate on the American Civil War Era*, 1999

All art is an organization of experience, whatever the form, and in that sense all the arts are kin; what form an artist chooses to demonstrate his soul, to parade his intelligence, is accidental and even unimportant.

—Shelby Foote, letter to Walker Percy, July 30, 1948

Confronting the Incommunicable: Narrative Strategies and the Battle of Shiloh

Bruce Catton, in the opening lines of a short article entitled "The Heather Is on Fire," comments on the endless fascination, and the ultimate frustration, experienced by those who take up the challenge of writing about "the incommunicable" experience of war. I quote it at length because Catton's description of the field of battle as a contingent meeting place of multiple

165

stories is similar to Shelby Foote's recognition that writing about the past is, inevitably and paradoxically, both a reduction and an enlargement.

> Follow a Civil War soldier through a battle and you find that you are studying two incomprehensible paths through space.
> One is the trajectory of the bullet that kills him: flat, direct, whining, going from here to there (200 yards, as likely as not) in a second or two and then stopping forever.
> The other is the trajectory of the man.
> It is infinitely complicated, unhurried, wandering down through the years with all sorts of twists, convolutions, false starts, unexpected dips and curves, and meaningless pauses. . . .
> If these two trajectories—that of the bullet and that of the man—meet, they both end, and one who looks on at a safe distance is likely to begin an unsatisfying speculation. The short life of the bullet's flight caused it to be at one particular point in space one foot above the top of a fence along Farmer Jones' cornfield, say, at precisely twenty-one minutes past nine o'clock on a certain Tuesday morning in September. The man's own flight, leisurely and whimsical, and all but purposeless, guided by forces whose complexity we can never understand, brought him from afar to that same place at exactly the same moment. If any of the infinite chances by which life is guided had made him veer one foot the other way or had delayed him one second, his trajectory would not have crossed the trajectory of the bullet and he would have lived. . . . Suppose, suppose, suppose . . . you are beginning to touch a mystery that is beyond earthly understanding, whether you want to speak of an inscrutable fate, divine Providence or a blind bumbling chance that makes a mockery of all our dreams. There is not any answer we can lay our hands on. (Catton, *Reflections* 157–58)

Yet, as Catton goes on to say, the unresolvable nature of this puzzle in no way invalidates making the attempt. Foote's artistic engagement with this paradox is evident in his fictional and historical versions of the Battle of Shiloh (April 6–7, 1862). Comparing his narrative approaches in each genre provides a unique opportunity to consider what David Cowart calls "the strange family resemblance between the fictive and the historical" (20).

The Narrative Framework of Shiloh

The penultimate section of *Shiloh* is devoted to the thoughts of the dozen soldiers who constitute G Company, part of Lew Wallace's division, and continues the momentum of the novel away from the shock of the first day's fighting. Here, in microcosm, Foote demonstrates the method of the narrative as a whole—a linear progression through the events of the Union advance composed entirely of the passing thoughts of the twelve combatants. Indeed, the ruminations of the first of these soldiers, Private Winter, underscore the paradoxical relationship between separateness and commonality that is the heart of the novel's theme and structure: "I used to think how strange it was that the twelve of us had been brought together by an event which separated brothers and divided the nation. Each of us had his history and each of the histories was filled with accidental happenings" (*Shiloh* 163). Winter's observation applies to the men of Company G, and also to the author's approach to narrative in the novel. Similarly, the conjunction of accident and larger design speaks to Foote's blending of the ideas of historical process and individual existential experience, as well as the elements of fact and fiction, within the framework of his novel. Out of this interplay comes the evenhandedness for which Foote is noted. *Shiloh* seeks to reconcile Stephen Crane's exclusive focus on the individual in *The Red Badge of Courage* (a "pure" fiction) with the documentary material Foote mentions in his bibliographical note ("pure" history). Paradoxically, by emphasizing the artifice, instead of realism, in his approach to the genre of historical fiction, Foote achieves a dual purpose—to humanize the history and authenticate the fiction.

The "Squad" section also includes a self-reflexive discussion of the method of Foote's narrative. Speculating about the writing of history, Corporal Blake—a folksy visionary—suggests that "books about war were written to be read by God Amighty, because no one but God ever saw it that way. A book about war, to be read by men, ought to tell what each of the twelve of us saw in our own little corner. Then it would be the way it was—not to God but to us" (*Shiloh* 164). As his compatriot Winter observes, such an attitude would satisfy only one part of the desire in men to understand: "People when they read, and people when they write, want to be looking out of that big Eye in the sky, playing God" (*Shiloh* 164). By acknowledging this debate, Foote calls attention to his own narrative strategies. In his dual role as novelist and historian, Foote employs the facts of the battle as a frame and control for the imaginative aspects of his encounter with the past. His narrative balances both the historical overview and the imaginative re-creation of individual experience, privileging neither. As White and Sugg suggest, Foote manages to have it "both ways" (70).

In establishing the parameters of the narrative structure of *Shiloh*, Foote took pains to underscore the central tension between "objective" and subjective viewpoints. The placement of a map at the outset of the work functions as a geographical and temporal frame for the action. In a literal sense, Foote charts the movements of the characters in a two-dimensional, "foreshortened" way—one that has sometimes been condemned as failed art in other of his works (for example, the obsessive mapping of Hector Sturgis in "Child by Fever" or the gargoyle-like perspective of Amanda Barcroft, the failed reader of *Love in a Dry Season*). Foote's map is a beginning, nothing more; it remains a broad sketch of the spatial and temporal limits of present action, skeletal in its aspect. Significantly, this bird's eye, "God-like" viewpoint reflects nothing of the larger troop movements on the field. The visual marking is reduced to incidents involving individual participants, the field within the field that Foote will employ in his fictional treatment of the battle. The map deliberately tells only part of the story; its blend of abstraction and particularity subverts our expectations of the usual illustrative function of maps in historical texts and suggests the dynamic of limitations central to Foote's narrative strategy.

The determinate elements of time and topography in *Shiloh* form an integral framework for each section. The novel begins at midday on Saturday, April 5, 1862, as the Confederate forces under General Albert Sidney Johnston approach from Corinth, Mississippi, and ends with the return of the army to the town late Tuesday night, April 8. Thus, the length of the action from Confederate advance to final retreat establishes the elapsed time in the novel. Similarly, Foote makes repeated references to the topographical frame of the field—a tableland situated between the rain-swollen Owl Creek on the north and the equally high backwater of Lick Creek on the south, with the Tennessee River at the Union rear—described geometrically as a "parallelogram" (*Shiloh* 44). In a note at the end of the book, Foote establishes an equivalent limitation with regard to the historical figures and material, stating that "[h]istorical characters in this book speak the words they spoke and do the things they did at Shiloh. Many of the minor incidents also occurred, even when here they are assigned to fictional persons; I hope the weather is accurate too" (*Shiloh* 225). Each of the seven

NARRATIVE STRATEGIES IN *THE CIVIL WAR*

sections consists of a monologue alternating Confederate and Union perspectives. (The penultimate one registers the thoughts of the Indiana squad
and swells the true number of monologues to seventeen.)

The only character given the distinction of having two sections is the
young southerner, Lieutenant Palmer Metcalfe, whose thoughts are represented in the opening and closing monologues. Metcalfe's experience, as
aide-de-camp to General Johnston, forms the bridge between the advance,
beginning on the Saturday, and the retreat, ending on Tuesday night. The
second of the monologues, that of Captain Walter Fountain, Adjutant, Fifty-
third Ohio, covers the time from 4:00 Sunday morning until shortly after
dawn when the Confederate attack takes place. These two sections are the
most complex of the monologues in structure and the most ambitious in
conveying the perspectives of the Confederate and Union forces at the
beginning of the action. The next four sections are devoted to the thoughts
of soldiers during the two-day battle and follow a tight chronological order
with only brief digressions: the monologue of Confederate Private Dade
(Sixth Mississippi Regiment) follows the battle from dawn until 2:30 P.M.
Sunday; the section devoted to Private Flickner, a cannoneer with the First
Minnesota Battery, covers the period from approximately 4:30 P.M. to midnight Sunday; Sergeant Jefferson Polly, a scout with Forrest's cavalry, traces
movements from midnight to dawn of Monday morning; and the last of
these four is the medley of twelve brief monologues of the Twenty-third
Indiana squad charting the Union advance from dawn Monday until the
end of fighting that evening. Lieutenant Metcalfe's last section forms an
ironic reprise as he picks up the thread of the narrative from General
Johnston's death to the arrival of the defeated army back in Corinth—having spent the remainder of the battle, like so many other Confederate soldiers in the confusion of the fighting, unattached. The chronological movement of events thus forms the backbone for a narrative structure whose
center is Foote's imaginative re-creation of the lived experience of the combat—the thematic "heart" of the novel being the revisionist depiction of
honor and courage presented in the Dade and Flickner sections.

The emotional and imaginative center of the novel is reached in
Flickner, and the last three chapters begin to complete its frame: spatially
by circling back to the road to Corinth, where the Confederates began; tem-
porally by describing the remainder of the fighting; and narratively by closing with Lieutenant Metcalfe. The monologues devoted to Scout Jefferson
Polly and the Indiana squad, chapters 5 and 6, provide incidents of the

battle untouched by previous sections. The construction of these chapters, increasing in formal complexity, also reinforces the shift from the immediacy of Dade and Flickner's experience. The momentum toward closure is anticipated by Foote's use of geometric descriptions of the field, specifically those of Metcalfe and Fountain. The linear temporal progression of individual experience is matched by circular spatial movements (the way the troops return to the points from which they began: e.g., Metcalfe's camping by his old fire and Sherman's troops bedding down Monday night in their original positions). These two forms coalesce with the central thematic motif: the pattern of descent and reemergence on individual levels with the elemental confrontations of Dade and Flickner and on a cultural level with Johnston's death (that "still point of the turning world" that marks the onset of the modern era). The motifs of doubling and the cultural parallels underline this shift in values and perspectives. The sensibilities that dominate the field at the conclusion of the novel—those of Forrest, Sherman, Corporal Blake, and members of the squad—enrich the pattern of correspondences and heighten the ironic implications of a nation forever afterward "torn on the bias."

The double agenda of the novel, with respect to the meeting of fiction and fact and the juxtaposition of Northern and Southern perspectives, is achieved by Foote's ability to open the ostensibly closed narrative. In the outer sections, he accomplishes this by the use of the flashback or narrative excursus. The most complex of these are linked, logically, to the better-educated of the characters: Metcalfe, Fountain, and Polly. In each case, the monologues include passages in which personal memory modulates into the atemporal voice of the historian. The interplay of narrative voices reflects Foote's complex balancing of his dual roles; it also creates the most problematic aspect of the book—a point that troubled the critic Allen Shepherd when he drew attention to the "unevenness" of the points of view in some of the monologues and objected to the sense of the "artificial" that these violations evoked in the reader (4–6). It can, however, be argued that these violations of the speaker's perspective by the intrusion of the historian's voice serve, like the conscious artifice of the forms in all of Foote's novels, to draw attention to the factual base upon which the imaginative components of the novel rest. As Foote has suggested, referring to one motivation for tackling the subject of Shiloh, "I was animated in part by revulsion to the historical novel" (*Conversations* 5). His own work, then, is a self-conscious exploration of the tensions within the genre.

The first excursus in Metcalfe's section introduces the history of the campaign in the West prior to the time of Shiloh, recounting the retreat through Tennessee to Corinth after the fall of Forts Henry and Donelson and the public outrage that tarnished the reputation of General Johnston. Here Foote provides the rationale for Metcalfe's assertion that the coming battle will be Johnston's "hour of vindication" (*Shiloh* 7), transferring the conflict from the realm of military strategy to that of a personal point of honor. Through Metcalfe's naïveté, established by such romantic details as his account of the Confederate battle plan, modeled after Napoleon's at Waterloo, Foote underscores from the outset that the strategies and tactics of the Southern generals were outmoded and makes subtle ironic play of the fact, ignored by Metcalfe, that the plan led to Napoleon's defeat. The intrusion of the historian's voice provides a sense of historical perspective, with the violation of the interior monologue contributing an ironic commentary on how history is lived and how it is understood. Metcalfe's ruminations also include a biographical sketch of General Johnston—a figure of legendary proportions logically familiar to a cadet with Metcalfe's family connections who had attended the Louisiana State Military Academy. Johnston's association with military tradition and the prevalent southern belief in a "gentleman's war" underscore another aspect of the novel's cultural concerns, specifically the predominance of the Cavalier myth. As the *Encyclopedia of Southern Culture* (1989) points out: "[T]he southern Cavalier began his career as a planter or the son of a planter and reached his maturity as a Confederate soldier" (3:503–4). This myth finds its embodiment in Johnston and represents the philosophical center of young Metcalfe's heritage.

Foote balances this vision of southern aristocracy and idealism with the introduction of Metcalfe's father, a one-armed veteran of the Mexican War who functions as an ironic counterpoint. In recounting an affair of honor involving Johnston, Metcalfe repeats his father's remark that "it would have been highly comical if it hadn't been deadly serious" (*Shiloh* 18). The father's sense of the absurd allows Foote to introduce a modern perspective on the cultural assumptions of the Southern leaders and their strategies. Indeed, the last of the interpolated sections of Metcalfe's first monologue—his romanticized memory of his mother and his dreams of military glory involving the capture of General Sherman—reinforce his unthinking absorption of Southern idealism. This adds to the irony of his post-battle allegiance to Colonel Nathan Bedford Forrest's vision of total

war. In fact, in the light of Metcalfe's father's assertions, Johnston's statement upon hearing small-arms fire early Sunday morning ("The battle
has opened, gentlemen. . . . It is too late to change our dispositions"
[*Shiloh* 29]) takes on ironic double meaning: the grand design of the flawed
battle plan is fixed, as are the temperaments, characteristics, and assumptions of the officers themselves. Having brought the army to the brink of
what Foote calls elsewhere "the first modern battle" (*CW* I.338), the intrusions of the historian's voice into Metcalfe's fictional consciousness suggest ironies inherent in the conflict between old and new orders.

The last chapter of the book—Metcalfe's reprise—recounts the loss of
this Cavalier self-image. The two major digressions of this final monologue,
entitled "Palmer Metcalfe, Unattached," stress the emerging power of the
previously discounted alternative voices. Here, the words of Metcalfe's
father, now identified as a "realist and straight thinker" (*Shiloh* 200), are
linked to the brutally frank remarks Metcalfe remembers Sherman making
in response to the secession of South Carolina: "'You are bound to fail,' he
said. 'In the end you'll surely fail'" (*Shiloh* 26–27). These echoes from the
past are now supported by Metcalfe's experience of the reality of war and
his first taste of the bitterness of defeat. Here too, in Metcalfe's reaction to
the death of Johnston and his shift of allegiance to the "newfangled" warfare of Forrest, Foote suggests the birth of the central myth of the postwar
South—that of the Lost Cause. Faced with the grisly results of Johnston's
failed grand design, Metcalfe endorses a new and even more deadly
model—one that recognizes the unconventional efficacy of the Forrest style
of fighting "by ear" (*Shiloh* 211) as the only response possible to the numerical and economic truths articulated by Sherman. The context and cost of
the war, after Shiloh, are irrevocably changed. The war will still be shaped
by the "dispositions" of the various commanders; yet the methods and values of Forrest, Sherman, and Grant are antithetical to the values represented by Johnston and Beauregard. Foote's point is made: this is no longer,
or never was, a chivalric tournament. In narrative terms, Metcalfe's monologues provide a fictional context for the introduction of the historical determinants—a procedure that reinforces the ironic double perspective operative throughout the novel.

The second section of *Shiloh* continues to elaborate this dual perspective by introducing an alternation between Southern and Northern points of
view. Devoted to the musings of Captain Walter Fountain (duty officer in
one of Sherman's outlying regiments) as he composes a letter to his wife

during the small hours of Sunday morning, this monologue provides a neat counterpoint to that of Lieutenant Metcalfe, both men being officers, both sharing a certain degree of education, and both having access to official and personal information about the army commanders. As in the case of Metcalfe, Fountain's monologue outlines the dispositions of the Union forces and includes a character sketch of the commanding officer. Fountain's section also carries forward the double agenda of the narrative; its epistolary structure highlighting the problematic nature of the "factual" data gleaned from surviving documents and the corresponding necessity for a balancing imaginative reconstruction. (It is a fact that Foote might have discovered when he read William Percy's memoirs. For when Percy looks back over his letters from the front, he finds they are "gauche outpourings, too hot and too cold, too eloquent in a distressingly amateurish fashion and too reticent, at once accurate and misleading. . . . I find they record all I have forgotten and omit all that I remember, all that made my stay at the front a test and a turning, the most memorable and maturing experience of my life. What soldiers write home about must be supplemented by what soldiers do not write home about, if one is to gain an inkling of why a soldier is more and less than a man" [214].) Interwoven with the sanitized and somewhat trivial news he includes in his letter home, Fountain's interior monologue conveys a considerable amount of information about Generals Grant and Sherman, the situation of the Union forces, and strategic and cultural assumptions representative of the Yankee soldiers. The incidental images establish parallels with Metcalfe's experience and stress similarities (particularly in relation to the "green" or untried nature of the men). Other correspondences point up differences in outlook—perhaps the oddest is the parallel reference to an armored vest. Metcalfe sees one discarded during the advance, "gleaming like old silver in the rain" (*Shiloh* 20), and finds little incongruity in such an archaic piece of military equipment because it fits with the chivalric and heroic conditioning of his imagination. Fountain, on the other hand, observes one of his compatriots wearing a similar vest and "clank[ing] when he walks" (*Shiloh* 56). Fountain comments on the incongruity of such armor and deems the matter humorous enough to record for his wife's amusement. Small details such as these begin to flesh out the more prosaic and utilitarian description of the attitude of the Union troops: more institutional and less inclined to effusions about abstractions such as duty and honor. Ironically, the event that supports Metcalfe's flights of heroic fancy, the Confederate victory at the First Battle of Manassas in

1861, is presented in an opposite guise when Fountain registers a sense of wounded professional pride at the Union defeat and thus foreshadows the hardening of Union purpose evident in the whole of the western campaign.

This Union resolve is conveyed through Fountain's musings on his commanding officer, Ulysses S. Grant. Foote creates a self-reflexive dimension to the text here—the intrusion of the historian's voice into Fountain's monologue is parallel to his self-censorship in his correspondence to his wife (a discrepancy between the record and the immediate reality). Coming from the same hometown as Grant, and combining this local memory with his own experience of the campaigns at Forts Henry and Donelson, Fountain provides the reader with a brief history of his general's transformation from "Useless" to "Unconditional Surrender" Grant. The portrayal matches, almost point for point, the profile of General Johnston created by Metcalfe— in terms of physical description as well as personal anecdotes about earlier military and civilian life. As Fountain's voice modulates into the historian's, details are provided about Grant's love of animals (*Shiloh* 35), his slovenly appearance (*Shiloh* 47), his lack of physical stature and military reputation (both as a West Point cadet and as a peacetime captain), his sudden mythologizing by the popular press as a result of the success of the Donelson campaign, and, finally, his subsequent political difficulties with his superior, General Halleck. The checkered past of General William Tecumseh Sherman, Grant's chief lieutenant on the field and Fountain's commander, is also sketched. As in the Metcalfe monologue, Foote employs these digressions to outline the Union campaign history and develop the contrasting perspectives of the two armies. Absent from the Union side is the chivalric overlay. Foote presents the Union forces in terms of their own flaws of complacency and inexperience. By withholding Sherman's Cassandra-like predictions about the South until Metcalfe's last section, Foote avoids a deterministic presentation of the conflict and allows the similarities and differences to coexist in a kind of generative ironic web, limited only by the temporal frame. In the flashbacks of these first two chapters, the historian's voice tends to supersede that of the character, gently accenting the tension between historical and immediate perspectives. Paradoxically, by drawing attention to the artifice of the novel's structure, Foote heightens the authenticity of the character's limited experiences.

Foote's creation, through these flashbacks, of a historical substructure for the fictional material extends to the last portrait of a ranking officer in the novel, that of Nathan Bedford Forrest. Introduced in the monologue of cavalry scout Jefferson Polly (chapter 5), Forrest's attributes, like those of his Union counterpart William Tecumseh Sherman (emerging in Metcalfe's last section), become the dominant models of the new warfare. In a fashion reminiscent of his treatment of Johnston and Grant, Foote provides a quick sketch of the seminal events of Forrest's life, details that temper the Forrest legend as an untutored military genius with the more prosaic reality of his role as an accomplished and respected citizen. Foote also provides two examples of Forrest's prose, each an advertisement in the *Memphis Appeal* for recruits to his regiment (one from before, and the other after, the battle), which emphasize the shift from a chivalric posture to a stress on self-reliance and Forrest's new philosophy of war: "I wish none but those who desire to be actively engaged.—Come on, boys, if you want a heap of fun and to kill some Yankees" (*Shiloh* 159). Gone is the pre-Shiloh rhetoric; now, war is about killing rather than principles, as Foote later affirms by appropriating both parts of Forrest's phrase as chapter titles for his treatment of this early part of the war in his history—"War means fighting. . . . And fighting means killing" (*CW* I.349). War retains glamour of a kind, but by having Metcalfe vow to fight Forrest's type of war under the shadow of Sherman's predictions about the South's limited industrial capacities and resources, Foote conveys the future cost and broader cultural implications of this battle for the nation as a whole.

The narrative digressions concerning the characters of the major historical figures thus occupy a central place in the framing sections that surround the main action of the novel. The monologues of the fictional characters give way to a wider historical perspective emphasizing the determinate nature of the past and the historian's overview of the broad cultural sweep of events. The general officers are used as doubles for the fictional witnesses/participants who embody the precepts that characterize differences between North and South. These pillars of the novel's structure (Metcalfe, Fountain, and Polly)—limited observers all, and in this respect historians in embryo—are displaced when the battle is actually joined, in favor of the more straightforward narrative flow and simpler temporal movements in the sections devoted to Dade, Flickner, and the Indiana squad. Foote's purpose, however, has been established: to render the complex interaction of a myriad of forces (past and present, cultural and personal) on the field of Shiloh and, also, to heighten the consciousness of the reader with respect to the necessarily conditional ("artistic") nature of historical truth.

The Armature of the Sculpture:
The Battle of Shiloh as Narrative History

When Foote writes, roughly five years later, the story of the same battle in volume 1 of *The Civil War,* the factual materials, even down to the statements recorded by various leaders, are much the same. The most notable alteration is his reversal of the novel's dominant trope: in *Shiloh,* the deep background provided by Metcalfe on Johnston (or Fountain on Grant, or Polly on Forrest) functions as a supporting substructure of assumptions, attitudes, and intentions that play against the dominants of geography, weather, and time, whereas in *The Civil War* this substructure is reversed into a narrative frame. Foote, then, approaches the question posed by Corporal Blake (How to work from the God's-eye view yet meet the aims of a history written for men?) from the opposite vantage in blocking out his historical narrative. As Foote suggests, "I would not want the reader to be too conscious of it, but there is a foundation, a skeleton that I hope supports like the armature in a piece of sculpture" (*Conversations* 123). By crafting a form that conveys an overview of the conflict yet retains a sense of the limited perspectives of the participants as they move through time (conditioned by their philosophical, political, or personal limitations), Foote creates a historical narrative capable of reproducing the subtleties and ironic nuances found in his fiction.

Commenting on Louis Rubin's observation that in Foote's work individual experience is subordinated to form, Robert L. Phillips offers an insightful suggestion about the implications this approach has for writing history:

> Character and situation work within form, but given the interest that Foote has had in history from the beginning of his writing career, his aesthetic decisions seem appropriate for they give the shape of the work a larger symbolic function. Form focuses the reader's responsive involvement on the shape of a completed action rather than on the unfolding of events. We are offered, in the narrative texture, patterns that the characters miss and by which their failures as human beings can be weighed. . . . It is an aesthetic that works particularly well for history, perhaps better than for fiction. . . . (237)

176

In many respects, the "narrative texture" of *The Civil War* displays considerable similarities to the principal methods evident in the fiction. Examining the Shiloh section of the history one can identify the familiar vortex shape in its architectonics, where the framing sections of the chapter create a deliberate narrowing of focus (the descent) toward the description of the battle itself and then the widening (emergence) from the maelstrom of combat. The process of events through time is reinforced not just through an attention to the verities of nature (day to night, seasonal changes, etc.) but also by Foote's attention to the way the military and political structures move in relation to events. The idea of national development, the maturation of the psyche of a people, through the impact of events, adds a complexity of scope to the history distant from the more contained depictions found in the novels.

As in the fiction, Foote's historical treatment employs the supporting frame to great effect; the "armature" of his narrative sculpture is constructed from the chronology of events and the hierarchy of command. For example, the frame of the Shiloh section of *The Civil War* begins with the command level of the western theater of operations, then dominated by the figure of General Henry Halleck. The narrative starts with this outermost circle, setting the events in the context of Halleck's political machinations after the Donelson campaign, and then moves gradually forward, in ever-tightening rings, toward the field itself. We witness Grant, during the month preceding the battle, fighting a rearguard action with his own commander, as Foote establishes the links between actions on the field and their repercussions in the larger military and political contexts. Neatly developing the relation between the hierarchy of command and the idea of historical process, Foote introduces the Shiloh section with a brief vignette outlining how the impact of a domestic tragedy of President Lincoln's—the death of his son Will—thwarts Halleck's ambitions for command of the West. The next section is devoted to the events of the first week in April and the preparations, or the lack of them, in both military camps. Here, Foote continues the alternation between Union and Confederate perspectives he employed in *Shiloh*.

As the sections progress toward the battle, each covers increasingly shorter time spans while the amount of space devoted to the material gets longer and more detailed—the foreshortened perspective modulates into close-ups of the action. The middle section, by far the most substantial, is devoted to the first day of the battle, Sunday, April 6. By opening the day

with Johnston and closing it with Forrest and Beauregard, Foote acknowledges the dominance of the South in that long first day's fighting—bracketing the Union activity in the narrative structure in much the same fashion as Grant's army was penned into Pittsburg Landing. The treatment
of Monday and Tuesday reflects the shift in initiative to the Union side
brought about by Buell's arrival, and Foote supports this by opening and
closing with the Union commanders, Grant and Sherman. The last section
is the one most completely removed from the immediate present, consisting
as it does of an accounting of the losses on both sides and the impact of
the battle on both Union and Confederate political spheres. The outermost
frame comes full circle with the inclusion of the retrospective comments of
the surviving commanders and also of politicians such as Halleck and
Jefferson Davis. This careful bracketing of events on the field tends to foreground the action of the battle itself and its impact on the participants,
while simultaneously acknowledging the relation of this one event to the
cultural upheaval represented by the Civil War as a whole.

In many small ways, Foote continually reinforces the reader's awareness of the chronology of the events. One technique is his displacement of
the map of Sunday's action until after the narrative recounting of the events
has taken place—the experience unfolds in story form before it can be
charted, or reduced, to the two-dimensional abstraction. Another example
of Foote's adherence to the ostensible present of the action is his delay in
explaining the significance of the name Shiloh ("the place of peace") until
after the first day's conflict, that is, until after the field merits this grim
irony. Foote's respect for the integrity of the immediate present is conveyed
by the stress he places on seemingly inconsequential incidents, such as the
passing of time on Sunday night, when the rhythm of the narrative slows in
response to the suspension of action on the field. Using the placement of
material as a form of commentary, Foote creates an ironic web of juxtapositions and parallels similar to the texture of his fiction. One example is the
description, in his own words, of Grant's initial confidence, which finds a
reprise in Beauregard's similar attitude on Sunday night, the ironic echoes
resonating across the opposing battle lines. Foote's narrative thus "discovers" in the events themselves, in the linear progression of the action, the
material that generates a subtle ironic commentary on the foibles and
accomplishments, the hubris and the pathos, of the participants. For instance, the description of the crippled Grant, riding into the field with a
crutch instead of a carbine, functions as a factual metaphor for the condi-

tion of his surprised army after the initial Confederate assault. Foote's eye for this sort of detail, and its telling placement in the text, is what constitutes the artist's paradoxical reduction and enlargement of our sense of the past. The artistic nature of such use of detail is, as Barbara Tuchman points out, at the heart of the idea of the historian as artist:

> I do not entirely go along with Webster's statement that fiction is distinct from fact, truth, and reality because good fiction . . . even if it has nothing to do with fact, is usually founded on reality and perceives truth—often more truly than some historians. It is exactly this quality of perceiving truth, extracting it from irrelevant surroundings and conveying it to the reader . . . which distinguishes the artist. What the artist has is an extra vision and an inner vision plus the ability to express it. He supplies a view or an understanding that the viewer or reader would not have gained without the aid of the artist's creative vision. (46)

Chronology plays a significant part in Foote's depiction of events in *The Civil War*. Time is an integral character in the drama. While chronological time exists as part of the narrative frame of *Shiloh* and functions as a baseline in the individual monologues, the novel places greater emphasis on the relativity of time in terms of individual experience and memory. The complexity of the structure of the individual monologues, with the exceptions of those—the foot soldiers' (Dade and Flickner)—at the novel's imaginative center, underlines humanity's problematic relation to the broad sweep of history. In *The Civil War* memory and, indeed, futurity are the prerogative of the historian and are used sparingly to establish the simultaneity of disparate events in brief asides or displaced into sections dealing with larger political concerns. Exceptions to this rule are used to convey a sense of the complexity of individual choice and action in relation to the immediate present. One example of the narrator's deliberate violation of chronology is Foote's interjection, into the middle of his depiction of the disarray of the Confederate advance by noon of the first day, of a description of Shiloh as the "first great modern battle" (*CW* I.338). Here, the hindsight of the historian intrudes into the action to provide a context for the battle unavailable to the participants and by doing so guards against the possibility of a charge of incompetence being rashly leveled at Johnston and Beauregard. The generals, after all, could not possibly know that the terms of war had changed. By marking this battle as a major shift in the military reality, Foote forestalls any superficial analytical conclusion that would violate the individual integrity of the participants. Generally, though, Foote's adherence to a chronological presentation is an acknowledgment of the human limitations of the historical figures and tends to work, as does any mature ironic vision, as a distancing and sympathetic device in relation to their successes and their failures. By this means, then, the history extends to the historical generals the same respect as men that Foote extended to the fictional characters in *Shiloh*. Their dominant traits or characteristics emerge as a function of their actions in time rather than being imposed from the beginning—they remain, despite their historical status, authentic characters able to grow, adapt, or dissolve, in accordance with events; figures able to "rear up on their hind legs," as Foote says, "the same way a character does in a novel" (*Conversations* 121).

Whether Foote employs the closed interior monologues of the Faulknerian tradition with the novel *Shiloh*, or trades this form for the discipline of the more conventional historical frame used later in *The Civil War*, his designs reinforce the ultimate mystery Bruce Catton raised about the insoluble riddle of historical trajectories. In each case, Foote develops the capacity of his narrative to support the reciprocal exchange between fiction and history, to assert—again, like Catton—that history and literature are "related art forms that depend on imaginative power and share the common purpose of understanding human motivation and achievement" (Belz 174), and by doing so to highlight the web of ironies inherent in human experience, limited as it is by our existence in time and space. As Phillips suggests: "Foote's fictional world and his vision of history might seem to give the impression that powerful historical forces exercise absolute control over human destiny, but this is not the case. These forces are not rigid laws that impose themselves on human action; they are what make life possible not what denies it" (236). On a number of occasions in interviews, Foote has asserted his conviction about the necessity for the writer to respect the integrity of factual data. Yet, as he also takes care to point out, "a fact is not a truth until you love it" (*Conversations* 248); until, that is, one places the fact within the paradoxically reducing and enlarging framework of art: "Most historians are, I am afraid, so concerned with finding out what happened that they make the enormous mistake of equating facts with truth. No great column of facts can ever pose as the truth. Truth is order imposed on those facts; truth is the breath of life breathed into facts. . . . The truth is the way you feel about it" (*Conversations* 124).

Writing about a historical event, about a battle as widely and closely chronicled as is Shiloh, imposes restrictions upon the breadth of invention possible—or at least the form for that invention. Similarly, since the conclusion of the conflict is generally known, any suspense must be generated by a concern for the individual characters and by an exploration of motivations. History, in this way, relies on the imaginative powers of the writer. As Tuchman suggests in reference to G. M. Trevelyan's definition of a historian as one who combines knowledge of the evidence with "the largest intellect, the warmest human sympathy and the highest imaginative powers": "[these last two elements] are a necessary part of the historian's equipment because they are what enable him to understand the evidence he has accumulated. Imagination stretches the available facts—extrapolates from them, so to speak, thus often supplying an otherwise missing answer to the 'Why' of what happened. Sympathy is essential to the understanding of motive" (47). By casting his frame in such a deliberate manner, accenting the spatial, temporal, and historical limitations, Foote continually reaffirms that the focus of his "humanistic history" (Williams 429) is the nature of the men themselves, as they succumb to, or surmount, the trials of circumstance and the whims of fate. It is a focus that John Keegan, in writing his groundbreaking *The Face of Battle: A Study of Agincourt, Waterloo and the Somme,* deemed absolutely essential to military history:

> . . . there is yet another element which [the historian] must add to everything he writes—an element compounded of affection for the soldiers he knows, a perception of the hostilities as well as the loyalties which animate a society founded on comradeship, some appreciation of the limits of leadership and obedience, a glimpse of the far shores of courage, a recognition of the principle of self-preservation ever present in even the best soldier's nature, incredulity that flesh and blood can stand the fears with which battle will confront it and which his own deeply felt timidity will highlight— if, in short, he can learn to make up his mind about the facts of battle in the light of what all, and not merely some, of the participants felt about their predicament, then he will have taken the first and most important step in understanding battle "as it actually was." (35)

By reaffirming the validity of historical narrative, Foote's work redresses an imbalance noted by Eric Foner in *Politics and Ideology in the Age of the Civil War* (1980) when he comments on the decline of history because of the fragmentation of historical scholarship under the sociological model: "The broadening of historians' concerns went hand in hand with a narrowing of their vision and the result was often specialized, even trivial, inquiries. American society was divided and subdivided so completely that the ideal of re-creating history as a lived experience seemed more remote than ever" (6). It is a point upon which Robert Penn Warren concurs when he suggests, in "The Use of the Past," that "The deepest value of history keeps alive the sense that men have striven, suffered, achieved, and have been base or generous—have, in short, been men" (37).

La Recherche du Temps Perdu: *Foote's Temporal Dialectic*

Commenting on Foote's debt to Proust, Louis Rubin points out that "The implications—more than that, the overtly voiced assumptions—of the French novelist's great work are that human existence in time must of its very nature prove unsatisfactory, since it is only a succession of material experiences lacking permanence and devoid of any meaning beyond that of ephemeral sensation. It is only through art—time regained—that the relationships between our otherwise perishable moments of existence in time can be recognized and joined together into a reality that may endure free of chronology" (*Tournament* n.p). As in Foote's fiction so too in his history; his writing in both genres illustrates how the present is tied to the past, how man's relation to the past is conditioned by his immediate experience, and how our sense of the past as an inaccessible "foreign country" can only be overcome by the agency of a self-conscious narrative art.

Foote's narrative acknowledges that the historian's shaping vision is inevitably conditioned by the present time of its composition and will inevitably be both an enlargement and a reduction. Conveying the limited perspectives of his characters in the immediate present is also an integral part of the texture of *The Civil War*. Foote's approach reflects the tension between the unifying impulse of the narrative in the present and the integrity of the limited perspectives of the characters in the past. White and Sugg call this process a "temporal dialectic" (111), an interplay between events in separate theaters of operation, as well as a reciprocal connection between military action and developments in the political arena. Commenting on an aspect of Proust's work that influenced him, Foote praises "how he moves that story, the whole time. No matter how many digressions there seem to be, that story is moving forward. . . . And it's that way all through Proust. He's nudging the story forward all the time. And that was the thing I had very much in mind while writing *The Civil War:* keep the story moving. Proust does that and he does it superbly. And the paradox is, he's thought to depart from the story so frequently. He never departs from the story" (*Conversations* 254–55). Once again, chronology is the touchstone, the essential armature. The sections and chapters in the history each have a temporal integrity yet contribute to the larger rhythms, the historical vision, and the textual memory, of the narrative. The narrative indicates through its intricate weave of incidents how the war generates its own particular memory and in doing so reshapes both the consciousness of the participants and the vision of the nation as a whole. The internal memory is an ironic counterpart for the textual memory (the one that includes the hundred years that passed since the war's end). The close reading of "Stars in Their Courses," which follows, illustrates, in microcosm, Foote's methods for attaining the narrative drive and the texture of the past that he admires in Proust.[*]

"Whatever lack of nerve or ingenuity had been demonstrated in Mississippi throughout the long hot hungry weeks that Vicksburg had shuddered under assault and languished under siege, there had been no shortage elsewhere in the Confederate States of either of these qualities on which the beleaguered city's hopes were hung" (*CW* II.428). Thus begins Foote's chapter on Gettysburg—often thought to be the most important, certainly the most symbolic, battle of the war. "Indeed," the next sentence continues, "a sort of inverse ratio seemed to obtain between proximity and daring, as if distance not only lent enchantment but also encouraged boldness, so far at least as the western theater was concerned" (*CW* II.428). These introductory sentences are important for a number of reasons. First, Foote achieves an effortless shift from the preceding treatment of the Vicksburg campaign to the simultaneous action in the eastern theater, leaving Vicksburg suspended in "unnatural" silence on the Fourth of July, 1863.

---

[*] Foote published two chapters extracted unaltered from *The Civil War* as separate books. The fifth chapter of volume 2, entitled *Stars in Their Courses: The Gettysburg Campaign, June–July 1863* (1994), and the fourth chapter from the same volume, entitled *The Beleaguered City: The Vicksburg Campaign, December 1862–July 1863* (1995), stand on their own and reflect Foote's consummate attention to structure throughout the work.

The two campaigns are thus separated by space yet joined in time and strategic importance. Second, Foote introduces this reciprocal relationship with an ironic emphasis on the "inverse ratio . . . between proximity and daring"—a motif that forms a subtext for this battle and, more generally, for Foote's sympathetic understanding of human fallibility when man attempts to master "fate." As we have seen before, Foote's conception of the "ordinances of time" informs his use of symmetries, balances, and "unknowable" ratios in the narrative. This web of correspondences supports the moral framework Foote assumes, and the ironic vision with which he questions it, throughout *The Civil War.*

The Gettysburg chapter (drawing on Phillips's discussion of the balanced structure of the entire trilogy) occupies the symbolic "still point" of the narrative—not a climax in the accepted sense of the word, but rather a privileged symbolic position that reflects the verdict of history. It exists both as part of the continuum of events, signaled by the following chapter's account of the retreat back to Virginia, and as a self-contained unit with an integrity and importance all its own. Foote reinforces this idea in a number of ways; one is the ironic echoes on the Fourth of July that the closing lines of the preceding chapter introduced when, from the east, General Joe Johnston notices a "strange thing":

> Today was the Fourth—Independence Day—but the Yankees over toward Vicksburg did not seem to be celebrating it in the usual fashion. On this of all days, the forty-eighth of the siege, the guns were silent for the first time since May 18, when the bluecoats filed into positions from which to launch their first and second assaults before settling down to the digging and bombarding that had gone on ever since; at least till now. Johnston and his men listened attentively, cocking their heads toward the beleaguered city. But there was no rumble of guns at all. Everything was quiet in that direction. (*CW* II.427)

Foregrounding the irony of "Independence Day" as the point of contact, Foote's narrative links these two events (one of which opened up the Mississippi and divided the Confederacy, the other of which effectively signaled the exhaustion of its offensive capabilities).

That the meaning of this silence from Vicksburg is withheld in the narrative until the outcome of Gettysburg is decided allows Foote to retain a focus on the immediate present in each case. We, as readers, await the closure initially denied at the end of chapter 4. Similarly, the dates are carefully chosen to reflect the chronological touchstones. By including the date May 18 (marking the beginning of the siege of Vicksburg) in this final paragraph, Foote introduces a connection to the Confederate strategy meetings that were taking place about that time in Richmond, a transition that provides him with a logical starting point for the forward momentum of decisions and actions culminating in the Battle of Gettysburg. This suspension respects, in a sense, the logic of war, where various grand designs, proffered by the likes of Beauregard, James Longstreet, and Lee, are seen first in all their pristine abstractness, as yet untouched by the vagaries of time and human fallibility. Where such plans exist throughout the narrative, Foote invariably foregrounds them in this fashion and marks the clear distinction between conception and execution.

The Confederate strategy anticipating Gettysburg plays a significant role in framing the depiction of the battle. As at the Battle of Shiloh, and throughout the war, Beauregard provides a mixture of insight and comic relief in his approach to strategy, being always ready with "inventive" (*CW* II.428), if somewhat impractical, solutions. Lee's suggestion carries the day, despite the very clear risks Foote takes pains to outline through the person of Postmaster General John H. Reagan. "In fact," as Foote suggests, reflecting that the weight of Lee's reputation was equal to or greater than that of his strategic argument, "'possible' became probable with Robert E. Lee in charge of an invasion launched as the aftermath of Fredericksburg and Chancellorsville, triumphs scored against the same adversary and against longer odds than he would be likely to encounter when he crossed the Potomac with the reunited Army of Northern Virginia" (*CW* II.431). Cabinet The Confederate cabinet and the public are "awed by his presence, his aura of invincibility" (*CW* II.432). The complexities of the immediate present are thus created out of this sense of textual memory and the presence of the past, just as the sense of fresh possibilities and new beginnings at the start of a campaign bespeaks an unscripted future. Foote balances the vagaries of chance in human affairs, and the stark reality of facts and statistics, by including evidence of man's endless capacity to dream and to believe.

If William Faulkner defined the postbellum southern sensibility in terms of that moment pregnant with possibility before the failure of Pickett's charge at Gettysburg ("For every Southern boy fourteen years old, there is the instant when it's still not yet two oclock on that July afternoon in 1863 . . ." [*Intruder* 194]), what Bernard DeVoto subsequently labeled "the everlasting If," then Foote extends and universalizes this attribute in treating all the participants of the war, each of whom is haunted by unrealized possibilities, each of whom must reconcile the intentions with the execution. In the closing scene of the chapter, Foote's sensitivity to this aspect of the human condition is crystallized in the character of Lee. Speaking to the cavalry officer Imboden, who has waited up until the early hours of the morning after Pickett's charge to meet the general, Lee voices his grief and weariness. Then, Foote suggests, Lee again

> fell silent, but presently he "straightened up to his full height" and spoke "with more animation and excitement" than Imboden had ever seen him display: "I never saw troops behave more magnificently than Pickett's division of Virginians did today in that grand charge upon the enemy. And if they had been supported as they were to have been—but, for some reason not yet fully explained to me, were not—we would have held the position and the day would have been ours." This last was a strange thing for him to say, for he himself had denied Hill permission to throw his whole corps into the assault. However, there was no mistaking the extent of his regret. "Too bad; too bad," he groaned; "Oh, too bad!" (*CW* II.581)

By including Lee in the narrative's pattern of expectation and disappointment, Foote manages to humanize this historically idealized figure (Thomas Connelly's "marble man") and dignify both his failings and his accomplishments relative to the degrees of success or failure found in other commanders.

Foote, having established the campaign as a Confederate initiative, structures the narrative to reinforce this aspect of the action. Despite the fact that Lee's army loses the battle, the Confederate forces take and retain the initiative—from the first encounter on McPherson's Ridge northwest of the village of Gettysburg, right up to Pickett's charge on the third day of combat and Lee's decision to withdraw. Accordingly, each of the sections are outlined, at the start, in "Confederate" time, as Lee and his troops determine events. Flashbacks from this "Confederate" present are used to reflect the generally reactive tenor of Meade's decisions. Consider, for example, Foote's presentation of the action on July 2, the second day of the battle. Here, Lee's activities from about 3:00 A.M. until the beginning of Longstreet's attack on the Union left about 4:00 P.M. are recounted in unbroken sequence (the exception being a brief aside at the beginning to report the gist of his late-night deliberations with Ewell). Just as Hood's division is beginning its advance, the perspective shifts to Meade and a recapitulation of his day, part of which is devoted to explaining the presence, just discovered by Hood, of Sickles's troops blocking their advance along the Emmitsburg Road. This distinction between active and passive in Lee and Meade, fitting for the two commanders, is abandoned once the action is joined—accounts of Confederate movements still precede Union activities, as is appropriate for the attacker, but the quick alteration of perspectives during the action proper carries little of the narrative's earlier implicit characterization of the generals. Instead, following a pattern introduced at the start of the history, Foote waits until the action is suspended that night to highlight the rationale for the narrative structure. Formulating their plans for the next day, he recounts, "the two reacted so literally in accordance with their native predilections—Lee's for daring, Meade's for caution—that afterwards, when their separate decisions were examined down the tunnel of the years . . . both would be condemned for having been extreme in these two different respects" (*CW* II.520–21).

Equal attention is paid to the points of exchange where Foote alters the perspective of the reader from Confederate to Union or vice versa. While providing balance to the narrative, these moments also create opportunities for Foote to introduce his ironic perspective. On the second day, for example, after recounting some of the frustrations of Longstreet's division commanders in getting their troops into position to attack the Union left, he brings the narrative, like the troops, to the point of departure, and then suspends the action when Union forces are discovered where they were not supposed to be.

> Southward the march continued, under cover of McPherson's Ridge, then around its lower end, eastward across Pitzer's Run and through the woods to Seminary Ridge, which here approached the Emmitsburg Road at the point desired. The head of the column—Law's brigade, which by now had spent twelve blistering hours on the march—got there shortly after 3 o'clock. This was not bad time for the distance hiked, but the better part of another hour would be required to mass the two divisions for attack. Worst of all, as Hood's

men filed in on the far right, confronting the rocky loom of Little Round Top, they saw bluecoats clustered thickly in a peach orchard half a mile to the north, just under a mile in advance of the main Federal line on Cemetery Ridge and directly across the road from the position McLaws had been assigned. This came as a considerable surprise. They were not supposed to be there at all, or at any rate their presence was not something that had been covered by Lee's instructions. (*CW* II. 493)

Once again the discrepancy between intent and execution is highlighted, but, more to the point, the section ends and the next begins, ironically, with the Union commander's own ignorance of the position of these troops. "Neither was their presence in the orchard covered by any instructions from their own commander," the opening sentence reads, and then continues: "In fact, at the time Hood's men first spotted them, Meade did not even know they were there, but supposed instead that they were still back on the ridge, in the position he had assigned to them that morning" (*CW* II.493). The following three pages are then devoted to recounting Meade's dispositions and activities over the course of the day, as well as providing the rationale behind Sickles's assumption of the initiative. By recapitulating this Federal activity, Foote concludes the section with the outbreak of gunfire that signals the Confederate attack—now in progress—and thus returns the narrative to its point of departure.

Foote's method of presenting the geographical attributes of the field suggests a continuation of the thematic tension between intention and reality or the discrepancy between the abstract and the concrete. Just as the campaign opens with the strategic considerations—the theoretical rationale for a particular course of action—and then progresses to the reality, so too the unfolding of the battle itself is presented in an increasing intimacy with the dictates of the field. Gettysburg is, initially, just one of a number of towns that figure in Lee's tactical considerations as he awaits news from the errant Jeb Stuart and studies "a large-scale map of western Maryland and southern Pennsylvania which Stonewall Jackson had had prepared that winter" (*CW* II.445). For one of his corps and one of his division commanders (A. P. Hill and Henry Heth, respectively), Gettysburg represents merely the rumor of a "supply of shoes" (*CW* II.465) overlooked by Early's men the week before. As the proximity of the armies increases, Foote takes advantage of the arrivals of key figures on the field to bring the terrain into sharper focus. Consider, for example, Lee's arrival during the first day's fighting along McPherson's Ridge "to see for himself what grounds there might be" (*CW* II.474) for his forebodings of disaster, his troops having been committed to battle in the absence of adequate reconnaissance. First, Foote outlines the present state of the contest, the immediate focal point of any general's attention, and then, as Lee follows the advancing Confederate forces to the rise called Seminary Ridge, the focus shifts to reveal his first impression of the field.

> Ahead of him, down the remaining half mile of the Chambersburg Pike, [the Union soldiers] were retreating pell-mell into the streets of Gettysburg, already jammed with other blue troops pouring down from the north, under pressure from Ewell, as into a funnel whose spout extended south. Those who managed to struggle free of the crush, and thus emerge from the spout, were running hard down two roads that led steeply up a dominant height where guns were emplaced and the foremost of the fugitives were being brought to a halt, apparently for still another stand; Cemetery Hill, it was called because of the graveyard on its lofty plateau, half a mile from the town square. Another half mile to the east, about two miles from where Lee stood, there was a second eminence, Culp's Hill, slightly higher than the first, to which it was connected by a saddle of rocky ground, similarly precipitous and forbidding. These two hills, their summits a hundred feet above the town, which in turn was about half that far below the crest of Seminary Ridge, afforded the enemy a strong position—indeed, a natural fortress—on which to rally his whipped and panicky troops, especially if time was allowed for the steadily increasing number of defenders to improve with their spades the already formidable advantages of terrain. Lee could see for himself, now that he had what amounted to a ringside view of the action, that his victory had been achieved more as the result of tactical good fortune than because of any great preponderance of numbers, which in fact he did not have. (*CW* II.477–78)

Lee's "ringside view" is still, however, incomplete; and Foote provides the next installment of the picture through the view of General Longstreet, who arrives after Lee has already decided to order Ewell's corps to the attack.

Foote's piecemeal presentation of the field, particularly with respect to the differing tactical attitudes of the generals, conveys something of the complexity of the immediate situation and underscores the fact that other possible options existed.

> While Lee explained what had happened so far today, and pointed out the hill aswarm with bluecoats across the valley, Old Peter took out his binoculars and made a careful examination of the front. A broad low ridge, parallel to and roughly three quarters of a mile east of the one on which he stood, extended two miles southward from Cemetery Hill to a pair of conical heights, the nearer of which, called Little Round Top, was some fifty feet taller than the occupied hill to the north, while the farther, called simply Round Top, was more than a hundred feet taller still. (*CW* II.479)

What follows is the famous fishhook analogy—a cliché of Gettysburg lore—for the geography of the battlefield, as Foote completes his survey of the area, modulating from the immediate to the historical. By dividing the presentation of the vista between Lee and Longstreet, he also illustrates how the focus of each reflects his attitude to the campaign as a whole, Lee favoring the aggressive thrust and Longstreet looking at the ground in terms of the "offensive-defensive campaign" he understood the army would pursue.

Foote's description, then, serves a number of purposes: it outlines the significant features of the terrain, and it subtly reflects the irreconcilable differences in the way these two commanders understand the nature of the campaign to be fought—Lee directing his gaze to the enemy's immediate position and possible vulnerability, Longstreet looking for opportunities to fight a defensive action. The text thus reinforces from within that history is not just determined but also rife with possibilities—"roads not taken." Foote, in this way, introduces the paradoxes that elevate the defeat to the level of tragedy. As he says to Walker Percy: "Youre right about it being sad; but only up to a certain point. There's a glory on beyond. There's paradox, as well: no paradox I know can compare with the one that shows Longstreet right, 100%, and Lee wrong, 100%. The poor damned impoverished South couldnt afford a general like Lee; he spilled blood like water. And yet it did afford him, at the cost of bankruptcy, and won glory in the process" (Letters, February 16, 1957). Foote's procedure is consistent throughout the chapter (as it is in the narrative as a whole), introducing new information in relation to the perspectives of different characters, eschewing the tidy introductory overview generally favored among historians.

Subtle variations can also be introduced by including the opposing viewpoint—in this case, confirming Lee's fears. While Lee is undoubtedly the Confederate hero of the piece, "clothed in glory" (*CW* II.433) and an "aura of invincibility" (*CW* II.432), his Union counterpart is General Winfield Scott Hancock, characterized after McClellan's coinage as "Hancock the Superb" (*CW* II.483). Foote sets this chivalric comparison in motion by a pointed matching of the time and manner of Lee and Hancock's arrivals on the field with a comparison of their first impressions—potential victory for the former, possible disaster for the latter. The actions of Hancock, who was dispatched by Meade following the news of Reynolds's death and cavalryman Buford's call for support, are virtually repetitions in miniature of Lee's during the advance.

> So Hancock set out. He rode part of the way in an ambulance, thus availing himself of the chance to study a map of the Gettysburg area, which he had never previously visited though he was born and raised at Norristown, less than a hundred miles away. Coming within earshot of the guns, which swelled to a sudden uproar about 3.30, he shifted to horseback and rode hard toward the sound of firing. At 4 o'clock, the hour that Lee climbed Seminary Ridge to find a Confederate triumph unfolding as his feet, Hancock appeared on Cemetery Hill, a mile southeast across the intervening valley, to view the same scene in reverse. "Wreck, disaster, disorder, almost the panic that precedes disorganization, defeat and retreat were everywhere," a subordinate who arrived with him declared. (*CW* II.482)

Following the preliminaries of acquainting himself with the tactical situation, Hancock glances around, "looking east and south along the fish-hook line of heights from Culp's Hill to the Round Tops" (*CW* ll.483), and decides to make a stand on this strong position. The elements noted in Lee's and Longstreet's perspectives—Culp's Hill and Little Round Top—are now reiterated with the addition of Hancock's assessment of their strategic importance. Our own knowledge of the ground keeps time with the observations and oversights of the participants (Hancock notes, but fails to act on, the necessity for adequate defenses on Little Round Top).

Revelations, such as Hood's surprised discovery of Sickles's men across the Emmitsburg Road or the absence of Union troops occupying the commanding position of Little Round Top (despite Hancock's original intentions), are then presented as they arise, maintaining the integrity of the tactical situations as they unfold. For example, when Confederate Colonel William Oates and his Alabama and Texas troops are sent to clear Union sharpshooters from the slope of Round Top during the second day of fighting, Foote seizes the opportunity to present another overview of the battlefield.

Unlike the lower conical hill immediately to the north, which had been cleared of timber in the fall and thus afforded an excellent all-round view of the countryside, this tallest of all the heights in Adams County—sometimes called Sugarloaf by the natives—was heavily wooded from base to crown, a condition detracting considerably from its tactical usefulness. Through the trees due north, however, just over a hundred feet below and less than half a beeline mile away, Oates could see the barren, craggy dome of Little Round Top, deserted except for a handful of enemy signalmen busily wagging their long-handled flags, while off to the left, on lower ground, smoke boiled furiously out of the rocks where the fight for the Devil's Den was raging at the tip of the left arm of the spraddled v drawn by Sickles, its apex in the Peach Orchard and its right arm extended for the better part of a mile up the Emmitsburg Road, south and west of the main Federal position along the upper end of Cemetery Ridge and on the dominant heights to the north and east, bend and barb of the fishhook Mead had chosen to defend. All this lay before and below the young Alabama colonel, who continued to look it over while his troops were catching their breath on the crest of Round Top. Victory seemed as clear to him, in his mind's eye, as the town of Gettysburg itself, which he could see through the drifting smoke, and the green fields rolling northward out of sight. He believed that with his present force he could hold this hilltop stronghold against the whole Yankee army, if necessary, so steep were the approaches on all sides, and if a battery of rifled guns could somehow be manhandled up here, piece by piece and part by part if need be, not a cranny of Meade's fishhook line would be tenable any longer than it would take a detail of axmen to clear a narrow field of fire. So he believed. (*CW* II.501–2)

Yet Oates is not given the opportunity to test his belief, and this vision of Confederate victory (as well as the descriptive overview of the progress of the battle—including the vortex of the fight for Devil's Den) disappears as he and his troops descend into the melee under orders to occupy Little Round Top. Once more, Foote takes care to move the action of the narrative forward, while also indicating how the participants move through a series of possibilities, choosing one, missing others. This sense of contingency is vital to the narrative's sense of "time regained."

The reader's increasing intimacy with the field at Gettysburg, created as the battle progresses through the cumulative impact of these various perspectives, is most narrowly focused and powerfully conveyed in Foote's portrayal of Pickett's charge. Foote provides first the Union impression of the advance, a mixture of gleeful expectation of revenge for Fredericksburg and an appreciation of the romantic pageantry of the charge: "Beautiful, gloriously beautiful, did that vast array appear in the lovely little valley," one New Yorker recalled (*CW* II.548). Then, stepping briefly back in time, dispensing with the romantic visions of military glory, Foote recounts the effects of the preceding artillery barrages and the trying wait Confederate troops endured as Union artillery shelled their hidden position. Finally, despite the obvious dangers, illustrated by the voiced reservations of such officers as Longstreet and Alexander, comes the order to advance. Having built the suspense to a fever pitch (not with respect to surprise, but instead by accenting the sense of grim inevitability), Foote opens the section depicting the charge from the soldier's perspective, and the dominant image is that of a revelation:

> By now—some twenty or thirty minutes after the Union guns stopped firing, and consequently about half that long since Alexander [the Confederate artillery commander] followed suit—much of the smoke had been diffused or had drifted off, so that for the attackers, many of whom had stepped at a stride from the dense shade of their wooded assembly areas into the brilliant sunlight that dappled the floor of the valley, the result was not only dazzling to their eyes but also added to their feeling of elation and release. "Before us lay bright fields and fair landscape," one among them would recall.
>
> It was not until the effect of this began to wear off, coincidental with the contraction of their pupils, that they saw at last the enormity of what was being required of them, and by then, although

the vista afforded absolute confirmation of their direst apprehensions, the pattern of exhilaration had been set. (*CW* II.552–53)

In ironic counterpoint to the impressions of the men caught, as one colonel described it, in "a wild kaleidoscopic whirl" (*CW* II.559), Foote sets the detached, if bitter, view of Longstreet himself, "perched atop [a] snake rail fence, observing through his binoculars the action on the ridge" (*CW* II.558).

> In point of fact, though Old Peter kept his binoculars trained on the flame-stabbed turmoil halfway up the enemy ridge, he watched the fighting not so much in suspense as to the outcome—for that had been settled already, at least to his own disgruntled satisfaction—as to study the manner in which it came about. Convinced that the attack had failed, even before the first signs of retreat were evident, he was mainly interested in seeing how many of his soldiers would survive it.
>
> But they themselves had no such detached view of the holocaust in which they were involved. (*CW* II.559)

This tension between immediacy and detachment is consistent throughout Foote's treatment; it is literally the situation of the participants but also comments on the roles of the historian and the reader. He employs this play on perspectives for ironic ends; it also militates against too easy and reductive readings of the complexity of the events in which the men were immersed. The technique finds its apotheosis in the Gettysburg campaign with Lee's retrospective remarks in the concluding paragraphs, as he recalls the charge of Pickett's men and the lost opportunity it represents. The tableau recognizes, by implication, the subsequent revisionist history linked to the idealization of Lee and the "Lost Cause," but here the narrative's focus remains on the man lost under the weight of the myth, the very human Lee of mistakes, regrets and, perhaps, self-deception. The strength of Foote's narrative rests on his exploration of such ironies and paradoxes, whether tied to gaps between conception and execution, or perception and reflection.

Commenting on Foote's history in *Twentieth-Century American Historians,* Clyde N. Wilson remarks:

> Foote's history is, as its subtitle implies, first and foremost a narrative, and chiefly a military narrative. . . . As a narrative, its virtues

are many. Perhaps no work has ever given a more justly proportional treatment to the different theatres of the war. . . . As storytelling, it reflects great artistry. It is possible to argue that no accounts of the great battles have ever equaled Foote's in their portrayal of relevant events and in their balance between the viewpoint and experiences of commanders and common soldiers. Another virtue is the writer's way of carrying the reader with him to well-known events, such as the Battle of Gettysburg. The reader does not so much think to himself that he is going to read about a battle as he is gradually, with a sense of surprise, swept into the event, just as the participants must have been. In no other modern military history is the reader so unconscious of the technique of presentation. (155)

Wilson's last sentence is perhaps the highest praise that can be offered to the storyteller—that the evidence of his craft, what Foote likens to the "armature in a piece of sculpture" (*Conversations* 123), is felt rather than intellectually perceived. Yet the marks of Foote's attention to "deep structure" (Cox 197) and narrative details abound throughout the text: an artistry that, like Proust's, works to continually move the story forward, "whether it's the telling of a little incident or the drawing of character or looking at life as to what it's all about, or . . . the nature of memory" (*Conversations* 254) or, as Foote suggests in summary, "the handling of a large-scale thing" (*Conversations* 254). With respect to the narrative's reflection of "the war as Foote envisions it," James M. Cox remarks: "He sees the whole cumulative force of the war as pushing forward; thus, the retroactive moves he perforce has to make in order to bring his war forward in all theaters of action are necessarily at variance with his deepest recognition of the war's forward thrust. Although there might be retreats on any given field, both sides went relentlessly forward not so much toward each other—though there were furious encounters of opposing forces—as in the powerful direction the war took, a direction beyond the management or even victory of either side" (197). Foote's search for the *temps perdu* of the Civil War finds its answer in the artistry of his narrative; for as Robert Penn Warren reminds us, the most obvious answer to the question "What does the study of the past offer?" is "so obvious that it is rarely given . . . that the past gives us a sense of time" (49). And, Warren continues, "in a primal way, in a gut way, the study of the past gives one a feeling for the structure of experience, for continuity, for establishing location on the shifting chart of being" (50). I would suggest

Foote's narrative, with its awareness of the paradoxes of time regained, with its generative ironic web, its deep structure, and its complex artistic texture, fulfills both Proust's and Warren's criteria.

"The Poetry of War":
Ironic Fraternities and Presidential Dialogue

Foote's presentation of the parallel development of Jefferson Davis and Abraham Lincoln—their lives provide the framework for the narrative as a whole—conveys many of the paradoxes and ironies inherent in his vision. This is especially true of his employment of their public statements ("reminiscent," James M. Cox suggests, "of the crafted speeches in Thucydides' history of the Peloponnesian War" [210]—with the caveat that Foote reproduces rather than writes them). This indirect, long-range debate involves the central issue of the conflict: is the Constitution organic in nature or static; does one support 1) the constructionist adherence to the law as embodied in the Constitution, or 2) the ability of that law, under the pressure of a moral imperative, to undergo change? Through the dialogue of the presidents, Foote creates an embodiment of the two unresolved aspects of the American psyche: Davis, the political idealist and "strict constructionist" (*CW* I.7), who stands on constitutional principle, and Lincoln, the political pragmatist, whose actions are shaped by a moral vision. The former is determined to preserve the constitutional status quo—paradoxically by beginning the nation anew. The latter is equally determined to shape the founding vision to his ends: first union and later emancipation. The dialectic between the words of these two characters, an exchange that participates in the ironic cast of the whole narrative, provides a background in political philosophy to the immediate action of the war.

Davis and Lincoln are one means whereby Foote conveys his sense of the manifold paradoxes that emerge from his contemplation of the past. Foremost among these is, perhaps, the evolution of the men themselves over the duration of the conflict: the narrative begins with a depiction of their quite different backgrounds and political positions; the story ends with both, by then martyrs to their respective causes, being translated out of the realm of fact and absorbed into the myth of modern America. After devoting the opening section of chapter 1 to a delineation of each man's character (through a presentation of his personal history up to the onset of the war), Foote then moves to suggest how each came to be understood in the popular consciousness. Both become "champions," caricatures, fictions, created by the polarized sentiments about what one side called a "revolution" and the other insisted was a "rebellion." Characteristically, Foote suspends the debate without resolution and asserts instead that "Whatever it [the conflict] was, it was plainly a fact" (*CW* I.163). The realities of the two leaders are similarly difficult to assert; instead, each becomes a "condition of the tournament," another "fact" that may or may not eventually find a satisfactory label.

> Between these two extremes, while the anti-Davis and anti-Lincoln cliques were respectively consolidating their opposition and sharpening their barbs, the mass of men who would do the actual fighting, and the women who would wait for them at home, took what came with a general determination to measure up to what was expected of them. It was their good fortune, or else their misery, to belong to a generation in which every individual would be given a chance to discover and expose his worth, down to the final ounce of strength and nerve. For the most part, therefore, despite the clamor of extremists north and south of the new frontier, each side accepted its leader as a condition of the tournament, and counted itself fortunate to have the man it had and not the other. Seen from opposite banks of the Ohio and the Potomac, both seemed creatures fit for frightening children into quick obedience. On the one hand there was Davis, "ambitious as Lucifer," with his baleful eyes and bloodless mouth, cerebral and lizard-cold, plotting malevolence into the small hours of the night. On the other there was Lincoln, "the original gorilla," with his shambling walk and sooty face, an ignorant rail-splitter catapulted by the long-shot politics into an office for which he had neither the experience nor the dignity required. (*CW* I.164)

Foote's procedure, given the unresolvable nature of such questions, is a relative one. He gauges each man by his opposite and not by some absolute scale. The relationship of the two presidents is an intricate web of connections and disconnections—antitheses that help generate a balanced and complex ironic perspective.

What they seemed to each other was another matter. Lincoln had recognized his adversary's renowned capabilities from the start, but it was not until well after Sumter—if then—that Davis, like so many of the northern President's own associates, including even his Secretary of State, began to understand that he was having to deal with an opponent not below but beyond the run of men. Their official attitude toward one another gave a certain advantage to the Southerner, since he could arraign his rival before the bar of world opinion, addressing him as a tyrant and "exposing" his duplicity; whereas Lincoln, by refusing to admit that there was any such thing as the Confederate States of America, was obliged to pretend that Davis, too, was nonexistent. However, it was a knife that cut both ways. Lincoln was not only denied the chance to answer charges, he was also relieved of the necessity for replying to a man who wasn't there. Nor was that all. Constitutionally, the Illinois lawyer-politician was better equipped for accepting vilification than the Mississippi planter-statesman was for accepting what amounted to a cut; so that, in their personal duel, the advantages of a cloak of invisibility were canceled, at least in part, by the reaction of the man who had to wear it. Davis wore it, in fact, like an involuntary hair shirt. (*CW* I.164)

In personal terms, Foote sees the contest as psychological, a battle with the self in its ultimate isolation. In social terms, the contest is presented in terms of Foote's sense of the changing conception of honor and morality (from the chivalric code to something closer to an individual response to existential angst, something akin to the Hemingway code).

The two figures reverse roles over the course of the narrative. Davis begins as the consummate southern gentleman, polished in manner, handsome in demeanor, cultivated, well educated, socially privileged, decorated as a war hero and articulate in the formal rhetoric of the day. His advocacy of states' rights as a sacred trust is presented with all the righteous vigor a "strict constructionist" (*CW* I.7) can muster. Lincoln, on the other hand, is notably lacking in the social polish or political accomplishment of his opponent, has little in the way of conventional good looks, and appears to hold expedient rather than principled positions with respect to the issues. Foote stresses, however, Lincoln's ability to adapt to the nature of the times—and to reflect these developments in uniquely "American" speech. Ideologically distant at the beginning of the story and physically separated throughout the war, Davis and Lincoln in Foote's narrative are, paradoxically, placed in direct and intimate relation to each other, and seem to effect a transference of traits over time. In the epilogue, the two presidents appear together—both embraced as important figures in the heritage of the modern nation. They become, in a sense, complementary aspects of a whole—a completeness that is directly tied to the artistry of Foote's narrative.

Anaximander's "ordinance of time" combines the law of temporal progression with a sense of moral purpose, a conception of justice existing above and beyond the workings of humanity. Foote's aesthetic representation of this totality informs his depiction of Davis and Lincoln—two figures presented as adherents to specific conceptions of the law, who each evolve, paradoxically, in direct relation to the chief characteristic of the opponent. In Davis's case, he begins as a stalwart supporter of the law as it is defined and limited by the Constitution. Over the course of Foote's narrative, under the press of circumstance, Davis undergoes a sea change with respect to this conception—altering his view from that of a "strict constructionist" (*CW* I.7), albeit unwillingly for the most part, to that of a political pragmatist, embracing, finally, a vision of America's future as "a consummation devoutly to be wished—a reunited country" (*CW* III.1058). From strict adherence to the letter of man-made law, Davis, given the last words of the narrative, moves toward something far less legalistic: "'Tell them—' He paused as if to sort the words. 'Tell the world that I only loved America'" (*CW* III.1060). Introduced as the advocate of a "superior morality" (*CW* II.15)—the tradition of honor and an adherence to the "system of government which our forefathers founded" (*CW* II.104), a government that "rests upon the consent of the governed" (*CW* I.65)—Davis stands, throughout most of the narrative, as the chief adherent of the law as defined and drafted by men. Foote makes the limitations of this constructionist position increasingly apparent—with a corresponding heightening of the ironies involved—as circumstances foist upon Davis the necessity to compromise his vision. Principle and application, in close proximity at the beginning of the Confederacy, are increasingly distant at the end. The situation leads finally to Davis's admission, when near the close of the war the arming of slaves is seriously considered, that necessity has overridden the principle of states' rights, and that "If the Confederacy falls . . . there should be written on its tombstone, Died of a Theory" (*CW* III.766). Davis becomes what Lincoln was said to be at the beginning: a political pragmatist whose principles must yield to the doctrine of necessity. Unlike the portrait of limitation and failure found in Allen Tate's *Jefferson Davis: His Rise and Fall*—a book Foote's work both acknowledges (in beginning as it does) and rejects (his view of Davis is far more sympathetic)—the vision in *The Civil War*, conditioned by the ordinances of time, enables Foote to incorporate the fact of Davis's transformation (and the reasons for it).

Foote's Lincoln, on the other hand, evolves in the opposite direction and with reference to his own definition of a higher morality—a law more attuned to principles outside and surpassing those enshrined in the Constitution. Lincoln, in a reverse progression from that of Davis, is presented initially as a political animal, a pragmatist whose positions, if not his principles, are continually adjusted in relation to present circumstances. Unlike his fairly constant representation of Davis's position, and the conventional rhetoric in which it is couched (terms that alter very little until the last sections of the narrative), Foote's treatment of Lincoln is as a complex character, attuned to the exigencies of the political arena. Lincoln's vision, his adherence to what he calls, early on in response to Stephen Douglas's Kansas-Nebraska Bill, his "ancient faith" that "all men are created equal" (*CW* I.27), is increasingly definitive and unyielding. If Davis lives in accordance to human law, then Lincoln, in Foote's narrative, is more closely aligned with what Walter Sullivan identifies in Foote's work as a as a "philosophical foundation" or "system older and better-established than any Southern code" (379). It was, Foote maintains, Lincoln's "particular talent" in his "long-range contest with Davis" to shift "the argument onto a higher plane" (*CW* I.805). Beginning with the law—time-bound and constitutional—Lincoln gradually redefines his position in relation to moral law, ordinances more clearly related to Anaximander's universal interplay of injustice and justice. Whereas Davis is forced, late in the war, to reconcile his principles with the demands of circumstance, Lincoln accepts this necessity at the outset.

> Loving the Union with what amounted in his own mind to a religious mysticism, he had overrated that feeling in the South; Sumter had cost him more than he had been prepared to pay for uniting the North. Through these months his main concern had been to avoid offending any faction—"My policy is to have no policy," he told his secretary—with the result that he offended all. Yet this was behind

him now; Sumter at least had gained him that, and this perhaps was the greatest gain of all. He was free to evolve and follow a policy at last.

Unlike Davis, in doing this he not only did not find a course of action already laid out for him, with his only task being one of giving it the eloquence of words and the dignity of a firm example; he could not even follow a logical development of his own beliefs as he had announced them in the past, but must in fact reverse himself on certain tenets which he had expressed in words that returned to plague him now and in the years to come. . . . He must raze before he could build, and this he was willing to do. (*CW* I.66–67)

The style with which these ideas are expressed is Foote's way of marking Lincoln's evolution. Against the single note of states' rights repeated through most of Davis's addresses, Foote sets Lincoln's "music," his evolving mastery of language as "a craftsman in the use of words" (*CW* I.806) and, through this art, his ability to transcend time.

In stylistic terms, Davis's rhetorical progression in Foote's narrative begins with the cultivated speech of an accomplished orator of his day, evident in the first pages when he rises to resign from the Senate: "We but tread in the paths of our fathers when we proclaim our independence and take the hazard . . . not in hostility to others, not to injure any section of the country, not even for our own pecuniary benefit, but from the high and solemn motive of defending and protecting the rights we inherited, and which it is our duty to transmit unshorn to our children. . . . [W]e will invoke the God of our fathers, who delivered them from the power of the lion [England], to protect us from the ravages of the bear [the Union]; and thus, putting our trust in God and in our own firm hearts and strong arms, we will vindicate the right as best we may" (*CW* I.5). Throughout the narrative, while his vehemence and bitterness may become more pronounced, the addresses retain their studied and formal character as they uphold the standard of states' rights. His last speech, however, spoken by a man just short of eighty addressing a gathering of young southerners, reflects an ardor tempered by time and experience and sounds a different note:

"Friends and fellow citizens," he began, and stopped. "Ah, pardon me," he said, "The laws of the United States no longer permit me to designate you as fellow citizens. I feel no regret that I stand before you a man without a country, for my ambition lies buried in the grave of the Confederacy." Then he went on to tell them what he had come to say. "The faces I see before me are those of young men; had I not known this I would not have appeared before you. Men in whose hands the destinies of our Southland lie, for love of her I break my silence to speak to you a few words of respectful admonition. The past is dead; let it bury its dead, its hopes and its aspirations. Before you lies the future, a future full of golden promise, a future of expanding national glory, before which all the world shall stand amazed. Let me beseech you to lay aside all rancor, all bitter sectional feeling, and to take your places in the ranks of those who will bring about a consummation devoutly to be wished—a reunited country." (*CW* III.1058)

This new simplicity of style marks a change reinforced by Foote when he assigns to Davis the final words of the narrative. Davis has come full circle, ending on the same note as Lincoln; and the heartfelt directness of the words, elevated past cliché by the reader's consciousness of what they cost, draws the two presidents—by this point, ghostly voices—together: "Tell the world that I only loved America."

In a complementary progression, Lincoln evolves from simplicity to eloquence. Where Davis's message and style seem accomplished but static until his final lines, Lincoln develops both his political vision and the manner of its expression. Where Davis struggles to reconcile his principles with the practical demands on his government as a result of the war, a process of accommodation that compromises both dimensions of his being, Lincoln develops from a political pragmatist into a moral philosopher. The two extremes of this alteration provide a counterpoint to Davis's; they form the moral framework for Foote's narrative and can be illustrated by two examples. The first is Foote's reproduction, in full, of the poignant simplicity of Lincoln's first stump speech in 1832, begun after a brief delay while he stepped down from the dais to break up a fight in the crowd.

"Gentlemen and fellow citizens," he said, "I presume you all know who I am: I am humble Abraham Lincoln. I have been solicited by many friends to become a candidate for the legislature. My politics are short and sweet, like the old woman's dance. I am in favor of a national bank. I am in favor of the internal-improvements system and a high protective tariff. These are my sentiments and political principles. If elected, I shall be thankful; if not, it will be all the same." (*CW* I.23)

Compare this with Foote's description of Lincoln's second inaugural address, begun after a sort of celestial benediction when he stepped forward and "sun broke through and flooded the platform with its golden light" (*CW* III.812). I quote this in full to reflect the evangelical and prophetic atmosphere of the speech as Foote re-creates it.

There was, as he maintained, "less occasion for an extended address" than had been the case four years ago, when his concern had been to avoid the war that began soon afterward. Nor would he much concern himself just now with purely military matters or venture a prediction as to the outcome, though his hope was high in that regard. "Both parties deprecated war; but one of them would make war rather than let the nation survive, and the other would accept war rather than let it perish. And the war came. . . . Neither party expected for the war the magnitude or the duration which it has already attained. Neither anticipated that the cause of the conflict might cease with, or even before, the conflict itself should cease. Each looked for an easier triumph, and a result less fundamental and astounding. Both read the same Bible and pray to the same God, and each invokes His aid against the other. It may seem strange that any men should dare to ask a just God's assistance in wringing their bread from the sweat of other men's faces; but let us judge not, that we be not judged. The prayers of both could not be answered; that of neither has been answered fully. The Almighty has His own purposes. 'Woe unto the world because of offenses! for it must needs be that offenses come; but woe to that man by whom the offense cometh!'"

"Bless the Lord!" some down front cried up: Negroes mostly, who took their tone from his, and responded as they would have done in church. Lincoln kept on reading from the printed text in a voice one hearer described as "ringing and somewhat shrill."

"If we shall suppose that American slavery is one of those offenses which, in the providence of God, must needs come, but which, having continued through His appointed time, He now wills to remove, and that he gives to both North and South this terrible war, as the woe due to those by whom the offense came, shall we discern therein any departure from those divine attributes which the believers in a living God always ascribe to Him? Fondly do we hope—fervently do we pray—that this mighty scourge of war may speedily pass away. Yet, if God wills that it continue until all the wealth piled by the bondman's two hundred and fifty years of unrequited toil shall be sunk, and until every drop of blood drawn from the lash shall be paid by another drawn with the sword, as was said three thousand years ago, so still it must be said: 'The judgments of the Lord are true and righteous altogether.'"

"Bless the Lord!" came up again through the thunder of applause, but Lincoln passed at once to the peroration. He was beyond the war now, into the peace which he himself would never live to see.

"With malice toward none; with charity for all; with firmness in the right, as God gives us to see the right, let us strive on to finish the work we are in; to bind up the nation's wounds; to care for him who shall have borne the battle, and for his widow, and his orphan—to do all which may achieve and cherish a just and a lasting peace, among ourselves and with all nations."

Thus ended, as if on a long-held organ note, the shortest inaugural any President had delivered since George Washington was sworn in the second time. (*CW* III.812–14)

Lincoln's progression is, in the reciprocal terms established by Foote's charting of his long-range dialogue with Davis, the reverse of the southern president's. Davis, at the beginning of the narrative, on the day before Lincoln's election, strikes "an organ tone that brought a storm of applause in his home state." It is a tone that swells quickly into a chivalric battle cry: "'I glory in Mississippi's star!' . . . 'But before I would see it dishonored I would tear it from its place, to be set on the perilous ridge of battle as a sign around which her bravest and best shall meet the harvest home of death'" (*CW* I.4). Having registered the intensity of southern feeling in this manner, Foote finds an answering and profounder reverberation in the vision put forward in Lincoln's speech; what begins as "a question of necessity—meaning Honor" (*CW* I.4) for Davis at the outset is translated over the course of the war, by Lincoln himself, into a mystical vision of redemption necessity of a higher order.

Davis's more limited chivalric code of honor is subsumed under Lincoln's own doctrine of necessity (*CW* I.710), which crystallizes in his mind at the time of the Emancipation Proclamation. The publication of the proclamation after Antietam marks the end of a long string of reverses, a period reflecting, so to speak, Lincoln's and the nation's dark night of the soul. His triumph, though, in Foote's eyes, is his "particular talent . . . [to shift] the argument onto a higher plane," a plane that renders impotent Davis's more limited doctrines of Honor and states' rights. In a way, Lincoln emerges in Foote's treatment as an embodiment of humanity's paradoxical position in relation to events, as possessor of a complexity of vision surpassing Davis's, despite the obvious virtues and integrity of Davis as a man. This awareness is marked near the end of volume 1 when Foote highlights Lincoln's role as a "literary craftsman" and, through the words of a White House visitor, suggests the nature of that genius: "Remarking 'the two-fold working of the two-fold nature of the man,' one caller at least had observed the contrast between 'Lincoln the Westerner, slightly humorous but thoroughly practical and sagacious,' and 'Lincoln the President and statesman . . . seen in those abstract and serious eyes, which seemed withdrawn to an inner sanctuary of thought, sitting in judgment on the scene and feeling its far reach into the future'" (*CW* I.804). Finally, the ever more prescient Lincoln provides a stark contrast to Davis, with his increasingly limited constructionist view. Foote makes this point when presenting Davis's morale-building speech in Montgomery, Alabama, after the fall of Atlanta, and then following it with a wry comment on this optimism. "There may be some men," Davis says, "who when they look at the sun can only see a speck upon it. I am of a more sanguine temperament perhaps, but I have striven to behold our affairs with a cool and candid temperance of heart, and, applying to them the most rigid test, am more confident the longer I behold the progress of the war. . . . We should marvel and thank God for the great achievements which have crowned our efforts" (*CW* III.608). By rejecting General Richard Taylor's gloomier prognostications, Foote remarks, Davis "refused to be daunted; like Nelson off Copenhagen, putting the telescope to his blind eye, he declined to see these specks upon the Confederate sun" (*CW* III.608). This mention, for symbolic purposes, of Davis's real physical infirmity—the only one of its kind in the narra-tive—underscores Foote's final sense of Davis's limitations in the long-range dialogue of the two leaders.

Lincoln, with his consciousness of the paradoxes of history, is aligned more closely with the vision of Foote's narrative as a whole. By recounting the president's December 1862 message to Congress in the concluding paragraph of volume 1, Foote establishes this connection with respect to Lincoln's broader vision. "We cannot escape history," the president re-marks. "We of this Congress and this Administration will be remembered in spite of ourselves. No personal significance or insignificance can spare one or another of us. The fiery trial through which we pass will light us down, in honor or dishonor, to the latest generation" (*CW* I.810). That the next volume of *The Civil War* introduces as an epigraph for the whole the quotation from Ecclesiasticus XLIV beginning, "All these were honoured in their generation . . ." reinforces this connection. The speech continues by presenting, in the form of a somewhat paradoxical expression, Lincoln's elevation of the contest to a higher plane: "We—even we here—hold the power and bear the responsibility. In giving freedom to the slave, we assure freedom to the free—honorable alike in what we give and what we pre-serve. We shall nobly save or meanly lose the last, best hope of earth. Other means may succeed; this could not fail. The way is plain, peaceful, generous, just—a way which, if followed, the world will forever applaud, and God must forever bless" (*CW* I.810).

Indeed, the paradoxes of human action in relation to the process of his-tory form a central theme of the narrative as a whole. The war begins with the paradox of the irreconcilable definitions of necessity and, by the end of volume 1, becomes a war for survival on equally paradoxical grounds. As Foote observes, commenting on the dedicatory nature of Lincoln's Decem-ber 1862 address:

> In issuing the Preliminary Emancipation Proclamation he had made certain there would be no peace except by conquest. He had weighed the odds and made his choice, foreseeing the South's reaction. "A restitution of the Union has been rendered forever impossible," Davis said. Lincoln had known he would say it; the fact was, he had been saying it all along. What he meant, and what Lincoln knew he meant, was that the issue was one which could only be settled by arms, and that the war was therefore a war for survival—survival of

the South, as Davis saw it: survival of the Union, as Lincoln saw it—with the added paradox that, while neither of the two leaders believed victory for his side meant extinction for the other, each insisted that the reverse was true. (*CW* I.805)

Indeed, by crafting a narrative structure that respects the integrity of each opposing perspective, allowing the paradoxes to stand, as it were, for each man's limitations amid the flow of events, Foote creates a powerful vehicle for the presentation of his ironic, humanist vision.

The second volume of *The Civil War* continues to develop this ironic perspective with respect to Davis's undoing. As the volume opens, Davis is on his first morale-boosting tour of the West, excoriating the northern government in a series of speeches and defending the central tenet of the southern cause, that of the "right to govern on the consent of the governed" (*CW* II.13). Following, as it does, Lincoln's eloquent defense of the principle of freedom at the end of volume 1, Davis's words take on a decidedly ironic cast: "The issue before us is one of no ordinary character. We are not engaged in a conflict for conquest, or for aggrandizement, or for the settlement of a point of international law. The question for you to decide is, Will you be slaves or will you be independent? Will you transmit to your children the freedom and equality which your fathers transmitted to you, or will you bow down in adoration before an idol baser than ever was worshiped by Eastern idolaters?" (*CW* II.14). It is telling, too, that Foote stresses at this point a theme that characterizes Davis's speeches until the end of the war—that "The question is only one of time" (*CW* II.15). Foote underscores Davis's more limited vision of time by establishing a counterpoint in Lincoln's association with what amount to statements of universal verities, a position reinforced when he rises to deliver the Gettysburg Address, with its avowal of a national vision "dedicated to the proposition that all men are created equal" and its call for "a new birth of freedom" (*CW* II.831–32). That the volume closes with Davis fighting a rearguard action against his fellow Confederates who would stand on the principle of states' rights at the expense of the war effort accentuates the increasingly untenable paradoxes of the southern position and Davis's more limited political vision.

As Foote suggests: "That was perhaps the greatest paradox of all: that the Confederacy, in launching a revolution against change, should experience under the pressure of the war which then ensued an even greater transformation, at any rate of the manner in which its citizens pursued their daily rounds, than did the nation it accused of trying to foist upon it an unwanted metamorphosis, not only of its cherished institutions, but also of its very way of life" (*CW* II.158). Where Davis is more and more dedicated to "harmonizing discord" (*CW* II.822) and is drawn from principle into politics, Lincoln's vision seems to rise above the political and temporal fray. In presenting the year-end addresses of both men at the close of volume 2 (and at the end of 1863), Foote contrasts Davis's growing reliance on past successes and old allegiances with Lincoln's focus on the theme of "reconciliation and suggestions for coping with certain edgy problems that would loom when bloodshed ended" (*CW* II.880). When Davis is forced to suspend habeas corpus throughout the South, losing the political high ground upon which his rhetoric is based, Foote notes the paradoxical implosion of the Confederate position—a constitutional war is now to be fought by the sacrifice of constitutional rights.

> [The war] was also, and first, a war for survival; but the ultraconservatives, including the fire-eaters who had done so much to bring it on, had been using the weapon of States Rights too long and with too much success, when they were members of the Union, to discard it now that they had seceded. They simply would rather die than drop that cudgel, even when there was no one to use it on but their own people and nothing to strike at except the solidarity that was their one hope for victory over an adversary whose reserves of men and wealth were practically limitless. It was in this inflexibility that the bill came due for having launched a conservative revolution, and apparently it was necessarily so, even though their anomalous devotion to an untimely creed amounted to an irresistible death-wish. But that was precisely their pride. They had inherited it and they would hand it down, inviolate, to the latest generation; or they would pray God "to sweep from the earth the soil, along with the people." (*CW* II.951)

When Davis must advocate a more pragmatic, Realpolitik approach to continuing the war effort, it is, as Foote so elegantly demonstrates, his misfortune to be undone by the very constructionist attitude that engendered his commitment to the cause at the outset.

At the beginning of the last volume, Davis and Lincoln are cast—the former seemingly unwittingly, the latter seemingly consciously as hostages of fortune. After yet one more lesson (the quick unraveling of Grant's grand strategy) about how "[i]n war, as in love—indeed, as in all such areas of so-called human endeavor—expectation tended to outrun execution" (*CW* II.757), Lincoln makes his wry admission that "I claim not to have controlled events, but confess plainly that events have controlled me" (*CW* III.138). Davis, meanwhile, is presented as a beleaguered leader, isolated amid the forced gaiety of "this fourth and liveliest of [Richmond's] wartime springs" (*CW* III.126); a scene of "parties and pleasurings" colored, in the recollections of a Richmond belle, by a sense of "foreshadowing, as in the Greek plays where the gloomy end is ever kept in sight" (*CW* III.126). Foote, it seems, concurs, when he casts Davis's foremost critic, the tenacious Edward A. Pollard, associate editor of the *Richmond Examiner,* as Thersites (*CW* III.95). Clearly, the fates are gathering around the shrinking borders of the Confederacy, and Davis is left with the small comfort of yet another paradox: "the tactical hope resulted from past Confederate defeats. Davis saw in every loss of territory—Nashville and Middle Tennessee, New Orleans, even Vicksburg and the Mississippi and the amputation of all that lay beyond—a corresponding gain, not only because what had been lost no longer required a dispersal of the country's limited strength for its protection, but also because the resultant contraction allowed a more compact defense of what remained" (*CW* III.102). Ironically, his hopes now rest on democratic exercise, the presidential election in the North. Increasingly, the gap between Davis's public statements about the southern defense of their "indefeasible rights" (*CW* III.624) is at odds with his own practice of curtailing those rights—the suspension of habeas corpus, the extension of conscription, the centralization of government power.

This ongoing presentation of Davis and Lincoln and their reversal of roles culminates in Foote's depiction of the Confederate president's cunning subversion of the peace initiatives of the Impossibilists. The episode conjures up distinct echoes of Lincoln's own victory over the Republican radicals around the time of the signing of the Emancipation Proclamation, when he outmaneuvered an attempt, fomented by Salmon Chase, to oust Secretary of State Seward from the cabinet (*CW* II.110–16). Where previously it was Lincoln who appeared Machiavellian in his adroit political maneuvers, and Davis who stood on principles of duty and loyalty, now Davis assumes the role of the "foxy, secretive and shifty" politician (*CW* III.772). Having determined that the necessity for resistance outweighs all theories and abstract political principles, Davis moves ruthlessly to discredit his opponents. As

Foote observes, employing imagery reminiscent of the parables of Aesop: "Each of the two Presidents thus had much to fret him while playing their game of high stakes international poker, and they functioned in different styles: different not only from each other, but also different each from what he had been before. During this diplomatic interlude, Lincoln and Davis— fox and hedgehog—swapped roles" (*CW* III.772). Lincoln becomes increasingly tied to the necessity for a complete victory to ensure the gains made by the Thirteenth Amendment, and absolutist in his position of support for this higher moral law; Davis, on the other hand, is learning, perhaps belatedly, the advantages of Realpolitik. The complementary nature of this reversal, with all its paradoxical resonances of accommodation and resolution in terms of man's relation to events, provides a strong subtext for Foote's pursuit of the same interplay with respect to the actions of men on the field of battle.

The opposing portraits of Davis and Lincoln at the start of the narrative serve as "Foote's prologue to the conflict . . . [and] equip him both narratively and thematically for his task of achieving balance between the eastern and western theatres of war" (Cox 194). But Foote's procedure is more than just a balance; in addition, it manifests a cumulative wholeness like that of *Follow Me Down*, in which the multifaceted nature of the narrative draws attention to the incompleteness of each perspective, and where the sum is greater than any of the parts. The inclusion of Beulah Ross's long flashback at the heart of the novel—the silenced speech available only to the reader—provides a final, and ironic, sense of the totality of the experience (an irony that encompasses even the accomplished storyteller Nowell Parker). In *The Civil War*, Foote draws attention to two similarly "silent" speeches, one from each of the presidents. In Lincoln's case, it is a speech he made in 1856, a presidential election year: "As a delegate to the state convention he caught fire and made what may have been the greatest speech of his career, though no one would ever really know, since the heat of his words seemed to burn them from men's memory, and in that conglomerate mass of gaping, howling old-line Whigs and bolted Democrats, Know-Nothings, Free Soilers and Abolitionists, even the shorthand reporters sat enthralled, forgetting to use their pencils" (*CW* I.29). At the other end of the narrative, when Davis is intent on rallying Confederate support for an increasingly desperate war effort, similar mention is made of an unrecorded speech delivered extempore to a gathering at the Metropolitan Hall in Richmond.

. . . he launched into an hour-long oration which all who heard it agreed was the finest he ever delivered. Even Pollard of the Examiner, his bitterest critic south of the Potomac, noting "the shifting lights on the feeble, stricken face," declared afterwards that he had never "been so much moved by the power of words spoken for the same space of time." Others had a similar reaction, but no one outside the hall would ever know; Davis spoke from no text, not even notes, and the absence of a shorthand reporter caused this "appeal of surpassing eloquence" to be lost to all beyond range of his voice that night. Hearing and watching him, Pollard experienced "a strange pity, a strange doubt, that this 'old man eloquent' was the weak and unfit President" he had spent the past three years attacking. "Mr Davis frequently paused in his delivery; his broken health admonished him that he was attempting too much; but frequent cries of 'Go on' impelled him to speak at a length which he had not at first proposed. . . . He spoke with an even, tuneful flow of words, spare of gestures; his dilated form and a voice the lowest notes of which were distinctly audible, and which anon rose as a sound of a trumpet, were yet sufficient to convey the strongest emotions and to lift the hearts of his hearers to the level of his grand discourse." (CW III.779)

Foote's inclusion of the silent speeches acknowledges that *The Civil War* participates in the incompleteness of human knowledge of the past. What remains, as compensation, is the aesthetic wholeness supplied by his narrative. Foote's portrait of the two leaders recognizes that they remain incomplete and ultimately unknowable, yet the narrative creates a self-conscious sense that the two figures presented in tandem are, as Foote says of the Emancipation Proclamation, a "container . . . greater than the thing contained" (*CW* I.708).

The parallels Foote establishes between Lincoln and Davis, and the ironic fraternal commentary they provide for each other over the course of the history, represents but a single thematic line in the multi-voiced symphony of *The Civil War*. The dialogue and counterpoint extends right down the chain of command, from generals to foot soldiers, with lively accents being added throughout by various civilian commentators. In this respect, Foote's narrative is a work that stands as an object lesson for historian Peter Burke's observation that fictional devices, such as heteroglossia, might "make civil wars and other conflicts more intelligible . . . [by allowing] the 'varied and opposing voices' of the dead to be heard again" (238). And it is this very aspect of Foote's narrative that James M. Cox praises when he suggests that "the range of voices in these volumes" (210) contribute greatly to the remarkable "texture of the narrative"—a texture that is "a translation of all his enormous reading of prior texts into a living and not merely a lively account of the action" (207).

Conclusion

"The painter's eye is not a lens, it trembles to caress the light"

A Novelist's Historiography

We are born with the dead:
    See, they return, and bring us with them.
    The moment of the rose and the moment of the yew-tree
    Are of equal duration. A people without history
Is not redeemed from time, for history is a pattern
    Of timeless moments.

—T. S. Eliot, *Little Gidding*, 1942

Everything I have to say about the writing of history was summoned up by John Keats in ten words in a letter, more or less like a telegram put on the wire nearly two hundred years ago. He said: "A fact is not a truth until you love it." You have to become attached to the thing you're writing about—in other words, "love it"—for it to have any real meaning. It is absolutely true that no list of facts ever gives you a valid account of what happened.

—Shelby Foote, "The Art of Fiction CLVIII," 1999

213

The last pages of *The Civil War* are organized around Jefferson Davis's emergence as the "embodied history of the South" (*CW* III.1055); with Davis's life as a template, Foote gradually widens the narrative focus to encompass the final years of the main characters. Writing these pages, Foote allows himself a gently ironic joke. As he recounts Davis's determination to record the history of the Confederacy, a resolve strengthened by the Confederate president's outrage at General Joseph E. Johnston's self-serving *Narrative of Military Operations Directed During the Late War Between the States* (1874), Foote outlines Davis's search for a suitable locale in which to undertake the rigors of composition: "Bustling Memphis, hot in summer, cold in winter . . . seemed unconducive to the peace he believed he needed for such work. Who could write anything there, let alone a full-fledged two- or three-volume history of the war?" (*CW* III.1051–52). This, of course, is precisely what Foote has just done, or is on the verge of doing, as he basks in the glow of his accomplishment while penning the final pages of his narrative in the early summer of 1974.

This fleeting reference puts a reader in mind of other implicit self-portraits found in the novels. For instance, Foote's relation to the narrator Asa in *Tournament*, as he juggles myth and memory; Foote as the ancient clerk in *Love in a Dry Season*, carefully entering notations by dip pen into a doomsday book; Foote as author/historian, balancing the soldier's and the God's-eye perspectives in *Shiloh;* or Foote surpassing the lawyer Nowell's skillful construction of an argument to a thesis in *Follow Me Down* by going him one better and including Beulah's "lost" monologue. In each case, the author indicates his own artistic involvement with the material of the story. In the history, this brief glimpse of Foote is a reminder of the distance and perspective he brings to the material: his own heritage as a southerner writing from the post-atomic vantage of the mid–twentieth century. It is a point Foote returns to in the last lines of the third "Bibliographical Note": "the conflict is behind me now, as it is for you and it was a hundred-odd years ago for them" (*CW* III.1065). "For Foote, as for any writer about the past," White and Sugg suggest, "the basic technique was to establish his own identifiable narrative voice, somewhat paradoxically introducing this into historiography, where the requirements of objectivity might seem to rule it out, having eschewed it in his fiction, where it seems that the novelist's license is not unrestricted, either" (110) The shaping vision of the narrator in *The Civil War*, as he makes the past "live again in the world around [him]" ("Novelist's" 220), includes a representation of the (short- and longer-term) memories of the participants, the creation of a textual memory for the reader and an acknowledgment of his own contemporary context— all of which suggests a self-conscious historiographical dimension to Foote's work.

The strength of Foote's narrative rests on his ability to re-create the lived memory of the participants; *The Civil War*, like *Jordan County*, involves the reader in this process of textual memory. In that novel, Foote moves us from the present into the past, deeper and deeper, creating an ironic tension through this reverse progression. Knowing what the future holds, even as the stories move into the more distant past, creates in *Jordan County* two levels of reader awareness: on one level exists the aesthetic dimension of Foote's historical reconstruction, while on the other level the integrity of a character's experience in the present is being maintained. In *The Civil War*, Foote develops a similar dynamic by respecting the temporal limitations of the historical figures, their immediate experience and memories, and the narrator's awareness of the present context of the readers. Present time in the narrative of the Gettysburg campaign, for example, is marked by the inclusion of events significant to the participants. The astonishingly brief period of time between major conflicts is employed as part of Foote's method. During the introductory pages, tracing the development of Confederate strategy, Foote notes the passage of time through references to Stonewall Jackson's death from his wounds at Chancellorsville (on May 10, 1863—the day Lee rejects Longstreet's proposal to relieve Vicksburg by reinforcing Bragg at Tullahoma) and then Jackson's burial, which coincides with Lee's arrival for the Richmond conference (*CW* II.429–30). Similarly, at a number of points throughout the chapter, the length of the campaign is charted by its distance from Chancellorsville (*CW* II.433, 436, 477, 525). While serving to reinforce the chronological progression of events, these reminders also suggest how previous experience shaped the consciousness, the attitudes, and the memories of the participants. Some examples of this lived memory are Lee's growing sense of the weakness of the command structure with the absence of Jackson, Meade's caution as a result of Hooker's disaster at Chancellorsville, and the legacy of defeat with which the Army of the Potomac lived for much of the war ("In the past ten months, the army had fought four major battles under as many different commanders—Bull Run under Pope, Antietam under

McClellan, Fredericksburg under Burnside, and Chancellorsville under Hooker—all against a single adversary, Robert Lee, who could claim unquestionable victory in three out of the four: especially the first and the last, of which about the best that could be said was that the Federal army had survived them" [*CW* II.446]).

Incidental references to earlier battles and campaigns also play a part in registering the impact of immediate memories on various decisions and actions. For example, by recollecting the victorious Confederate frontal assault on the entrenched Union position at Turkey Hill during the Battle of Gaines Mill in the Peninsula campaign, at the same moment that Lee formulates the orders that will result in Pickett's charge (*CW* II.521), Foote reinforces the level of confidence and expectation such triumphs had inaugurated. Conversely, the Union troops who wait behind the stone wall to receive Pickett's charge are understandably eager to exact a price equivalent to a "Fredericksburg in reverse" (*CW* II.485, 555). Recounting the seeming inability of the Confederates to exploit the opportunities presented during the series of assaults on the second day of fighting, Foote offers an explanation again based on the "lived" experience of the text: "The truth was, the army had slipped back to the disorganization of the Seven Days, except that here at Gettysburg there was no hardcore tactical plan to carry it through the bungling. . . . There was, as always, no lack of Confederate bravery, and the army's combat skill had been demonstrated amply by the fact that, despite its role as the attacker, it had inflicted even more casualties than it had suffered, yet these qualities could not make up for the crippling lack of direction from above and the equally disadvantageous lack of initiative just below the top" (*CW* II.513–14). Along with the theoretical explanation comes the reminder that the Seven Days were, after all, barely more than a year in the past; a year, moreover, characterized, as Foote mentions earlier, by a "string of victories" (*CW* II.477).

The broader temporal frame within which the reader is placed includes these memories of "lived" experience, as well as attributes outside the present memory of the participants. The Battle of Gettysburg, leaving aside its symbolic and historical importance, is presented as "the bloodiest battle of the war to date" (*CW* II.520, 525), a climax or culmination made understandable by Foote's presentation of the somewhat generic aspects of Civil War battlefields. This contest gathered together elements and aspects of many that preceded it and carried forward the recollection of those earlier events. Gettysburg has its peach orchard as did Shiloh; it has its stone wall atop Cemetery Ridge and the tragic echoes of Fredericksburg; the wheat-field across which Pickett's troops moved under withering gunfire carries forward memories of the unsuccessful Confederate charge at Malvern Hill or the slaughter in the cornfield at Antietam. The list could be extended, but the point is that Foote's narrative, working in a cumulative fashion, con-veys much of the horror and the irony of the Civil War through the reap-pearance of these features, increasingly invested with the consciousness of the valor and sacrifice they represent. The litany can seem, occasionally, quite numbing; this, too, is a legitimate effect in re-creating the experience of the past.

The continuity between these past battles and more contemporary twentieth-century experience is also part of Foote's vision. In *Jordan County* we are presented with this double consciousness of past and future; so too in *The Civil War* Foote sparingly suggests connections with future events. Outlining the inadvertent destruction created in the Union rear by the over-shooting of the Confederate cannonade prior to Pickett's charge, Foote con-cludes his description with an observation that anticipates both the slaugh-ter immediately to follow and, lest the reader become too complacent, a reference to even greater wholesale destruction awaiting future generations.

> All in all, though it was more or less clear already that the gray artillerists were going to fail in their attempt to drive the blue de-fenders from the ridge, they had accomplished much with their faulty gunnery, including the disruption of army headquarters, the wounding of the chief of staff, and the displacement of the artillery reserve, not to mention a good deal of incidental slaughter among the rearward fugitives who had not intended to take part in the fighting anyhow. Unwittingly, and in fact through carelessness and error, the Confederates had invented the box barrage of World War One, still fifty-odd years in the future, whereby a chosen sector of the enemy line was isolated for attack. (*CW* II.543)

Each battle, like the war itself, is understood as part of the cumulative process of history, along with the wry and ironic acknowledgment that "pro-gress" means one generation's error is another's approved tactics. As with the pillars of smoke and fire that appear at intervals throughout the narra-tive, connecting an Old Testament image with intimations of contemporary apocalyptic destructiveness, Foote insists on the continuity between past events and contemporary sensibilities—on history as a continuum and not progress.

One of the revealing devices Foote employs in his treatment of time and memory is the displacement of the annual dates to the top of each page. A reader immersed in the text, like the men fighting the war, exists in a world of days and weeks, rather than a perspective of years (until each particular "season" is over, signaled by the onset of winter weather, the retiring of armies into winter quarters, and then a narrative shift to the world of the commanders, where larger strategic concerns and plans for the next year dominate). Evidence of time's passing is typically presented through the relationship between events in the present and those already past, whether by a careful marking of the anniversaries of battles or the counting of days from the outset of the particular campaign or action. In *The Civil War* the sensibilities and consciousnesses of the participants are shaped by the developing memory of their war experience—as are those of the readers. The narrative becomes a sort of world unto itself that refashions the perceptions of individuals as they adjust, or fail to adjust, to the changes in the immediate context of the war. The text, in effect, functions as its own memory, chronicling the alterations in perspective over the duration. One example might serve to illustrate how Foote suggests the symbiotic relationship between the war and the larger cultural shifts—an ironic vision of the situation of men, as dwellers in time, when memory of the past is ignored. In the following passage, taken from volume 1, Foote describes General McClellan's return, with his newly refurbished Army of the Potomac, to the site of the Battle of Bull Run:

> Presently, crossing Bull Run by Blackburn's ford, they came onto the scene of last year's smoky, flame-stabbed panorama. It was a sobering sight, for those who had been there then and those who hadn't: the corpse of a battlefield, silent and deserted except perhaps for the ghosts of the fallen. Shell-blasted, the treetops were twisted "in a hundred directions, as though struck by lightning," one correspondent wrote. Manassas Junction lay dead ahead, the embers of it anyhow, at the base of a column of bluish-yellow smoke, and off to the right were the tumbled bricks of Judith Henry's chimney, on the hill where the Stonewall Brigade had met the jubilant attackers, freezing the cheers in their throats, and flung them back; Jeb Stuart's horsemen had come with a thunder of hoofs,

hacking away at the heads of the New York Fire Zouaves. All that was left now was wreckage, the charred remains of a locomotive and four freight cars, five hundred staved-in barrels of flour, and fifty-odd barrels of pork and beef "scattered around in the mud." McDowell was there, at the head of his corps, and one of his soldiers wrote that he saw him weeping over the sunbleached bones of the light-hearted berry-picking men he had led southward under the full moon of July.

McClellan was not weeping. This field held no memories for him, sad or otherwise, except that what had happened here had prompted Lincoln to send for him to head the army he found "cowering on the banks of the Potomac" and later to replace Scott as chief of all the nation's armies. He went to bed that night, proud to have taken without loss the position McDowell had been thrown back from after spilling on it the blood of 1500 men. Next day he was happy still, riding among the bivouacs. But the day that followed was another matter. He woke to find his time had come to weep. (*CW* I.266)

In this way, with the description of a seemingly innocuous event of little military significance, Foote illustrates both a central aspect of McClellan's character, his arrogant self-confidence, and the creation of a new set of cultural memories.

The inclusion of Lincoln's Gettysburg Address accomplishes on a larger scale the process embodied by McClellan's experience. The redefinition of the nature of the American vision in Lincoln's assertion of the centrality of the Declaration of Independence over the Constitution contained in the Gettysburg Address plays a central role in demonstrating how the events on the field generate a new conception of the American cultural identity. Garry Wills's reading of Lincoln's speech in *Lincoln at Gettysburg: The Words That Remade America* establishes quite clearly the scope of the cultural realignment Lincoln accomplished in a mere 272 words. In fact, it is Lincoln—the epic's consummate memorialist—who introduces this theme into Foote's *The Civil War* in the closing lines of the first inaugural address: "Though passion may have strained, it must not break our bonds of affection. The mystic chords of memory, stretching from every battlefield and patriot grave to every living heart and hearthstone all over this broad land, will yet swell the chorus of the Union when again touched, as surely they will be, by the better angels of our nature" (*CW* I.40). To a great extent, much of Foote's strategy in *The Civil War* is directed toward chronicling the emergence of a new set of cultural memories, a new mythic past, that shapes the modern era of the United States. As Michael Kammen points out in *Mystic Chords of Memory: The Transformation of Tradition in American Culture* (1991): "Between 1861 [Lincoln's election] and 1907 [the year of Henry James's reference to the "chord of remembrance" in *The American Scene*] American memory began to take form as a self-conscious phenomenon" (100).

Although a kind of twilight descends on the narrative in this final chapter, the apocalyptic imagery is not abandoned. Consider, for example, its title, "Lucifer in Starlight," which refers to Davis's figure as a president without a country, a rebel angel in perpetual exile (the phrase is from George Meredith's poem about Lucifer's resurgent pride quenched by a vision of the "army of unalterable law" and makes an intriguing connection to Anaximander's ordinance of time). Employing Anaximander and Ecclesiasticus (chapter 44, the passage beginning "Let us now praise famous men . . . ," is the epigraph for volumes 2 and 3) as guiding lights, Foote's *The Civil War* conveys a similar impulse toward a more inclusive view of historical narrative. The narrative seeks to embody the events that brought the modern United States into being (the transformation from a plurality of states into a single nation): "Before the war," Foote observes in an interview, "people had a theoretical notion of having a country, but when the war was over, on both sides they knew they had a country. . . . Before the war, it was said, 'The United States are. . . .' Grammatically, it was spoken that way and thought of as a collection of independent states. After the war, it was always 'The United States is . . .'—as we say today without being self-conscious at all. And that sums up what the war accomplished. It made us an 'is'" (Ward, *Civil War* 273). The reality of the war begins to recede into the past, becoming part of the cultural memory of the new America, the modern nation referred to in the singular as the United States.

The narrative of *The Civil War* registers how the cataclysm of fratricidal conflict is transmuted into words—a process begun during the war itself, with the Gettysburg Address as a stellar example. Historian Alice Fahs, in *The Imagined Civil War*, also comments on the link between the matter of the war and the written tradition: "The sense that the war had created an inexhaustible supply of stories, that there were innumerable 'incidents and anecdotes' of the war to be collected and told, energized popular literature both during and after the conflict. This understanding of the storied abundance of the war was one of the chief legacies of popular Civil War literature. No other war in American history has had this profound sense of narrativity associated with it, centered around the abiding faith that every individual experience of the war was not only worthy of but demanded representation" (311). The epilogue of Foote's narrative is, in fact, a mediation on time, memory, and the power and limitations of language to recapture the past. The erosion of certain "facts" begins almost immediately. Foote tells, for example, of how the rebel yell—impossible to recreate when warlike conditions did not apply—"perished from the sound waves" (*CW* III.1046). On a more elevated level, Foote recounts a Memorial Day address given by the younger Oliver Wendell Holmes in 1884; with its intimations of future conflicts and conflagrations, and its echoes of the Lincoln music, Holmes's words suggest the transformative power of language and memory. Commenting on how Memorial Day was for him—a thrice-wounded veteran—and his listeners "the most sacred of the year," Holmes continues:

> But even if I am wrong, even if those who are to come after us are to forget all that we hold dear, and the future is to teach and kindle its children in ways as yet unrevealed, it is enough for us this day is dear and sacred. . . . For one hour, twice a year at least—at the regimental dinner, where the ghosts sit at table more numerous than the living, and on this day when we decorate their graves—the dead come back and live with us. I see them now, more than I can number, as once I saw them on this earth. The generation that carried on the war has been set aside by its experience. Through our great good fortune, in our youth our hearts were touched with fire. It was given to us to learn at the outset that life is a profound and passionate thing. While we are permitted to scorn nothing but indifference, and do not pretend to undervalue the worldly rewards of ambition, we have seen with our own eyes, beyond and above the gold fields, the snowy heights of honor, and it is for us to bear the report to those who come after us. (*CW* III.1047)

The apocalyptic fire is translated into myth and memory—into language, into art. Indeed, historian David W. Blight finds that Holmes's artistry made him one of the most articulate of those advocating a reconciliatory vision: "a story of how in American culture romance triumphed over reality, [and] sentimental remembrance won over ideological memory" (4). Blight characterizes Holmes's art as contributing to a "grand evasion" (70) in cultural memory, an attempt to avoid addressing the realities of race and disenfranchisement by supplanting the continuing struggle with images of a nation (at least its white members) reunited in mutual heroism. It is telling, then, that the last example of this kind of memory in Foote's text is offered by another artist manqué figure; in this case, to a certain extent, the quotation becomes an ironic comment on all such attempts—Foote's own included—at make the past live again (and the dangers of a romanticized version of events). The writer is Sergeant Berry Benson, "a South Carolina veteran from McGowan's brigade, Wilcox's division, A. P. Hill's corps, Army of Northern Virginia." Foote picks up the story:

> In time, even death itself might be abolished. Sergeant Berry Benson . . . saw it so when he got around to composing the Reminiscences he hoped would "go down amongst my descendants for a long time." Reliving the war in words, he began to wish he could relive it in fact, and he came to believe that he and his fellow soldiers, gray and blue, might one day be able to do just that: if not here on earth, then afterwards in Valhalla. "Who knows," he asked as his narrative drew toward its close, "but it may be given to us, after this life, to meet again in the old quarters, to play chess and draughts, to get up soon to answer the morning roll call, to fall in at the tap of the drum for drill and dress parade, and again to hastily don our war gear while the monotonous patter of the long roll summons to battle? Who knows but again the old flags, ragged and torn, snapping in the wind, may face each other and flutter, pursuing and pursued, while the cries of victory fill a summer day? And after the battle, then the slain and wounded will arise, and all will meet together under the two flags, all sound and well, and there will be talking and laughter and cheers, and all will say: Did it not seem real? Was it not as in the old days?" (*CW* III.1048)

Reliving the war in his own narrative, and recounting this story at its close, Foote acknowledges the fallibility of his medium, the seductive nature of the romantic impulse, and the dangers inherent in attempting to recapture the past. In fact, Foote's return to fiction with *September September,* set close to the start of the Civil Rights movement, suggests his own consciousness of the unwritten coda to the war—the tragedy of Reconstruction as it failed, so completely, to legitimize the rights of African Americans.

In his meditation on the nature of cultural memory (and human fallibility), Foote suggests, "Memory smoothed the crumpled scroll, abolished fear, leached pain and grief, and removed the sting from death" (*CW* III.1047), and the artist works to reintroduce those elements, reconcile them with the bloodless myths, and transform both into art. Responding to an interviewer's comment that he takes a "colder and more realistic look at the South than did Faulkner, who was more a creator of myths," Foote remarks: "I think I do that too. But I do think that a quality of very great writing is that it converts tales into myths" (*Conversations* 224). His consciousness of this attribute of historical writing is further supported by a quotation from Northrop Frye penciled into the margin of the manuscript of his essay "The Novelist's View of History": "'In a sense, the historical is the opposite of the mythical, & to tell the historian that what gives shape to his book is a myth would sound to him vaguely insulting.' And yet, he adds, 'When a historian's scheme gets to a certain point of comprehensiveness it becomes mythical in shape, & so approaches the poetical in its structure'" (Papers, Series 2.3, 87–88). The purpose of history, of narrative history in particular, Foote suggests, involves redressing the balance between the experiential realities (the apocalyptic fire) and the memorial or purgative one.

"Style," Proust said, "is in no way a decoration as some people believe; it is not even a matter of technique; it is—as colour is with painters—a quality of vision . . ." (Gay 5). Peter Gay, employing Proust's famous dictum as a starting point for his discussion in *Style in History,* goes on to suggest that a writer's style is an "unmistakable signature . . . the cultivated manner . . . [whereby] the writer instructively expresses his personal past as well as the culture's ways of thinking, feeling, believing and working" (7). Foote's history, with its attention to structure, its acknowledgment of the conditional nature of past experience, its self-conscious reflections, and its goal of harmonization, demonstrates an adherence to the Proustian ideal. It is interesting to note in this context that Barbara Tuchman, commenting on how invaluable she found Proust's writings when working on her history of the Dreyfus affair, says that "for source material I want something I can see. When you read Proust you see Paris of the nineties, horse cabs and lamplight, the clubman making his calls" (40). Where Tuchman turned to

Proust for his subject matter, Foote turns to Proust as a stylistic guide, adopting his means and not his matter, and by doing so creates a complex interplay between the concrete and the abstract, between the texture of the past and the perspective of the present, in writing his version of the Civil War. By self-consciously approaching the writing of history as art, by registering his own "quality of vision," Foote gives mythic shape to the past, acknowledging through his method the paradoxical nature of cultural memory—the reality that such hindsight, as David Lowenthal maintains, is always both a reduction and an enlargement (217). "The rationale of history," David Cowart suggests,

> . . . coincides with that of art, for each promotes a cultural self-knowledge commensurate with and complementary to that personal self-knowledge traditionally viewed as one of the major objects of humanistic study. But every culture expresses itself more definitely through its artists than through its historians. Homer and Sophocles do more to define their civilization than do Herodotus or Thucydides, and Mark Twain and Walt Whitman capture the American spirit better than does Francis Parkman. Artists, after all, speak to the cultural memory with greater authority than do historians. Artists provide the myths by which any cultural body defines itself, the myths that historians mistakenly seek to unravel. (25)

Foote, in these terms, is the exception that proves the rule, straddling as he does in *The Civil War* the easy distinction Cowart makes between the creative writer and the historian. The particular virtue of Foote's vision, like that of Vermeer in Robert Lowell's "Epilogue," whose "painter's eye is not a lens, / it trembles to caress the light," is most aptly expressed in the Shakespearean echoes at the end of the poem: "We are poor passing facts, / warned by that to give / each figure in the photograph / his living name" (127).

Ken Burns, in an interview included in the centenary issue of the *American Historical Review*, responded to a question about Foote's role as the "central voice" of his documentary *The Civil War* by saying: "I didn't pick him to be the central voice. He picked himself. The film picked him. We interviewed . . . many, many, many, scholars, people, experts . . . most of whom . . . could not give a sense of what happened during the Civil War. . . . What Shelby had was both a rigorous intellectual relationship to the war but also an ability to place it in a narrative context" (761). The factual material Burns gleaned from these numerous interviews with scholars contributed greatly to the project, but only as background incorporated into the script, because "[they] told us in a way that couldn't be used. They never ended a sentence. . . . And so I had to go with someone who knew how to tell stories" (761). A little later in the interview, Burns employs another analogy for this process of Foote's "self-selection":

> And so, finally, you trade for Babe Ruth, and you get rid of a lot of minor players . . . [in favor of the one who] covers all of the intellectual points but then also brings in art, humor, literature, feeling, affection. All of those things came with what Shelby said. And it was funny in the scholarly [consulting] meeting. Twenty-four scholars we had: C. Vann Woodward, Robert Penn Warren, Ira Berlin. [Yet] people at the end of this three-day conference were turning and saying, "But Shelby, what actually happened?" Because he knew what happened . . . not just that Antietam was significant. . . . He felt it and, in fact, perhaps lived it. And that's the communication, and that's the great mission. (763)

While Burns also acknowledges the very real contributions of the other scholars and their work to his film, his anecdote is, nevertheless, an indicative one, pointing as it does to the still-vexed question of the relationship between academic and popular history. Twenty-two years earlier, a similar balance is struck in Foote's "The Novelist's View of History," when, after illustrating the literary flaws in Kenneth P. Williams's *Lincoln Finds a General,* Foote pauses to praise its merits as an academic work that is "accurate, hard-gutted, definitive as to facts . . . [and] extremely useful" to the composition of his narrative (222).

The point both Burns and Foote make—in keeping with remarks by other artist-historians such as Bruce Catton and Allen Nevins—is that history, if it is to be a living part of cultural memory, must also live as art. As David Lowenthal suggests, regarding the contribution of narrative history to cultural memory: "Understanding the past demands some location of people and things; a chronological framework clarifies, places things in context, underscores the essential uniqueness of past events. . . . The pearls of history take their value not merely from being many and lustrous, but from being arranged in a causal narrative sequence; the narrative lends the necklace of time meaning as well as beauty" (224). Foote has maintained this idea throughout his career: "There is no reason why the historian should not be an artist, too; and all art is mutual. . . . [The historian] can learn even from a writer of fiction, who is nothing if he is not an artist in pursuit of truth" ("Novelist's" 224). And truth, in Foote's view, comes from a reciprocity between the factual materials and the writer's dedication to style, from a love of subject inexorably wedded to a "quality of vision." As the art of *The Civil War: A Narrative* demonstrates: "A fact is not a truth until you love it" (*Conversations* 248).

Works Cited

Appleby, Joyce, Lynn Hunt, and Margaret Jacob. *Telling the Truth about History.* New York: Norton, 1994.

Belz, Herman. "Twentieth-Century American Historians and the Old South: A Review Essay." *Civil War History* 31.2 (June 1985): 171–80.

Blight, David W. *Race and Reunion: The Civil War in American Memory.* Cambridge, Mass.: Harvard U P, 2001.

Brinkmeyer, Robert H. "The Foote/Percy Letters." *Virginia Quarterly Review* 74.1 (Winter 1998): 197–204.

Burke, Peter. "History of Events and the Revival of Narrative." In *New Perspectives on Historical Writing,* edited by Peter Burke. Cambridge: Polity Press, 1991. 233–46.

Burns, Ken. "Historical Truth: An Interview with Ken Burns." By Thomas Cripps. *American Historical Review* 100.3 (June 1995): 741–64.

Cash, W. J. *The Mind of the South.* 1941. Reprint, New York: Vintage, 1991.

Catton, Bruce. *Prefaces to History.* Garden City, N.Y.: Doubleday, 1970.

———. *Reflections on the Civil War,* edited by John Leekley. Garden City, N.Y.: Doubleday, 1981.

Chadwick, Bruce. *The Reel Civil War: Mythmaking in American Film.* New York: Knopf, 2001.

Cobb, James. *The Most Southern Place on Earth: The Mississippi Delta and the Roots of Regional Identity.* New York: Oxford U P, 1992.

Cohn, David. *Where I Was Born and Raised.* Boston: Houghton, Mifflin, 1948.

Conrad, Joseph. "Preface to *The Nigger of the 'Narcissus.'*" 1898. In *Norton Anthology of English Literature,* edited by M. H. Abrams et al. 5th ed. Vol. 2. New York: Norton, 1986. 1810–13.

Cotkin, George. *Reluctant Modernism: American Thought and Culture 1880–1900.* New York: Twayne, 1992.

Cowart, David. *History and the Contemporary Novel.* Carbondale and Edwardsville: Southern Illinois U P, 1989.

Cox, James M. "Shelby Foote's Civil War." In *Recovering Literature's Lost Ground: Essays in American Autobiography.* Baton Rouge: Louisiana State U P, 1989. 191–214.

Cullen, Jim. *The Civil War in Popular Culture: A Reusable Past.* Washington: Smithsonian Institution Press, 1995.

Eliot, T. S. "The Dry Salvages." 1941. In *Collected Poems 1909–1962*. 1963. London: Faber and Faber, 1974. 205.

Fahs, Alice. *The Imagined Civil War: Popular Literature of the North and South, 1861–1865*. Chapel Hill: U of North Carolina P, 2001.

Faulkner, William. *Absalom, Absalom!* 1936. In *Novels, 1936–1940*, edited by Joseph Blotner and Noel Polk. New York: Library of America, 1990.

————. *Intruder in the Dust*. 1948. In *Novels, 1942–1954*, edited by Joseph Blotner and Noel Polk. New York: Library of America, 1994.

Foner, Eric. *Politics and Ideology in the Age of the Civil War*. New York: Oxford U P, 1980.

Foote, Shelby. "The Art of Fiction CLVIII: Shelby Foote." *The Paris Review*. Interview by Carter Coleman, Donald Faulkner and William Kennedy. 41.151 (Summer 1999): 48–91.

————. *The Beleaguered City: The Vicksburg Campaign, December 1862–July 1863*. New York: Modern Library, 1995.

————. *The Civil War: A Narrative, Vol. 1: Fort Sumter to Perryville*. New York: Random House, 1957.

————. *The Civil War: A Narrative, Vol. 2: Fredericksburg to Meridian*. New York: Random House, 1963.

————. *The Civil War: A Narrative, Vol. 3: Red River to Appomattox*. New York: Random House, 1974.

————. *Conversations with Shelby Foote*, edited by William C. Carter. Jackson and London: U P of Mississippi, 1989.

————. *The Correspondence of Shelby Foote and Walker Percy*, edited by Jay Tolson. New York: Norton, 1997.

————. *Follow Me Down*. New York: Dial, 1950. Reprint, New York: Vintage, 1993.

————. Introduction to *The Red Badge of Courage: An Episode of the American Civil War*, by Stephen Crane. New York: Modern Library, 1993. vii–li.

————. *Jordan County: A Landscape in Narrative*. New York: Dial, 1954. Reprint, New York: Vintage, 1992.

————. *Love in a Dry Season*. New York: Dial, 1951. Reprint, New York: Vintage, 1992.

————. Lectures. Rec. 1966–67. Audiocassette. The Mississippi Valley Collection. John Willard Brister Library. U of Memphis, Memphis, Tenn.

————. Letters. ms. Series 1. (Correspondence) and Subseries 2.3. (Shorter Writings). Shelby Foote Papers. Southern Historical Collection. Wilson Library. U of North Carolina at Chapel Hill. Chapel Hill, N.C.

————. "The Novelist's View of History." *Mississippi Quarterly* 17 (Fall 1964): 219–25.

————. *September September*. New York: Random House, 1977. Reprint, New York: Vintage, 1991.

————. *Shiloh*. New York: Dial, 1952. Reprint, New York: Vintage, 1992.

———. *Stars in Their Courses: The Gettysburg Campaign, June–July 1863.* New York: Modern Library, 1994.

———. *Tournament.* New York: Dial, 1949. Reprint, with a foreword by Louis D. Rubin Jr. and a preface by Foote. Birmingham: Summa, 1987.

Garrett, George. "Foote's *The Civil War*: The Version for Posterity?" *Mississippi Quarterly* 28 (Winter 1974–75): 83–92.

Gay, Peter. *Style in History.* 1974. Reprint, New York: Norton, 1988.

Gignilliat, John L. "Douglas Southall Freeman." In *Twentieth-Century American Historians,* edited by Clyde N. Wilson. Dictionary of Literary Biography, no. 17. Detroit: Gale Research, 1983. 157–69.

Gray, Richard. *The Life of William Faulkner: A Critical Biography.* Oxford, England: Blackwell, 1994.

———. *Writing the South: Ideas of an American Region.* 2nd ed. Baton Rouge: Louisiana State UP, 1997.

Harrington, Evans, and Ann J. Abadie, eds. *The South and Faulkner's Yoknapatawpha: The Actual and the Apocryphal.* Jackson: U P of Mississippi, 1977.

Holman, C. Hugh. *The Immoderate Past: The Southern Writer and History.* Athens: U of Georgia P, 1977.

Horwitz, Tony. *Confederates in the Attic: Dispatches from the Unfinished Civil War.* New York: Pantheon, 1998.

James, Henry. "The Art of Fiction." 1884. In *The Norton Anthology of American Literature,* edited by Nina Baym et al. 3rd ed. Vol. 2. New York: Norton, 1989. 456–70.

Jenkins, Keith. *On "What Is History?": From Carr and Elton to Rorty and White.* London and New York: Routledge, 1995.

———. *Re-thinking History.* London and New York: Routledge, 1991.

Johnson, Paul. *A History of the Modern World: From 1917 to the 1990s.* 1983. Rev. ed. London: Weidenfeld and Nicolson, 1991.

Kammen, Michael. *Mystic Chords of Memory: The Transformation of Tradition in American Culture.* 1991. Reprint, New York: Vintage, 1993.

Keegan, John. *The Face of Battle: A Study of Agincourt, Waterloo and the Somme.* 1976. Reprint, London: Pimlico, 1992.

Kreyling, Michael. *Figures of the Hero in Southern Narrative.* Baton Rouge: Louisiana State U P, 1987.

LaCapra, Dominick. *History & Criticism.* Ithaca: Cornell U P, 1985.

Lowell, Robert. "Epilogue." In *Day by Day.* New York: Farrar, Straus and Giroux, 1977. 127.

Lowenthal, David. *The Past Is a Foreign Country.* Cambridge and New York: Cambridge U P, 1985.

Malvasi, Mark G. *The Unregenerate South: The Agrarian Thought of John Crowe Ransom, Allen Tate, and Donald Davidson.* Baton Rouge: Louisiana State U P, 1997.

Matthews, John T. *The Sound and the Fury: Faulkner and the Lost Cause.* Boston: Twayne, 1990.

McMurray, Richard M. "Allen Nevins." In *Twentieth-Century American Historians,* edited by Clyde N. Wilson. Dictionary of Literary Biography, no. 17. Detroit: Gale Research, 1983. 315–27.

McPherson, James M. *Battle Cry of Freedom: The Civil War Era.* New York: Oxford U P, 1988.

Moore, L. Hugh, Jr. *Robert Penn Warren and History: "The Big Myth We Live."* The Hague: Mouton, 1970.

Murray, Peter. "The Historical Narrative." In *Companion to Historiography,* edited by Michael Bentley. London and New York: Routledge, 1997. 851–67.

O'Brien, Michael. *Rethinking the South: Essays in Intellectual History.* 1988. Athens: U of Georgia P, 1993.

Percy, Walker. "Stoicism in the South." In *Signposts in a Strange Land,* edited by Patrick Samway. New York: Farrar, Straus and Giroux, 1991. 83–88.

Percy, William Alexander. *Lanterns on the Levee: Recollections of a Planter's Son.* 1941. Reprint, with an introduction by Walker Percy, Baton Rouge: Louisiana State U P, 1973.

Phillips, Robert L. *Shelby Foote: Novelist and Historian.* Jackson: U P of Mississippi, 1992.

Reardon, Carol. "Bruce Catton." In *Twentieth-Century American Historians,* edited by Clyde N. Wilson. Dictionary of Literary Biography, no. 17. Detroit: Gale Research, 1983. 98–102.

Robertson, James I., Jr. Review of *The Civil War: A Narrative,* by Shelby Foote. *Civil War History* 22.2 (June 1975): 172–75.

Rollyson, Carl E., Jr. *The Uses of the Past in the Novels of William Faulkner.* Ann Arbor: UMI Research P, 1984.

Rubin, Louis D., Jr. "Old-Style History." *New Republic* 171.22 (November 30, 1974): 44–45.

Shepherd, Allen. "Technique and Theme in Shelby Foote's *Shiloh.*" *Notes on Mississippi Writers* 5 (Spring 1972): 3–10.

Simpson, Lewis. *The Brazen Face of History: Studies in the Literary Consciousness of America.* Baton Rouge: Louisiana State U P, 1980.

———. "Shelby Foote and Walker Percy: Art and God." *Southern Literary Journal* 30.2 (Spring 1998): 91–121.

Singal, Daniel Joseph. *The War Within: From Victorian to Modernist Thought in the South, 1919–1945.* Chapel Hill: U of North Carolina P, 1982.

———. *William Faulkner: The Making of a Modernist.* Chapel Hill: U of North Carolina P, 1997.

Sullivan, Walter. "The Continuing Renascence: Southern Fiction in the Fifties." In *South: Modern Southern Literature in Its Cultural Setting,* edited by Louis D. Rubin Jr. and Robert D. Jacobs. Garden City: Doubleday, 1961. 376–91.

Tolson, Jay. *Pilgrim in the Ruins: A Life of Walker Percy.* 1992. Chapel Hill: U of North Carolina P, 1994.

Tuchman, Barbara W. *Practicing History: Selected Essays.* New York: Knopf, 1981.

Tulloch, Hugh. *The Debate on the American Civil War Era.* Manchester: Manchester U P, 1999.

Ward, Geoffrey C., with Ric Burns and Ken Burns. *The Civil War: An Illustrated History.* New York: Knopf, 1990.

———. "Telling How It Was." *American Heritage* 38.8 (December 1987): 14, 18.

Warren, Robert Penn. "The Use of the Past." In *New and Selected Essays.* New York: Random House, 1989. 29–53.

Watson, Ritchie Devon. *Yeoman Versus Cavalier: The Old Southwest's Fictional Road to Rebellion.* Baton Rouge: Louisiana State U P, 1993.

White, Hayden. "Historical Text as Literary Artifact." In *Tropics of Discourse: Essays in Cultural Criticism.* Baltimore: Johns Hopkins U P, 1978. 82–99.

White, Helen, and Redding S. Sugg Jr. *Shelby Foote.* Boston: Twayne, 1982.

Williams, T. Harry. "Freeman, Historian of The Civil War: An Appraisal." *Journal of Southern History* 21.1 (February 1955): 91–100.

Williams, Wirt. "Shelby Foote's Civil War: The Novelist as Humanistic Historian." *Mississippi Quarterly* 24 (Fall 1971): 429–36.

Williamson, Joel. *William Faulkner and Southern History.* New York: Oxford U P, 1993.

Wills, Garry. *Lincoln at Gettysburg: The Words That Remade America.* New York: Simon & Schuster, 1992.

Wilson, Charles Reagan, et al., eds. *Encyclopedia of Southern Culture.* 4 vols. Chapel Hill: U of North Carolina P, 1989.

Wilson, Clyde N. "Shelby Foote." In *Twentieth-Century American Historians,* edited by Wilson. Dictionary of Literary Biography, no. 17. Detroit: Gale Research, 1983. 154–56.

Woodward, C. Vann. *The Burden of Southern History.* 3rd ed. Baton Rouge: Louisiana State U P, 1993.

———. "The Great American Butchery." *New York Review of Books* 22 (March 3, 1975): 12.

———. *Origins of the New South, 1877–1913.* Baton Rouge: Louisiana State U P, 1951.

Wyatt-Brown, Bertram. *The House of Percy: Honor, Melancholy, and Imagination in a Southern Family.* Toronto: Oxford U P, 1994.

Index

Singal, Daniel: aristocratic culture, 11–12,
  16, 156; the South and modernism, xiii,
  17, 18, 29–30
Stars in Their Courses (Foote), 183n.
  See also *Civil War: A Narrative, The*;
  Gettysburg, The Battle of
Stevens, Wallace, 23
Sullivan, Walter, 26, 84, 200

Tacitus, xii; artist-historian, xv
Tate, Allen, 11, 17, 80; Jefferson Davis
  biography and, 200
Textual memory, 135, 147, 179–80, 183,
  185; in *The Civil War: A Narrative*,
  215–23; cultural memories and, 219–23
Tolson, Jay, 5, 6, 7, 8, 9
Tournament: 18, 34, 35, 37, 72, 81, 101,
  110–11, 127; artist manqué in, 75,
  81–82, 214
  —Asa Bart as narrator, 61, 72, 75–81,
    83, 89, 127, 214; Palmer Metcalfe and
    81–82
  Florence Bart (daughter) in, 62, 64;
  Florence Bart (wife) in, 61–62, 63–64;
  Hugh Bart Jr. in 61, 77
  —Hugh Bart in, 34, 64, 72, 85, 110–11,
    127; compared to Issac Jameson,
    39–41; as failed narrator, 80–81; the
    failed dynastic ambitions of, 60–62;
    and history, 75–81; and the modern
    condition, 39–43; and Solitaire,
    39–41, 61–62
  decline of planter-aristocrat in, 39–43;
  modern condition in, 42–43, 80–81;
  familial relationships in, 61–62; female
  characters in, 62–68; narrative structure
  of, 75–81

Tuchman, Barbara, 147, 164, 179, 181;
  Proust and, 223–24
Tulloch, Hugh, 165
Turner, Frederick Jackson, 110
Two Gates to the City (Foote), 3, title of
  unfinished novel, xvi; opening sentence
  of, 5

Vermeer, Jan, loss and, xiv; drama in, xii,
  xvii; limitations and, 73–74; in Lowell
  poem, 224

Warren, Robert Penn, ix, as modernist, xiii,
  17, 18; on role of history, xi–xii, xv–xvi,
  182, 195–96
Washington, Booker T., 53, 58, 106
Watson, Richie Devon, 12, 16, 138–39
White, Hayden, 22–23, 24, 25, 70
White, Helen and Redding S. Sugg Jr.,
  connection of novels to history, 100, 168;
  Foote's temporal dialectic, 182; on *Love
  in a Dry Season*, 94, 97, 98; narrative
  voice, 72, 110; on Parker Nowell, 92–93;
  on Beulah Ross, 83; on *Tournament*, 75
Wilson, Clyde, 194–95
Williams, K.P. 147–48, 225
Williams, Raymond, 31
Williams, Wirt, 133, 143, 181
Williamson, Joel, on southern idealism,10;
  on Faulknerian universe, 14–15
Wills, Garry, 219
Woodward, C. Vann, on *The Civil War:
  A Narrative*, xv; on irony and history,
  25–26; on the Lost Cause, 10, 18
Wyatt-Brown, Bertram, 7– 8, 16, 138

DATE DUE
